The Druids
and King Arthur

The Druids and King Arthur

A New View of Early Britain

Robin Melrose

McFarland & Company, Inc., Publishers
Jefferson, North Carolina, and London

Illustrations by Diana Gardner

LIBRARY OF CONGRESS CATALOGUING-IN-PUBLICATION DATA

Melrose, Robin.
    The Druids and King Arthur : a new view of early Britain /
Robin Melrose.
        p.   cm.
    Includes bibliographical references (p.   ) and index.

    ISBN 978-0-7864-5890-5
    softcover : 50# alkaline paper ∞

    1. Druids and Druidism. 2. Arthur, King. 3. Great
Britain — History — Anglo-Saxon period, 449–1066. I. Title.
BL910.M45   2011
942.01′ 4 — dc22   2010043915

British Library cataloguing data are available

Front cover: The rider-god known as the Thracian Horseman,
found on the Lincolnshire/Nottinghamshire border, near the
village of Brough (Roman Crocolana). British Museum.

Manufactured in the United States of America

McFarland & Company, Inc., Publishers
    Box 611, Jefferson, North Carolina 28640
    www.mcfarlandpub.com

Table of Contents

Introduction   1

Chapter 1 • The Dragon Star   5

Chapter 2 • The Severed Head and the Bone Cave:
   Religion in Roman Britain   18

Chapter 3 • Arthur's Voyage: *The Spoils of Annwn*   42

Chapter 4 • Magic Mounds, Sea People and Shape-Shifters:
   The Wonderful World of the *Mabinogion*   66

Chapter 5 • Mounds, Mounds, Mounds: Rubbish Heaps,
   Hillforts and the Prehistory of Southern England   86

Chapter 6 • Visitors from the East   114

Chapter 7 • Brutus of Troy Town   155

Chapter 8 • Arthur, King of Wessex?   168

Chapter Notes   193
Bibliography   203
Index   211

Introduction

Many books have been written about the Druids, and even more have been written about King Arthur. However, this book is not really about the Druids or King Arthur, but about where the people we call the Druids came from, where the story of Arthur came from, and the role played by the Druids and Arthur in the creation of a new order after the end of Roman rule. To understand the beliefs of the Druids, we will be looking at the religion of Roman Britain, an Old Welsh poem called *The Spoils of Annwn*, and four medieval Welsh tales known as the *Mabinogion*. To understand where the Druids originated, we will be investigating the archeology and history of Salisbury Plain, the site of Stonehenge, and surrounding areas from 2300 B.C. until the arrival of the Celts; and we will be exploring legends of the foundation of Britain, the cult of the Thracian Horseman, the oracle of Dodona who listened to the rustling of oak leaves, the lore and legends surrounding the star Arcturus and Arcas the mythical founder of Arcadia, and some basic principles of prehistoric astronomy. From this rich brew we will demonstrate that the Druids originated from central or eastern Europe in around 850 B.C., bringing with them the cult of an underworld deity, a belief in reincarnation, and a keen interest in astronomy. In the final chapter we will show that while the Druids tried to protect the people of Britain from the comet that appeared in A.D. 539 and the outbreak of plague that followed it with the monster-slaying Arcturus/Arthur, at the same time a descendant of the families that had ruled Salisbury Plain for so long joined forces with another Briton to establish the Kingdom of Wessex and so maintain a continuity that was only broken by the Norman Conquest in 1066. The Druids are usually interpreted as "oak-seers," but I will argue that they were in fact "doorkeepers" who, with their knowledge of the doors to the underworld and the celestial realms, ruled over the people of southern England for over a thousand years and guided them through the transition from Roman Britain to Saxon England.

In researching this book, I have drawn on the works of a large number of writers and scholars from the dawn of European literature to the present day. As far as primary sources go, I have relied on numerous classical Greek and Roman authors, from Homer and Hesiod to Julius Caesar, Pliny the Elder and Tacitus, for their insights into the Druids, the Celts and a host of other subjects. For insights into early British religion, mythology and history, I have consulted works in Latin, including Nennius's *History of the Britons* and Geoffrey of Monmouth's *History of the Kings of Britain*, and works in Welsh, including the mysterious and haunting poem *The Spoils of Annwn*, which has an early mention of Arthur, and the mythological tales of the medieval Welsh *Mabinogion*, which may provide the key to early British history as well as further information on the Druids and Arthur.

As for secondary sources, I am indebted to the work of the archeologist Barry Cunliffe, who has not only carried out excavations of important sites like the hillfort of Danebury in Hampshire, but has in all his writings tried to put a human face to the people whose dwelling-places he has excavated, and brought alive the prehistory of southern England. Another scholar whose work has contributed to this book is Miranda Green: her output on the Celts has been prodigious, and I have frequently turned to her two books on Celtic art and the role of animals in Celtic life and myth for guidance. I have also made considerable use of John Koch's *Celtic Culture: A Historical Encyclopedia*, an indispensable work for someone with an interest in the Celts.

But this book is not only about the Celts, and *The All-Knowing God*, by the Italian scholar Raffaele Pettazzoni, first published in 1955, has proved an invaluable resource in understanding the religion of the Thracians and the Thracian Horseman. Graham Anderson's *King Arthur in Antiquity* has proposed a number of Greek, Macedonian and Scythian sources for the mythology of Arthur and opened up some novel lines of research; Thomas McEvilley, in *The Shape of Ancient Thought*, has provided a plausible framework for the Druid belief in reincarnation; and both Richard Hinckley Allen (*Star Names: Their Lore and Meaning*) and F. Graham Millar ("The Celestial David and Goliath") have made me understand how the Druids and the prehistoric people of southern England may have viewed the heavens. Finally, in the Arthurian sections I have relied on the work of Frank D. Reno (*Historic Figures of the Arthurian Era*) for the historical background to Arthur, Thomas Green (*Concepts of Arthur*) for the mythological Arthur, and Barbara Yorke (*Wessex in the Early Middle Ages*) for the early history of Wessex.

Ultimately I have used all these writers and scholars very much in my own way, drawing conclusions that those among them who are still alive might well disagree with. In coming to these conclusions, I had a number of eureka moments: one when I read in Gibbon's *Decline and Fall of the Roman Empire* about the comets in the 530s and the ensuing plague, and linked that to the story of how Uther Pendragon got his name; another when I read in Cunliffe's *Iron Age Communities* that the All Cannings Cross pottery of Wiltshire could have been brought there by people from eastern France about 800 B.C.; and a third when I read in Cunliffe about the horse-and-dog burials at Danebury and discovered they might have a Druid connection. The conclusions I have drawn may well be wrong, but I have tried to provide solid evidence for them wherever that was possible, and weave all the disparate elements into a coherent narrative that tells the story of southern England from the time of Stonehenge to the founding of the kingdom of Wessex in the 6th century A.D., accounting for the Druids and the story of Arthur. At times I have resorted to etymology (the history of the origins of words) to prove a point — I have a professional interest in language — using the *Indo-European Etymological Dictionary* of the great German philologist Julius Pokorny, and Ranko Matasovic's *Etymological Lexicon of Proto-Celtic*, as well as Koch's excellent etymological notes. Sometimes when history, literature and archeology are silent on a particular point, language is the only resource we have for peering into the past. Words have a story to tell, if only we can find a way of making them talk, and I am always happy to hear any story that will unlock the secrets of the distant past. My greatest regret, as a student of language, is that, as languages have disappeared from southern England, so many stories have been lost, so many ways of understanding the world have vanished. This book has been written in an attempt to recover these lost stories, these vanished ways of viewing the world. If I have succeeded in this endeavor, then it has all been worthwhile.

Chapter 1

The Dragon Star

The Son of the Dragon Star

Around A.D. 1136 the Welsh priest Geoffrey of Monmouth published his work *Historia Regum Britanniae* (*History of the Kings of Britain*), which launched the literary career of one of Britain's most famous sons, King Arthur. Geoffrey's *History* is a rich source for the legendary history of Britain, and we will return to it frequently in the course of our investigation, but for the moment I want to focus on Arthur and his father, Uther Pendragon. According to Geoffrey,[1] Uther got his name Pendragon when "there appeared a star of wonderful magnitude and brightness, darting forth a ray, at the end of which was a globe of fire in form of a dragon, out of whose mouth issued forth two rays; one of which seemed to stretch out itself beyond the extent of Gaul, the other towards the Irish Sea, and ended in seven lesser rays." Troubled by the star, Uther ordered Merlin to be called, and Merlin explained the star in these terms: "The star, and the fiery dragon under it, signifies yourself, and the ray extending towards the Gallic coast portends that you shall have a most potent son, to whose power all those kingdoms shall be subject over which the ray reaches. But the other ray signifies a daughter, whose sons and grandsons shall successively enjoy the kingdom of Britain." When Uther became king, he remembered Merlin's explanation of the star and

> commanded two dragons to be made of gold, in likeness of the dragon which he had seen at the ray of the star. As soon as they were finished, which was done with a wonderful nicety of workmanship, he made a present of one to the cathedral church of Winchester, but reserved the other for himself, to be carried along with him to his wars. From this time, therefore, he was called Uther Pendragon, which in the British tongue signifies the dragon's head; the occasion of this appellation being Merlin's predicting, from the appearance of a dragon, that he should be king.

Geoffrey's explanation of the meaning of Pendragon is not correct — it actually means "Chief Dragon" — but it does not detract from what is a great story. But is it only a story? Edward Gibbon, in *The History of the Decline and Fall of the Roman Empire*,[2] records that in the fifth year of the reign of the Eastern Roman Emperor Justinian (A.D. 527–A.D. 565), in the month of September,

> a comet was seen during twenty days in the western quarter of the heavens, and which shot its rays into the north (A.D. 531). Eight years afterwards (A.D. 539), while the sun was in Capricorn, another comet appeared to follow in the sagittary; the size was gradually increasing; the head was in the east, the tail in the west, and it remained visible above forty days. The nations, who gazed with astonishment, expected wars and calamities from their baleful influence; and these expectations were abundantly fulfilled.

Abundantly fulfilled because in A.D. 542 an outbreak of plague reached Constantinople from Egypt — the so-called Plague of Justinian, which may have killed up to 100 million people across the world, and reduced the population of the eastern Mediterranean by a quarter.

Geoffrey's description of the "star of wonderful magnitude" sounds rather similar to Gibbon's description of the comet of A.D. 539. It is unclear whether Geoffrey would have read Procopius, the Byzantine Greek historian who wrote a history of Justinian, but we can take it that the event Geoffrey describes is genuine, and it tells us a great deal not only about Uther, but also about his son Arthur.

Geoffrey, of course, did not invent Arthur — he had been known since at least the time of *Historia Brittonum* (*History of the Britons*), a work attributed to the Welsh monk Nennius and written around A.D. 830. Arthur is mentioned twice in this work, the first time[3] in relation to a series of twelve battles against the Saxons, the second time[4] in a list of marvels or wonders. Many of the battles are in places that cannot be identified, but those that can be located range widely over the island of Britain: the site of the seventh battle, Coit Celidon, is the Caledonian Forest, which once covered the uplands of Scotland; the ninth battle was waged at the City of Legions, either Caerleon, near Newport in Wales, or Chester in Cheshire; and the twelfth battle was at Mons Badonicus (Mount Badon), thought to be somewhere in Oxfordshire or Wiltshire (see Chapter 8).

The first marvel that mentions Arthur is in a region called Buelt (Builth Wells, in Powys, eastern Wales). Nennius says there is "a mound of stones there and one stone placed above the pile with the pawprint of a dog in it. When Cabal, who was the dog of Arthur, was hunting the boar Troynt, he impressed his print in the stone, and afterwards Arthur assembled a stone mound under the stone with the print of his dog, so it is called Carn Cabal." The second wonder is in the region called Ercing (now in western Herefordshire): "A tomb is located there next to a spring called Licat Amr; and the name of the man who is buried in the tomb was called Amr. He was the son of Arthur the soldier, and Arthur himself killed and buried him in that very place. Men come to measure the grave, and find it sometimes six feet in length, sometimes nine, sometimes twelve, sometimes fifteen."

These two chapters from Nennius provide a good summary of the early Arthur, part warrior, part wonder-worker. A better picture of this early Arthur can be built up if we look at Welsh texts composed before the time of Geoffrey of Monmouth, or at least not influenced by Geoffrey's Arthur. For a fuller discussion of these texts, the reader is directed to Thomas Green's *Concepts of Arthur*, and to his excellent website http://www.arthuriana.co.uk, where much of the following information was gleaned (see in particular "A Bibliographic Guide to Welsh Arthurian Literature"). One of the earliest references to Arthur is in the *Marwnad Cynddylan* (*The Death-song of Cynddylan*), composed immediately after the death of Cynddylan, ruler of Powys, in A.D. 655. In this poem it is suggested that Cynddylan and his brothers might be seen as "whelps of great Arthur, a mighty fortress." A similar reference to Arthur is also found in *Y Gododdin*, composed sometime between A.D. 800 and A.D. 1000 to commemorate warriors who died fighting the Angles of Deira and Bernicia at a place called Catraeth in about A.D. 600: it is said that the warrior Gwawddur "fed black ravens on the rampart of a fort, although he was no Arthur."

Both of these references seem to depict Arthur as a peerless warrior, but this is only one aspect of the early Arthur. In the enigmatic poem *The Spoils of Annwn*, attributed to Taliesin and possibly composed in A.D. 800 or earlier, Arthur appears as part of a group of people, including the poet himself, making a journey to Annwn, the Welsh Otherworld (this poem will be considered in detail in Chapter 3). It is unclear what Arthur's role is in this journey — all we know is that, in the words of the mournful refrain, "except seven none rose" from Annwn.[5]

More aspects of Arthur emerge in *Pa gur yv y porthaur?* (*What man is the gatekeeper/porter?*), composed sometime between A.D. 800 and A.D. 1000. In this poem,[6] Arthur is interrogated by a gatekeeper or porter who will not let him in unless he vouches for those traveling with him. His companions include Mabon son of Modron, who figures in our discussion of the next early Arthurian work; Manawydan son of Llyr, who appears in two branches of the Welsh mythological work known as the *Mabinogion* (see Chapter 4); and Cai, better known as Sir Kay, Arthur's foster-brother and one of the first Knights of the Round Table. Cai tells us that Arthur "caused blood to flow/ In the hall of Wrnach [or Afarnach]/ Fighting with a witch"; and on "the heights of Eidyn/ He fought with champions [or dog-heads]." Arthur then informs us of Cai's exploits: when "he would drink from a horn,/ He would drink as much as four"; he "slew nine witches"; he "went to Ynys Mon/ To destroy lions"; but "Little protection did his shield offer/ Against Palug's Cat." There are also accounts of what sound like real battles, but we get the impression that Arthur and Cai did not only fight historical foes, but also were also pitted against witches and monsters.

This impression is reinforced in the last early Arthurian work we will consider, *Culhwch and Olwen*.[7] This work is thought to have been composed in the late 11th century, and is the longest of the Arthurian tales predating Geoffrey of Monmouth. The hero of the story is Culhwch — "Pig-Run," because he was born in a swine's burrow — and the story begins when Culhwch's stepmother tells him that he is destined to marry Olwen, daughter of the giant Ysbaddaden. Culhwch instantly falls in love with Olwen, and rides off to see his cousin Arthur to ask him to help him find her. We learn that Arthur's court is at Celliwig ("Forest-Grove") in Cornwall, and we are introduced to Arthur's courtiers, whom Culhwch calls on for help one by one. This list of warriors he calls on is very long and at times downright silly, as if the copyist had got bored and decided to have some fun, and includes some obscure names as well as some interesting ones. Among the interesting names are Cai, mentioned also in *Pa gur*; Bedwyr, also mentioned in *Pa gur* (the Sir Bedivere of Arthurian romances); Gwyn son of Nudd, who is usually associated with the Otherworld — his father Nudd is the Celtic god Nodons or Nodens (see Chapter 2); Gwalchmei son of Gwyar, who is the Sir Gawain of later literature; Gwenhwyvar Chief of Queens, the Guinevere of later tradition, whose name is usually translated as "White Phantom" or "White Fairy"; and Lludd Llaw Eraint ("Lludd Silver-Hand"), the god Nodons, and the Welsh equivalent of the Irish Nuada, the first king of the Tuatha De Danann ("Peoples of the Goddess Danu"), a race of people in Irish mythology, thought to represent the deities of pre–Christian Ireland.

Arthur then orders some of his warriors, including Cai and Bedwyr, to help Culhwch find the giant Ysbaddaden and his beautiful daughter, and they set off. Eventually, of course, they find Ysbaddaden, and Culhwch asks for the hand of his daughter Olwen. However, the giant is reluctant to grant Culhwch's request, since he is destined to die on the day Olwen marries. After three days he finally agrees that Culhwch and Olwen can marry — but only if Culhwch fulfills a long list of impossible-sounding tasks. The first task is carried out immediately — Cai kills the giant Gwrnach and carries off his sword — then they return to Arthur's court.

The rest of the tale is taken up by several of the tasks, most notably the hunt for the great boar Twrch Trwyth, and the preparations that must be made before this hunt can be successfully undertaken. The hunt for the great boar is impossible without the dog Drudwyn, and the only person who can hunt with Drudwyn is Mabon son of Modron, so Arthur and his men set off first to find Mabon. Mabon is the Celtic god Maponos ("Divine-Son"), and Modron is the goddess Matrona ("Divine-Mother") — see Chapter 2 for further discussion — and he is a prisoner somewhere, after being taken from his mother when he was three nights old. In order to find Mabon, Cai and Arthur's "interpreter" Gwyhyr must seek his whereabouts from a series of ever older animals: the Ousel of Cilgwri, the Stag of Redynvre, the Owl of Cwm Cawlwyd, the Eagle of Gwern Abwy, and the oldest of all, the Salmon of Llyn Llyw, who tells them that Mabon is imprisoned in the walls of Gloucester. Cai and Gwrhyr inform Arthur, who storms Gloucester with his warriors and frees Mabon.

A number of tasks are carried out before the hunt for the great boar is described, and one of these in particular stands out as significant not only to the story of Arthur, but to British and Welsh mythology in general. Ysbaddaden had asked Culhwch to get the cauldron of Diwrnach Wyddel (Diwrnach the Irishman), the steward of Odgar the son of Aedd, king of Ireland, to boil the meat for his marriage feast. To fulfill this task, Arthur sent an embassy to ask for the cauldron, but the request was refused, so he boarded his ship Prydwen and sailed to Ireland, where Bedwyr slew Diwrnach and seized the cauldron. We will return to this important cauldron in Chapters 2 and 3.

The hunt for the great boar probably has its roots in Celtic mythology and is even referred to in *Historia Brittonum*, Chapter 73, where the boar is called Troynt, and Arthur's dog, as in *Culhwch and Olwen*, is Cabal, which, curiously, means "Horse." In *Culhwch and Olwen* this hunt is a momentous event, with Arthur summoning all his warriors from "the three islands of Britain," France, Armorica, and Normandy. This mighty force then sails to

Ireland and reaches the place where the great boar is living with his seven young pigs. The battle wages for over a week, and we learn that Twrch Trwyth was once a king transformed into a boar for his sins. The battle then switches to the island of Britain — the great boar can obviously swim — and Twrch Trwyth slays a large number of Arthur's warriors, and Arthur and his men in turn kill a number of the great boar's piglets. In the end they manage to achieve their objective — to get the comb, and the razor, and the scissors, which are between the two ears of Twrch Trwyth, but the great boar escapes into the deep sea off Cornwall.

The Star Watchers

The early Welsh material on Arthur shows that he and his men were not only mighty warriors, but regularly did battle with various monsters and giants. But this book is not only about Arthur — it also investigates that mysterious priesthood called the Druids. The Druids and Arthur may seem to have little in common, but there is a link between the two: Arthur's father, according to Geoffrey of Monmouth, was a man who was inspired by a comet, and the Druids counted among their many accomplishments an interest in astronomy.

All our knowledge of the Druids comes from classical writers. Perhaps the most extensive description of them comes from Julius Caesar, in the book he wrote about his campaigns in Gaul and Britain, *Commentarii de Bello Gallico* (*Commentaries on the Gallic War*). He says of the Druids[8]:

> Throughout all Gaul there are two orders of those men who are of any rank and dignity: ... of these two orders, one is that of the Druids, the other that of the knights. The former are engaged in things sacred, conduct the public and the private sacrifices, and interpret all matters of religion. To these a large number of the young men resort for the purpose of instruction, and they [the Druids] are in great honor among them. For they determine respecting almost all controversies, public and private; and if any crime has been perpetrated, if murder has been committed, if there be any dispute about an inheritance, if any about boundaries, these same persons decide it; they decree rewards and punishments; if any one, either in a private or public capacity, has not submitted to their decision, they interdict him from the sacrifices. This among them is the most heavy punishment. Those who have been thus interdicted are esteemed in the number of the impious and the criminal: all shun them, and avoid their society and conversation, lest they receive some evil from their contact; nor is justice administered to them when seeking it, nor is any dignity bestowed on

them. Over all these Druids one presides, who possesses supreme authority among them. Upon his death, if any individual among the rest is pre-eminent in dignity, he succeeds; but, if there are many equal, the election is made by the suffrages of the Druids; sometimes they even contend for the presidency with arms. These assemble at a fixed period of the year in a consecrated place in the territories of the Carnutes, which is reckoned the central region of the whole of Gaul. Hither all, who have disputes, assemble from every part, and submit to their decrees and determinations. This institution is supposed to have been devised in Britain, and to have been brought over from it into Gaul; and now those who desire to gain a more accurate knowledge of that system generally proceed thither for the purpose of studying it.

From this we learn that the Druids functioned as judges in Gaul, that there was a supreme Druid, that there was a general assembly of Druids held in the territories of the Carnutes, who lived between the Seine and Loire in present-day France, and, most significantly, that the institution was devised in Britain, where Gauls went to study the finer points of Druidism.

Caesar continues in Chapter 14:

The Druids do not go to war, nor pay tribute together with the rest; they have an exemption from military service and a dispensation in all matters. Induced by such great advantages, many embrace this profession of their own accord, and [many] are sent to it by their parents and relations. They are said there to learn by heart a great number of verses; accordingly some remain in the course of training twenty years. Nor do they regard it lawful to commit these to writing, though in almost all other matters, in their public and private transactions, they use Greek characters. That practice they seem to me to have adopted for two reasons; because they neither desire their doctrines to be divulged among the mass of the people, nor those who learn, to devote themselves the less to the efforts of memory, relying on writing; since it generally occurs to most men, that, in their dependence on writing, they relax their diligence in learning thoroughly, and their employment of the memory. They wish to inculcate this as one of their leading tenets, that souls do not become extinct, but pass after death from one body to another, and they think that men by this tenet are in a great degree excited to valor, the fear of death being disregarded. They likewise discuss and impart to the youth many things respecting the stars and their motion, respecting the extent of the world and of our earth, respecting the nature of things, respecting the power and the majesty of the immortal gods.

Here we are told that the Druids learn by heart a great number of verses, that to become a Druid requires twenty years of training, that they believe "souls do not become extinct, but pass after death from one body to another," and that they "impart to the youth many things respecting the stars and their motion, respecting the extent of the world and of our earth, respecting the nature of things."

In Chapter 17 Caesar says:

> They worship as their divinity, Mercury in particular, and have many images of him, and regard him as the inventor of all arts, they consider him the guide of their journeys and marches, and believe him to have great influence over the acquisition of gain and mercantile transactions. Next to him they worship Apollo, and Mars, and Jupiter, and Minerva; respecting these deities they have for the most part the same belief as other nations: that Apollo averts diseases, that Minerva imparts the invention of manu-factures, that Jupiter possesses the sovereignty of the heavenly powers, that Mars presides over wars.

This is an example of what is called *interpretatio Romana*, in which Romans took the gods of conquered people and interpreted them as Roman gods. We will return to the gods Caesar mentions in Chapter 2 and throughout the book, but for the moment it will be enough to say that Mercury (the Greek Hermes) was the messenger of the gods and the god of trade, profit and commerce; Apollo was the god of light and the sun, of prophecy, archery, medicine, healing, music, poetry and the arts; Mars was the god of war; Jupiter was the king of the gods; and Minerva was the virgin god-dess of warriors, poetry, medicine, wisdom, commerce, crafts, magic, and the inventor of music.

The final piece of information that Caesar gives us is in Chapter 18: "All the Gauls assert that they are descended from the god Dis, and say that this tradition has been handed down by the Druids. For that reason they compute the divisions of every season, not by the number of days, but of nights; they keep birthdays and the beginnings of months and years in such an order that the day follows the night." Dis or Dis Pater is the Roman god of the underworld, whose functions were later taken over from Pluto or Hades, and will be explored further in Chapter 2 and in subse-quent chapters.

The next classical writer to offer observations on the Druids is the Greek historian Diodorus Siculus, who flourished in the 1st century B.C. and who, as his name indicates, was born in Sicily. In his *Historical Library*,[9] he is discussing the Gauls:

> Among [the Gauls] are also to be found lyric poets whom they call Bards. These men sing to the accompaniment of instruments which are like lyres,

and their songs may be either of praise or of obloquy. Philosophers, as we may call them, and men learned in religious affairs are unusually honoured among them and are called by them Druids. The Gauls likewise make use of diviners, accounting them worthy of high approbation, and these men foretell the future by means of the flight or cries of birds and of the slaughter of sacred animals, and they have all the multitude subservient to them. They also observe a custom which is especially astonishing and incredible, in case they are taking thought with respect to matters of great concern; for in such cases they devote to death a human being and plunge a dagger into him in the region above the diaphragm, and when the stricken victim has fallen they read the future from the manner of his fall and from the twitching of his limbs, as well as from the gushing of the blood, having learned to place confidence in an ancient and long-continued practice of observing such matters. And it is a custom of theirs that no one should perform a sacrifice without a "philosopher"; for thank-offerings should be rendered to the gods, they say, by the hands of men who are experienced in the nature of the divine, and who speak, as it were, the language of the gods, and it is also through the mediation of such men, they think, that blessings likewise should be sought. Nor is it only in the exigencies of peace, but in their wars as well, that they obey, before all others, these men and their chanting poets, and such obedience is observed not only by their friends but also by their enemies; many times, for instance, when two armies approach each other in battle with swords drawn and spears thrust forward, these men step forth between them and cause them to cease, as though having cast a spell over certain kinds of wild beasts.

From this we learn that there are lyric poets in Gaul called "bards," as well as philosophers called "Druids." The Gauls, he says, also make use of diviners, and practice human sacrifice (Caesar also mentions this), but cannot carry out any sacrifices unless a Druid is present. He also claims that if a Druid steps between two warring armies, the armies will immediately cease hostilities.

Another Greek historian who touches on the Druids is Strabo (64 B.C.–A.D. 24). In his *Geography*,[10] Strabo writes:

Among all the Gallic peoples, generally speaking, there are three sets of men who are held in exceptional honour; the Bards, the Vates and the Druids. The Bards are singers and poets; the Vates, diviners and natural philosophers; while the Druids, in addition to natural philosophy, study also moral philosophy. The Druids are considered the most just of men, and on this account they are entrusted with the decision, not only of the private disputes, but of the public disputes as well; so that, in former times, they even arbitrated cases of war and made the opponents stop when they were about to line up for battle, and the murder cases, in particular, had been turned over to them for decision. Further, when there is a big yield from these cases, there is forthcoming a big yield from the land too, as they think. However, not only the Druids, but others as well, say that men's souls, and also the universe, are indestructible, although both fire and water will at some time or other prevail over them.

What Strabo tells us is not very different from the information provided by Caesar and Diodorus Siculus, except that we learn from Strabo that the "diviners" of Diodorus Siculus are called "Vates."

Two early Christian writers also have something to say about the Druids. Hippolytus of Rome (c. A.D. 170–c. A.D. 236), who was one of the most prolific writers of the early Church, wrote of the Druids[11]: "The Keltic Druids apply themselves thoroughly to the Pythagorean philosophy, being urged to this pursuit by Zamolxis, the slave of Pythagoras, a Thracian by birth, who came to these parts after the death of Pythagoras, and gave them the opportunity of studying the system." Hippolytus may have linked the Druids to the Greek philosopher Pythagoras (c. 570 B.C.–c. 495 B.C.) because, like the Druids, Pythagoras and his followers believed in reincarnation. Zamolxis, said by Hippolytus to be the slave of Pythagoras, was actually a god of the Getae, or Thracian Dacians, tribes that occupied regions south and north of the lower Danube.

Clement of Alexandria (c. A.D. 150–A.D. 215) was a Christian theologian who does not mention the Druids directly, but has some interesting points to make[12]: "Alexander, in his book *On the Pythagorean Symbols*, relates that Pythagoras was a pupil of Nazaratus the Assyrian..., and will have it that, in addition to these, Pythagoras was a hearer of the Galatae and the Brahmins." The Alexander that Clement is referring to is Alexander Polyhistor (c. 100 B.C.–c. 40 B.C.), who wrote a large number of ethnogeographic and philosophical works. Nazaratus the Assyrian may be Zoroaster, the ancient Iranian prophet who founded the religion known as Zoroastrianism, and the Galatae or Galatians are a Celtic tribe who settled in Anatolia (now Turkey) around 270 B.C. Although Clement does not mention the Druids, he does refer to Pythagoras, linked by Hippolytus to the Druids, and claims in addition that Pythagoras was inspired by Zoroaster, the Celtic Galatians and the Brahmins, the priestly caste of India.

Another intriguing snippet of information comes to us from Pomponius Mela, who wrote *De situ orbis* (*Description of the world*) in around A.D. 43. In one passage in Book 3.2.18–19, quoted by John Koch,[13] Pomponius writes: "[The Druids] claim to know the size of the earth and cosmos, the movements of the heavens and stars, and the will of the gods.

They teach, in caves or hidden groves, many things to the nobles in a course of instruction lasting up to twenty years." Most of this is repeating what Caesar had written a century earlier, but the claim that they carried out their teaching "in caves or hidden groves" is new.

More about the practices of the Druids can be found in the *Natural History* of Pliny the Elder (A.D. 23–A.D. 79)[14]:

> I must not omit the veneration shown to mistletoe by the provinces of Gaul. The Druids (the name they give to their priestly caste) hold nothing more sacred than mistletoe and the tree on which it grows, provided it is a hard-oak. They also choose groves of hard-oak for its own quality, nor do they perform any sacred rites without leaves from these trees, so that from this practice they are called Druids after the Greek word for oak. For they believe that anything growing on oak trees is sent by heaven and is a sign that the tree has been chosen by God himself.
>
> Mistletoe, however, is rarely found on hard-oaks, but when it is discovered, it is collected with great respect on the sixth day of the moon. Then, greeting the moon with a phrase that in their own language means "healing all things," the Druids with due religious observance prepare a sacrifice and a banquet beneath a tree, and bring two white bulls whose horns are bound for the first time.
>
> A priest in a white robe climbs the tree and with a golden sickle cuts the mistletoe, which is caught in a white cloak. Then they sacrifice the victims praying that God may make his gift propitious for those to whom he has given it. They think that mistletoe given in a drink renders any barren animal fertile and is an antidote for all poisons.

Further Druid practices in the gathering of medicinal plants are revealed by Pliny when he is discussing *selago*, also known as *lycopodium* ("wolf's foot") or fir club moss[15]:

> Similar to savin is the herb known as "selago." Care is taken to gather it without the use of iron, the right hand being passed for the purpose through the left sleeve of the tunic, as though the gatherer were in the act of committing a theft. The clothing must be white, the feet bare and washed clean, and a sacrifice of bread and wine must be made before gathering it: it is carried also in a new napkin. The Druids of Gaul have pretended that this plant should be carried about the person as a preservative against accidents of all kinds, and that the smoke of it is extremely good for all maladies of the eyes.

The Druids' veneration of oak-trees and mistletoe is by now well known, but several other points are less well known and worth mentioning. Pliny tells us that the Druids will not perform any sacred rites "without leaves from these trees"; they collect the mistletoe "on the sixth day of the moon";

they cut the mistletoe with a "golden sickle"; they sacrifice two white bulls after gathering the mistletoe; and they gather selago "without the use of iron."

The reports of all these classical writers seem to raise more questions than they answer, and the last writer to be considered is no different. The late 4th-century Roman historian Ammianus Marcellinus, in his *Roman History*, gives us this very curious history of the Gauls[16]:

> The ancient writers, in doubt as to the earliest origin of the Gauls, have left an incomplete account of the matter, but later Timagenes, a true Greek in accuracy as well as language, collected out of various books these facts that had been long forgotten; which, following his authority, and avoiding any obscurity, I shall state clearly and plainly. Some asserted that the people first seen in these regions were Aborigines, called Celts from the name of a beloved king, and Galatae (for so the Greek language terms the Gauls) from the name of his mother. Others state that the Dorians, following the earlier Hercules, settled in the lands bordering on the Ocean. The Drysidae [i.e. Druids] say that a part of the people was in fact indigenous, but that others also poured in from the remote islands and the regions across the Rhine, driven from their homes by continual wars and by the inundation of the stormy sea. Some assert that after the destruction of Troy a few of those who fled from the Greeks and were scattered everywhere occupied those regions, which were then deserted. But the inhabitants of those countries affirm this beyond all else, and I have also read it inscribed upon their monuments, that Hercules, the son of Amphitryon, hastened to destroy the cruel tyrants Geryon and Tauriscus, of whom one oppressed Spain, the other, Gaul; and having overcome them both that he took to wife some high-born women and begat numerous children, who called by their own names the districts which they ruled.

Timagenes was a Greek historian who flourished in the 1st century B.C., and wrote a *History of Alexander* and a *History of the Gauls*, now lost; Hercules or Heracles is the Greek demi-god and hero; the Dorians are one of the three tribes of ancient Greece; Amphitryon was the apparent father of Heracles (his real father was in fact Zeus, the king of the gods); and Geryon was a fearsome giant who lived at the western end of the Mediterranean, whose cattle Hercules had to steal in his Tenth Labor.

There are several intriguing details here. Ammianus was apparently getting some of his history from the much earlier Timagenes, so there may be something in what he says. He tells us that the first inhabitants of Gaul were Celts, though some assert that Dorians may also have settled there; the Druids, he says, claim that part of the people were indigenous, but others came from "remote islands" (possibly Britain or even Ireland), and from "the regions across the Rhine" (that is, from what the Romans called Germania); some of the inhabitants may be descendants of those who fled the destruction of Troy; and finally, he claims that some Gauls may be descended from Hercules, who married a Gaulish noblewoman and fathered a number of children by her. Ammianus seems to support Caesar's contention that the Druids originated in Britain, and also suggests a connection between Gaul and Troy. This last suggestion, which mirrors the Roman claim that Rome was founded by descendants of the Trojan hero Aeneas, will be further addressed in Chapter 5 and beyond when we come to look at the prehistory of southern England.

"Caves and Hidden Groves"

Pomponius Mela told us that the Druids carried out their instruction in caves and hidden groves, and this seems to reflect the content of their teachings: a cave sounds like an ideal place to be initiated into the mysteries of the underworld god that Caesar called Dis Pater, and a hidden grove would have been a good place to study the natural world, including the collection and use of plants like mistletoe and selago, and to learn about the "movements of the heavens and stars." In this book I will be attempting not only to discover what some of these teachings might have been, but also to discover where the Druids came from, and what this can tell us about Arthur. I hope to show that the comet that gave Uther Pendragon his name also gave us Arthur, and that Arthur was one of the last gifts that the Druids gave to the British people. One of the last because I will demonstrate that the greatest of the Anglo-Saxon kingdoms may have been founded by the British, and that England itself may therefore be a legacy of this mysterious priesthood.

Chapter 2

The Severed Head and the Bone Cave

Religion in Roman Britain

The Conquest of Britain and the Shape of Roman Britain

The Romans invaded and occupied Britain in A.D. 43, and Britain remained part of the Roman Empire until around A.D. 410, when the Roman legions withdrew from the island. The invasion of A.D. 43 was not the first Roman contact with Britain: Julius Caesar had twice led his forces to the island in 55 B.C. and 54 B.C., as part of his Gallic wars. Caesar believed that Britons were supporting the campaigns of the Gauls against him, and that Belgae from Gaul were fleeing to Belgic settlements in Britain (the Belgae were probably Germanic tribes ruled by a Celtic elite and living in what is today northern France, Belgium, Luxembourg and Germany west of the Rhine). So Caesar may have wished to cut off this support; if so, the first invasion of 55 B.C. was unsuccessful, since the Roman forces gained a beachhead on the Kent coast, but achieved little else.

The second invasion of 54 B.C. was more successful. Caesar was accompanied by Mandubracius, the king of the Trinovantes, a tribe inhabiting what is now Essex and Suffolk; Mandubracius had sought Caesar's help after his father had been deposed by the British chief Cassivellaunus. Caesar marched inland from Kent, crossed the Thames, possibly at Westminster, and besieged Cassivellaunus at his hillfort in Hertfordshire. Mandubracius was restored to power, and Cassivellaunus surrendered, agreeing to pay an annual tribute to Rome. And both Cassivellaunus and even Mandubracius entered into British and Welsh legendary history, as we will see later in our discussion of the *Mabinogion*.

Caesar left no troops in Britain, and it was not until A.D. 43 that the

Romans set about occupying the island. The invasion was met with resistance from Togodumnus and Caratacus, sons of the late king of the Catuvellauni, Cunobelinus. (The Catuvellauni inhabited the modern counties of Hertfordshire, Bedfordshire and south Cambridgeshire, and were probably the tribe to which Cassivellaunus belonged.) The Catuvellauni were defeated in two battles on the rivers Medway and Thames, but Caratacus survived and continued to resist the Romans. He joined two tribes in east Wales called the Silures and Ordovices, and they were defeated in A.D. 51 by the Roman governor Publius Ostorius Scapula. Members of his family were captured, but Caratacus managed to escape. He fled north to the Brigantes, but their queen Cartimandua was loyal to the Romans and handed him over in chains.

The Silures continued to resist the Roman occupation, and were not finally conquered until about A.D. 76. Meanwhile, the Druids make their first appearance in British history. The Romans obviously considered them a threat, since in A.D. 60 Gaius Suetonius Paulinus destroyed the Druid center at Mona, now known as Anglesey, in north Wales. The confrontation between the Romans and Druids is famously described by the Roman historian Tacitus (c. A.D. 56–c. A.D. 117) in his *Annals*[1]:

> On the shore stood the opposing army with its dense array of armed warriors, while between the ranks dashed women, in black attire like the Furies, with hair disheveled, waving brands. All around, the Druids, lifting up their hands to heaven, and pouring forth dreadful imprecations, scared our soldiers by the unfamiliar sight, so that, as if their limbs were paralyzed, they stood motionless, and exposed to wounds. Then urged by their general's appeals and mutual encouragements not to quail before a troop of frenzied women, they bore the standards onwards, smote down all resistance, and wrapped the foe in the flames of his own brands. A force was next set over the conquered, and their groves, devoted to inhuman superstitions, were destroyed. They deemed it indeed a duty to cover their altars with the blood of captives and to consult their deities through human entrails.

However, Gaius Suetonius Paulinus was unable to consolidate his conquests in Wales, because he had to deal with the uprising led by Boudica, also known as Boadicea. She was queen of the Iceni tribe of what is now Norfolk, the wife of Prasutagus, an Icenian king who had ruled as a nominally independent ally of Rome. When he died, he left his kingdom jointly to his daughters and the Roman Empire, but his will was ignored: the kingdom was annexed as if conquered, Boudica was flogged and her daughters raped. The uprising that followed is described by Tacitus in his

Annals, and also by another Roman historian Cassius Dio (c. A.D. 160–c. A.D. 230) in his *Roman History.* According to Cassius Dio,[2] before joining battle, Boudica made a stirring speech to her assembled troops: "When she had finished speaking, she employed a species of divination, letting a hare escape from the fold of her dress; and since it ran on what they considered the auspicious side, the whole multitude shouted with pleasure, and Boudica, raising her hand toward heaven, said: 'I thank thee, Andraste, and call upon thee as woman speaking to woman.'" This must be one of the earliest references to British religious practice, and has Boudica calling on Andraste, the Icenian goddess of victory, who may be related to Andarta, a warrior goddess worshipped in southern Gaul.

These troops included the Iceni and the Trinovantes, and they destroyed Camulodunum (Colchester in Essex), formerly the capital of the Trinovantes, but by then a *colonia* (a settlement for discharged Roman soldiers) and the site of a temple to the former emperor Claudius, and routed a Roman legion sent to relieve the settlement. On hearing news of the revolt, Suetonius hurried to Londinium (London) and, concluding he did not have the numbers to defend it, evacuated and abandoned it. It was burnt to the ground, as was Verulamium (St. Albans in Hertfordshire). It is thought that between 70,000 and 80,000 people were killed in Camulodunum, Londinium and Verulamium. Suetonius, meanwhile, regrouped his forces in the West Midlands, and despite being heavily outnumbered, defeated Boudica in the Battle of Watling Street, somewhere between Londinium and Viroconium (Wroxeter in Shropshire). According to Tacitus, Boudica poisoned herself, while Cassius Dio says she fell sick and died, and was given a lavish burial.

The destruction of the Druid groves at Mona and the suppression of Boudica's revolt was of course not the end of the Roman conquest of Britain. The Romans pushed north and attempted to bring Scotland into the Empire, but never succeeded, and the northern border of the Empire became Hadrian's Wall, begun in A.D. 122 well short of the Scottish border. But what did Roman Britain look like? In order to understand religion in Roman Britain, we need to know a little of how Britain was organized and administered.

In general Britain was organized along tribal lines, taking the tribes, as the Romans found them or perceived them, as the basic administrative units. The following table gives the tribes of Britain in Roman times, together with the territory they occupied and the name of the Roman capital and any other town in the territory, going from south to north.

Tribe	Territory	Capital and Other Towns
Dumnonii	Devon and Cornwall	Isca Dumnoniorum (Exeter in Devon)
Durotriges	Dorset, south Wiltshire, south Somerset	Durnovaria (Dorchester in Dorset); Lindinis (Ilchester in Somerset)
Belgae	Southern Hampshire	Venta Belgarum (Winchester in southern Hampshire); Magnus Portus (Portsmouth); Sorviodunum (Old Sarum)
Atrebates	Northern Hampshire, Surrey	Calleva Atrebatum (Silchester in northern Hampshire); Cunetio (Mildenhall)
Regnenses	West Sussex	Noviomagus Reginorum (Chichester)
Cantiaci	Kent	Durovernum Cantiacorum (Canterbury)
Catuvellauni	Hertfordshire, Bedfordshire, Buckinghamshire, Oxfordshire	Verulamium (St. Albans in Hertfordshire); Durocina (Dorchester-on-Thames)
Trinovantes	Essex and Suffolk	Camulodunum (Colchester in Essex)
Iceni	Norfolk	Venta Icenorum (Caister Saint Edmunds in Norfolk)
Dobunni	Gloucestershire, north Somerset	Corinium Dubonnorum (Cirencester in Gloucestershire); Aquae Sulis (Bath); Glevum (Gloucester)
Silures	Monmouthshire, Breconshire, Glamorganshire	Venta Silurum (Caerwent in Monmouthshire); Isca Silurum (Caerleon, north of Newport)
Demetae	Pembrokeshire, Carmarthenshire	Moridunum (Carmarthen); Luentinum (Dolocauthi Gold Mines)
Cornovii	Staffordshire, Shropshire, Cheshire	Viroconium Cornoviorum (Wroxeter in Shropshire); Deva Victrix (Chester)
Corieltauvi	East Midlands	Ratae Corieltauvorum (Leicester); Lindum Colonia (Lincoln)
Brigantes	North of England, Midlands	Eboracum (York)
Parisii	East Yorkshire	Petuaria (Brough)
Carvetii	Cumbria, north Lancashire	Luguvalium (Carlisle)

Religion in Southern Britain: Temples

There are a number of ways we can investigate religion in Roman Britain: we can look at the archeological remains of Romano-British temples; we can explore sacred spaces other than temples; and we can draw on the evidence provided by religious images. For reasons which will become apparent in the course of this book, we will restrict this examination largely to southern Britain, more specifically to an area stretching from Gloucestershire in the north through Wiltshire and Somerset to Dorset in the south, focusing on temples, sacred spaces and religious images that help to give us a coherent picture of religion in this important area of Britain. To start with, I'll be concentrating on six important temples in our target area.

Uley, Gloucestershire

The first Romano-British temple I want to look at is the temple at Uley in Gloucestershire, in the territory of the Dobunni (see Maps 1 and 2). Uley now is a small village situated in a wooded valley in the Cotswold escarpment, but in Roman times the settlement and temple were on West Hill, above the modern village of Uley to the south and overlooking the Severn Valley to the west. The nearest towns to Uley were the *colonia* of Glevum 12 miles to the north, and the tribal capital Corinium 16 miles to the east. To the southeast the Fosse Way (the Roman road from Exeter to Lincoln) connected Bath and Cirencester, while the road running southwest from Gloucester passed along the Severn Valley below West Hill. According to Oxford University's Centre for the Study of Ancient Documents (CSAD)[3]—which specializes in the study of curse tablets, which were found in large numbers at Uley—the site was a center of worship before Roman times. In "Uley: History," the CSAD website says:

> Beneath the Roman temple are the remains of an earlier shrine, a square timber structure in a subrectangular ditched enclosure, constructed in the half century preceding the Roman conquest.... A temple was constructed in stone in the early second century A.D., [and] continued to be maintained and modified for almost three hundred years.... An aisled timber building with a semicircular annex was erected on the site of the temple during the fifth century and was rebuilt in stone in the early sixth century. These structures have been interpreted as a church and baptistery, but the form and parallels of the buildings are uncertain. Carefully buried outside the annex was the head of the cult statue of Mercury from the temple, which must have been curated for at least a century after the collapse of the building.

The god that Mercury represented must have been very important to the Dobunni for Christians to have kept the head of a pagan deity (see Figure 1).

Map 1: Some important Roman towns and settlements in southern England, showing the modern counties of Wiltshire, Hampshire, Somerset, Dorset, Gloucestershire and Oxfordshire.

The CSAD website notes ("Uley: deity") that the votive deposits (sacrifices) associated with the pre–Roman sanctuary

> give some clue to the character of the pre–Roman deity. The presence of weapons suggests a martial aspect. In the Roman period the identity of this local god ... seems to have been assimilated with the Roman deity Mercury. Mercury is named on curses, stone altars and metal plaques and represented in statues and figurines. The major cult statue probably stood within the *cella* (inner chamber of the temple). The god was nude and slightly larger than life-size, accompanied by a ram and cockerel at his feet.

We do not know the name of the god worshipped at Uley before the Romans came, but the Roman god Mercury is widely believed to be the equivalent of the Celtic god Lugus. Alexei Kondratiev[4] discusses the evidence we have for Lugus and his Roman counterpart Mercury, starting with place-names. The name *Lugudunon*, says Kondratiev,

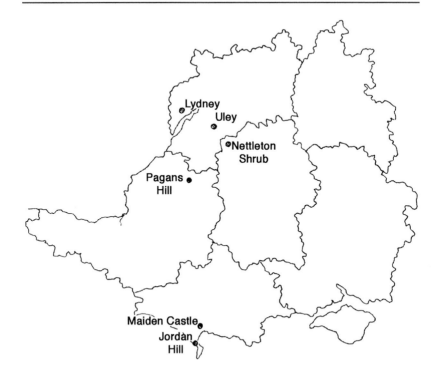

Map 2: Some important Roman temples in southern England, showing modern counties of Wiltshire, Hampshire, Somerset, Dorset and Gloucestershire.

was given to a very large number of sites (Lyons, Loudun, Laon, Liegnitz, probably Leiden, etc.) from the later Iron Age. In Old Celtic *dunon* means "fort" (the word has modern cognates in Irish *dún* "fort" and Welsh *din[as]* "city"), but the *Lugu-* element can only be explained by a proper name. We have no dedications to a god by that name at those sites, but a famous dedication to the *Lugoues* by the shoemakers' guild of Uxama (Osma) in Spain; another inscription mentioning the *Lugoues* from Avenches in Switzerland; and dedications to *Lugubus Arquienobus* from Orense and Lugo in Galicia (northwest Spain) all indicate that the name Lugus was indeed known. Interestingly, in all these cases the name is given in the plural, as though it referred to a group of divinities rather than to a single god.

As we saw in Chapter 1, Julius Caesar in his *Commentaries on the Gallic War*, Book 6, Chapter 17, said that the Gauls "worship as their divinity, Mercury in particular, and have many images of him, and regard him as the inventor of all arts, they consider him the guide of their journeys and marches, and believe him to have great influence over the acquisition

of gain and mercantile transactions."
This may explain why there are so few
dedications to Lugus in Roman times,
but so many to Mercury throughout the
Romanized Celtic world: well over 400
dedications to "Mercury" or one of his
common native titles have been found.
His importance in Gaul and Britain far
exceeded anything that the role of Mercury in Roman religion could have war-
ranted.

Representations of "Mercury," like
the one at Uley, often depict him with
his usual classical attributes, but as Kondratiev points out, he also has four traits
which are peculiar to the Celtic world.
He is linked with high places (for example, the Arverni, from the Auvergne
region of France, had a gigantic statue
of "Mercury" seated atop their sacred

Figure 1: Head of the statue of
Mercury from the Roman tem-
ple at Uley in Gloucestershire.
British Museum.

mountain, the Puy-de-Dôme); he is often represented with three heads;
he is often linked to the antlered god called Cernunnos, of whom more
later; and in the Belgic lands, particularly the Rhineland, "Mercury" is
armed with a spear and accompanied by his consort Rosmerta, "The Great
Provider," a goddess of fertility, who will be discussed later in this chapter.
Kondratiev believes that in these specific representations "Mercury" and
Rosmerta

> are particularly linked to the concept of sovereignty. In Iron Age society
> the cohesion of a group around a chieftain was secured and given a sacred
> recognition by the means of a communal feast, in which a ritual drink
> served by the goddess of the land (a role played by a priestess or by the
> chieftain's consort) was shared, binding all the participants to their land,
> their ruler, and each other. Rosmerta was the divine keeper of the drink of
> sovereignty, while the spear-wielding "Mercury" was the archetype of all
> rulers, the Otherworldly protector of the earthly king.

The origin of the name Lugus is much debated. It was earlier thought
to derive from the Indo-European root *leuk-* "light," which gives Latin
lux and English *light*, but as Kondratiev points out, it may well be derived
from the Indo-European root *leugh-* or *lugh* "oath," which give Old *Irish*

lu(i)ge and Welsh *llw*. In support of this, he cites the famous Gaulish text found at Chamalières in 1971. This text, which is "the script of a magico-religious ritual for obtaining the help of Arvernian Maponos in a military revolt, concludes with the thrice-repeated formula '*Luge dessumiis* [= *dexumiis*]' ('By an oath I make them ready'), where the echo of the god's name in the expression *luge* could hardly have failed to impress itself on a Celtic-speaker's ear."

Lydney Park, Gloucestershire

The second temple I want to consider is the temple at Lydney Park in Gloucestershire, built within the ramparts of an old hillfort, and close to Iron Age and Roman iron mines. It was close to the main Roman road that ran from Gloucester (Glevum), 18 miles to the east, to the legionary fortress of Caerleon and to Venta Silurum (Caerwent), the capital of the Silures, 12 miles to the southwest.

The temple is generally thought to have been built some time after A.D. 364, and is dedicated to the god Nodens or Nodons, who gave rise to the mythological characters Gwyn son of Nudd and Llud Llaw Eraint that we saw in our earlier discussion of *Culhwch and Olwen*. The website of the Centre for the Study of Ancient Documents (CSAD) confirms ("Lydney: deity and cult") that

> the presiding deity at Lydney is named as Nodens on the single curse tablet from the site, and on two other metal plaques from the site as M(ars) Nodons and Nudens Mars. The god is also referred to in an abbreviated form (MN) on a mosaic. The name "Nodens" is Celtic and its etymology may suggest a possible association with catching or trapping. The god is perhaps also associated with the river Severn and its tidal bore. Nodens is only otherwise attested on two statuettes found near Lancaster.
>   Amongst the votive objects found at the site are dog figurines, some highly schematic, one amongst the most accomplished pieces of bronze sculpture from Roman Britain.

CSAD hypothesizes that the dog figurines (see Figure 2) may be related to hunting, or be associated with healing — though as we'll see in this chapter, dogs can also be associated with the underworld — and notes: "A curative role for the temple might also explain the presence of two possible offerings to the god, the bone representation of a woman and a hollow bronze arm. The discovery of an oculist's stamp (to be stamped into cakes of eye medicine) also suggests the presence of a healer."

Nettleton Shrub, Wiltshire

This Romano-British temple is in the northwest corner of Wiltshire, 10 miles northeast of Aquae Sulis (Bath), to the west of the Fosse Way which ran from Corinium (Cirencester) to Aquae Sulis, Lindinis (Ilchester) and Isca Dumnoniorum (Exeter). Three temples have been discovered at Nettleton, dating from around A.D. 69 to around A.D. 360. There is a rectangular temple (Nettleton 1), 63 ft. by 21 ft., "aligned roughly north-south with its rear built into the valley side. Finds from this site included a small bronze candlestick in the form of a cockerel; fragments of stone slabs bearing sculpted reliefs, smaller than life-size, depicting scenes [interpreted as Diana and Hound and Mercury and Rosmerta]; and glassware, samian and coarse pottery and many bronze coins dating from Hadrianic times to the late-4th century."[5]

Then there is an octagonal temple (Nettleton 3) "built on the site of an earlier, possibly pre–Roman, circular temple (Nettleton 2). The two successive temples or shrines were enclosed within a walled precinct or *temenos*. Several construction phases have been identified," including a 2nd-century circular shrine, a 3rd-century octagonal stone podium, and the 4th-century octagonal temple.[6]

From an altarstone it appears that the temple was dedicated to Apollo Cunomaglus ("Apollo the Hound-Lord"), though at one point in the 4th century alternate chambers were blocked and the plan of the building took on a cruciform aspect, implying that it was used as a church, before reverting to pagan worship.[7] These changes of use reflect the history of 4th-century Rome: Christianity became the official religion of Rome under Constantine around A.D. 313, then paganism was briefly restored when Julian became Emperor in A.D. 355. And all this was happening just at the time when Roman control over Britain was beginning to weaken, as shown by the rise of Magnus Maximus, the Iberian general who was proclaimed Western Roman Emperor by British troops in A.D. 383, and who ruled over

Figure 2: Bronze statuette of a dog, said to be an Irish wolfhound, from the Roman temple at Lydney Park in Gloucestershire.

Gaul, Britain and Spain until A.D. 388, when he was executed at the command of the Roman Senate.

But who was Cunomaglus? He is not known outside this Wiltshire shrine, but the pairing with Apollo and the link to Diana suggest that he was a god of hunting and healing, while the presence of a possible Mercury and Rosmerta relief suggests a link to Lugus.

Pagans Hill, Somerset

This temple is in north Somerset, near the present-day village of Chew Stoke, on a promontory overlooking the River Chew. According to the CSAD website ("Pagans Hill: History and Buildings"), "the coins recovered during the excavation suggest that the temple complex was built in the later third century A.D.... Occupation continued throughout the fourth century, with a possible interruption in the middle of the century, and perhaps ceased in the early fifth century, the latest datable coin being of the emperor Arcadius (A.D. 383–408)." It is not clear what deity was worshipped at the temple. The CSAD website ("Pagans Hill: deity and cult") says that a clue comes from

> four sculptural fragments, parts of the torso of a seated dog with a jewelled collar perhaps originally c. 0.8m in height. Believed at the time of excavation to date to the 15th or 16th centuries, re-evaluation suggests a Roman date. Dogs are sometimes associated with the god Apollo in healing cults across the Roman world, being perhaps suitable spirit guides to those in the grip of a healing trance.

As the CSAD website points out, the temple at Pagans Hill was octagonal, like the one at Nettleton Shrub, and since the cult at Pagans Hill seems to have been linked to dogs, it is tempting to speculate that Cunomaglus was worshipped at both sites.

Maiden Castle, Dorset

Maiden Castle is an Iron Age hillfort one and a half miles south of Durnovaria (Dorchester) in the territory of the Durotriges. A temple complex was built on the hill in the late 4th century A.D., nearly two hundred years after the hillfort was abandoned. The English Heritage website devoted to Maiden Castle says that the temple "consisted of a central room, surrounded by a passage called an ambulatory, with a portico open to the weather. Close to the temple was an oval hut, thought to have functioned as a shrine. This was built directly over an Iron Age hut, and may show continued use of an earlier ritual building. A two-roomed building adjacent to the temple is believed to have been a priest's house."

Perhaps the most interesting find at this temple site was the statue of a three-horned bull which the excavator, Sir Mortimer Wheeler, named as Tarvos Trigaranus. Tarvos Trigaranus, the "Bull with Three Cranes," is best known from the bas-relief called the Pillar of the Boatmen, which once stood in a temple in Lutetia (modern Paris). The bas-relief shows the bull with three cranes perched on his back, standing under a tree. On an adjacent panel, the Gaulish god Esus is shown cutting down a tree (possibly a willow) with an axe. A similar representation, this time with no inscription, is found on a pillar from Trier in Germany where a man with an axe cuts down a tree in which are sitting three birds and a bull's head. Anne Ross, in *Pagan Celtic Britain*, as quoted by David Blamires,[8] says that there are several tales and traditions both in Scotland and in Ireland of the transformation of women, especially those of a parsimonious nature, into cranes. Ross suggests that since the crane (or heron) is a metamorphosis undergone or adopted only by women, the three cranes of Tarvos Trigaranus might be "especially concerned with otherworld goddesses, being both the form and symbol taken by them."

Jordan Hill, Dorset

This temple is 8 miles south of Durnovaria (Dorchester), in the territory of the Durotriges, and was probably built in the 4th century, on a hill overlooking Weymouth Bay. However, according to the Visit Weymouth website, "finds such as animal bones and bull horns suggest the site had also been used during Iron Age times." Only the temple foundations and the base of the walls remain, which are over 3 feet thick and enclose an area of less than 265 square feet. This site is interesting for a find in the southeast corner of the structure — a shaft around 12 feet deep "containing 2 urns, a spearhead and a sword in a stone cist at its base. Above this cist were deposited 16 layers of ash and charcoal, each containing the remains of a bird along with a coin and separated from the next layer with roofing slabs." Some sources say the birds included buzzard, raven, starling and crow, but Green[9] says they were all ravens.

As Kondratiev shows, Lugus was connected in some way with ravens. In the text *De Fluviis*, attributed to the Greek historian Plutarch (c. A.D. 46–A.D. 120), the writer gives us some information about Lugdunum (Lyons, the "Fort of Lugus"). We are told that at the time of the founding of the city certain ravens flew down from the sky, and were interpreted as a good omen. These were not ordinary ravens, but had some white feathers in their plumage; and they became the focus of a prophetic shrine where, after an inquirer had made an offering of food on an elevated platform, a priest would divine the answer to his query from the behaviour of the ravens as they went after the food. The main role of these ravens was therefore ... one of Otherworldly contact, which was made possible by their unusual appearance: although they were traditional examples of blackness, they nevertheless contained their opposite (whiteness) within themselves, and could thus offer passage between seemingly opposed realms, even as Lugus/"Mercury" facilitates such passages. Representations of the unnamed *genius loci* of Lugdunum (almost certainly Lugus himself, since he has typical "Mercury" attributes) show him accompanied by ravens.

Religion in Southern Britain: Other Sacred Spaces

Alveston Cave, Gloucestershire

The first sacred space I want to look at is a cave near Alveston, a village in South Gloucestershire, a mile south of Thornbury and 13 miles north of Bristol, not far from the Severn Estuary and from the Lydney Park temple, and therefore in the territory of the Dobunni (see Map 3). Bones were discovered in the cave in 1998, and in 2001 the archeology program *Time Team* carried out an investigation there.[10] The *Time Team* website explains the finds: "The cavers' finds included a large number of bones: animal, including many dog bones, and human, including a skull and femur. These were to be added to by similar bones unearthed during *Time Team*'s excavation. Some showed the distinctive signs of having been butchered at around the time of death. Others showed clear signs of the people they belonged to having been suddenly and violently killed."

During their investigation of the cave, the *Time Team* archeologists "came to the conclusion that these people from around two millennia ago had indeed met sudden deaths and had indeed then been butchered and eaten. With radiocarbon dating of the bones from the cave suggesting that they were all buried around 2,000 years ago, at the very end of the Iron Age or beginning of the Roman occupation, *Time Team* was looking at evidence for the most recent case of cannibalism yet found in Britain by archaeologists." As the *Time Team* website goes on to point out, clues as to why these bones were placed in the cave came from the other finds.

These included numerous dog bones, as well as the occasional cattle bone, a possible vertebra of a bear and wooden twigs. Mark Horton said: "This was a highly structured deposit that can only have got there as a result of some form of ritual activity. This region was an important centre for underworld cults during the later Iron Age, some of which survived into the Roman period — in particular the Celtic Hound God, Cunomaglus, was represented as a dog guarding the underworld in local temple sculpture."

It seems from this that Cunomaglus was associated with an underworld cult which, in the Iron Age at least, may have included human sacrifice and even cannibalism.

Other Ritual Shafts

Mark Horton refers to an "underworld cult" in the Gloucestershire region, and it is worth pausing to ask what he means by that. As the finds at Jordan Hill show, ritual shafts were obviously important in Roman times, but in fact they have a long history in southern Britain. As Jodie Lewis says,[11] at Wilsford Shaft, Normanton Down, near Stonehenge, "a monument previously interpreted as a simple pond barrow was found to cover an artificial shaft, 100 feet deep and 6 feet in diameter. A range of deposits were recovered, the earliest being Bronze Age in date, comprising a shale ring, amber beads and bone pins, along with animal bone and organic materials." The Wiltshire Council website says[12] that Wilsford Shaft could have been constructed as early as 2300 B.C., and quantities of "wooden tubs, bowls, scoops, amber beads, bone pins, thong and rope, and pottery of Deverell-Rimbury affinity" were found there, with a date of around 1450 B.C.

Ashbee, who excavated the shaft, argued (says Lewis) that the ring, beads and pins should be interpreted as votive deposits, of a type similar to those found as grave furniture in Wessex in the Early Bronze Age. He stresses that there is a very strong possibility that "many shafts may exist adjacent to the major round barrow cemeteries of Wessex and that the chthonic 'cult' of the Iron Age and Roman periods may well have a much earlier origin."

We will be exploring ritual shafts in more detail in Chapter 5, so for the moment I'll restrict myself to saying that ritual shafts continued to be used in the area around Stonehenge into Roman times. Wessex Archaeology have excavated a Romano-British village at Butterfield Down near Amesbury, not far from Stonehenge. This village, they say,[13] was founded in the 2nd century A.D. but was at its largest in the 3rd and 4th centuries.

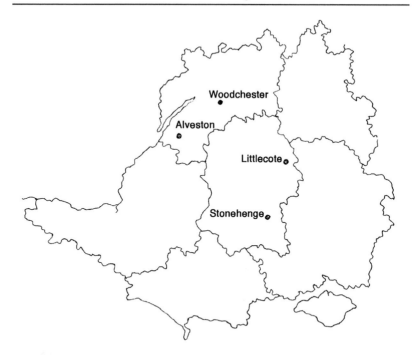

Map 3: Other sites of religious activity in southern England in prehistoric and Roman times, in the modern counties of Wiltshire and Gloucestershire.

> Houses and yards lined the trackways that met in the centre of the village. One of the tracks ran between the Roman towns of Durnovaria (Dorchester) to the south-west and Calleva Atrebatum (Silchester) to the northeast. The rectangular houses were made of timber and probably had thatched roofs.... Votive shafts about 10 feet deep and sited at the edge of the village were used to communicate with the gods of the underworld. Offerings to the gods were placed in the shafts. Near the centre of the village there are traces of a building built of stone. It is possible that this building was a temple. A small metal model of a bird may have decorated the end of a priest's sceptre.

The bird at the end of the priest's sceptre is unidentified, but it recalls the ritually deposited birds at Jordan Hill, and the importance of birds in Romano-British religion.

Orpheus Mosaics

One classical figure closely associated with the underworld is Orpheus, who is said to have traveled to the underworld after the death of his wife

Eurydice and softened the hearts of Hades and Persephone with his music. There are at least two Orpheus mosaics in southern Britain, one at Woodchester Roman villa in Gloucestershire, the other at Littlecote Roman villa in Wiltshire.

In *The Romans at Woodchester*, Graham Thomas, a local historian, discusses[14] the villa and its mosaic. Building probably began during the reign of Hadrian (A.D. 117–A.D. 138), and the villa was built and rebuilt over two centuries or more. Giles Clarke believes[15] that it was unlikely to have had an "official" function. He argues that more likely, the villa was built and lived in by the descendants of the local pre–Roman tribal leader. We don't know why it was built there, but Woodchester was not far from three important Roman towns, Aquae Sulis (Bath), Corinium (Cirencester) and Glevum (Gloucester), and was already on the path of an ancient road that ran between Gloucester and Bath.

As Clarke says,[16] the area immediately surrounding Woodchester is remarkably rich archeologically: there are at least seven other villas within a five-mile radius. The great mosaic was made around A.D. 325 by craftsmen from Corinium, with the main design based around Orpheus and his relationship with nature.

The villa was first excavated in the 1790s by Samuel Lyson, who published the results of his work in *Account of the Roman Antiquities Discovered at Woodchester in the County of Gloucester*. He also found a number of very fine marble sculptural fragments, including the headless statue of Diana Luna, the moon goddess, with the sacrificial bull at her feet, which are now in the British Museum. The quality of the carving is exceptional for statues found in British villas and these finds indicate the luxurious character of the villa.

As Katherine Dunbabin says,[17] Woodchester was a villa "of exceptional size and grandeur, at least twenty of whose rooms were decorated with mosaics." The Orpheus pavement occupied the central hall, c. 50 square feet. The center here was

> an octagon originally containing representations of fish, possibly with a fountain basin or similar feature. Orpheus was therefore moved into the next encircling ring, where he sat playing his lyre in the midst of a procession of birds. A second ring, separated by concentric borders, contained the beasts, walking against a plain white ground, with small trees between them — the beasts included a gryphon, a bear, a leopard, a stag, a tigress, a lion, a lioness, a boar, a dog and an elephant. Beyond this was an outer ring, with a fleshy scroll, growing from the head of Ocean. This circle is contained in a square, with four column bases in its corners; in the span-

drels are pairs of water-nymphs, shown, unusually, against a dark background.

Littlecote Roman villa is in Littlecote Park, near Ramsbury, Wiltshire, in the Kennet Valley. In Roman times, it would have been close to the Roman fortified *vicus* (settlement) of Cunetio, on the banks of the River Kennet, and at the crossroads formed by two major Roman roads — east-west from Calleva Atrebatum to Aquae Sulis, and southeast to northwest from Venta Belgarum to Corinium. The settlement, says Wikipedia, "may have begun life as a small short-lived military establishment guarding a crossing of the River Kennet. This was replaced by local circular farming huts around A.D. 70 and a Roman-style rectangular building fifty years later.... After another fifty years, this was replaced by a large two-storeyed winged corridor villa with integral bath suite. This building went through a number of changes over the subsequent centuries, notably a major rebuilding around A.D. 270."

Around A.D. 360, "agricultural activity seems to have ended and the complex acquired a religious use. A large barn was converted into a court-yard and a very early triconch ('three-shells') hall was built alongside with its own bath suite. Upon its floor was laid a now famous Orpheus mosaic, first discovered in 1727 by the Steward of the Littlecote Park estate." This change of use, from villa to shrine, has been associated with the pagan revival under the Emperor Julian, which dates from A.D. 362. Many of the buildings were demolished or fell into decay around A.D. 400, shortly after the Theodosius made Christianity the official state religion.

Martin Henig describes the mosaic as follows.[18] The central theme of the mosaic, he says, is

> Apollo equated with Orpheus, accompanied by Orpheus' regular attribute of a fox surrounded by personifications of the seasons (riding upon animals) which belong with Apollo. Heads of Sol in the apses also refer to Apollo, but the Sun's rays project almost to the edge of the panel and may also be interpreted as pecten (scallop) shells, recalling the belief in the voyage of the soul over the sea to the Blessed Isles. The other section of the mosaic is mainly geometric, but a panel with sea-panthers again evokes the marine *thiasos* (the ecstatic retinue of Dionysus/Bacchus), while a pair of facing panthers, one on each side of a chalice, is a well-known Bacchic device. The mystery at Littlecote seems to have exploited the close relationship between Bacchus (Dionysus), Orpheus and Apollo, and to have been connected with salvation.

Some further explanation is required here. Henig says elsewhere[19] that Bacchus or Dionysus was a savior-god who was "envisaged as leading the dead to a life of triumph, just as he had once rescued Ariadne, the daughter of King Minos of Crete, on Naxos and carried her away with him to share the delights of the *thiasos*." The Blessed Isles exist in both Greek and Celtic mythology as a blissful paradise for heroes and other favored mortals, and according to Toynbee,[20] the scallop-shell symbolizes the soul's journey across the ocean to this paradise. And of course, Apollo, in the form of Apollo Cunomaglus, was worshipped not far away from Littlecote in the temple of Nettleton Shrub.

Religious Images

This survey of religious images and inscriptions will start in the north of the target region, in Gloucestershire, the territory of the Dobunni. I mentioned earlier that in Gaul the Gaulish Mercury is often accompanied by a goddess of fertility called Rosmerta, and although there are no dedications to Rosmerta in Britain, there are images thought to be those of Rosmerta. There is an image on a relief in Gloucester (Glevum) (from the Shakespeare Inn, Northgate Street) which has been identified as Rosmerta and Mercury (see Figure 3): Mercury has his cockerel, caduceus and winged hat, while Rosmerta has a "curious sceptre in one hand and a ladle in the other, poised over a cylindrical wooden, iron-bound bucket on the ground."[21] In another image, from Bath (Aquae Sulis), "Mercury is conventional, with *petasos* (winged hat), purse and *caduceus*. Apart from Rosmerta's own 'caduceus' (which may instead be a wand of authority), she rests her right hand on a cylindrical receptacle — box, casket, or bucket. The Celtic character of the couple is enhanced by the presence of three minute *genii cucullati* at the base of the stone"[22] (see Figure 4). The mother-goddess is also associated with war, according to Green. At Daglingworth near Cirencester (Corinium), an image of the Dubonnic mother-goddess "sits with three hooded godlets, two of whom bear swords."[23] A relief from Kingscote, 3 km east of Uley, "associates a throned goddess who holds bread or fruit with a warrior."[24]

The *genii cucullati* ("hooded spirits") are found in religious sculpture throughout the Celtic world, from Austria to Britain. Green notes[25] that the British *genii cucullati* are rather different from their continental counterparts: "They are characterized by their triplicate form, though single ones occasionally occur; they are invariably dwarves and their phallicism is not stressed. However, there are overt fertility associations. Thus, the gods are frequently in company with the mother-goddesses, especially in the territory of the Dobunni, and they often carry eggs." They are found in both the north and the south of Roman Britain. At Housesteads (Vercovicium, on Hadrian's Wall), "the trio, who come from a small 3rd century shrine in the *vicus* of the fort, are swathed in heavy cloaks reaching to their feet"; the face of the central god is masculine while the other two may be feminine — or one may be older, and the other two may be youths.

The southern British *genii cucullati*, says Green, are "more varied in their associations. They are linked with healing springs at Springhead, Kent, ... and at Bath (Aquae Sulis)."[26] Healing may again be their function at Lower Slaughter, Gloucestershire, where "two schematized groups of *cucullati*, one with a worshipper, are depicted and where the context of the well may imply a curative-water association. But the group with the devotee are associated with the symbols of a rosette and two ravens, which may have otherworld associations."[27] The Dobunnic *cucullati* are firmly linked with the mother-goddess. On a relief from Corinium (Cirencester) a triplet of hooded spirits receives something from a goddess called Cuda (which Green claims denotes *prosperity*).[28] Another relief from Corinium depicts the *cucullati* in company with a mother nursing a cake or fruit; and "two of the spirits carry swords as if to defend her."[29] On another stone "a mother-goddess bears fruit and the accompanying *cucullatus* an egg; and two triads at Wycomb, near Uley, also bear these fertility symbols."[30] The link between the *genii cucullati* and the mother goddess is reinforced by the fact that the mother-goddesses also appear in threes (see Figure 5).

These images from the territory of the Dobunni are significant for our understanding of British religion and later Welsh mythology. The bucket or tub associated with the mother-goddess has been interpreted as a cauldron,[31] and given the link between the *cucullati* and fertility, healing and the Otherworld (the Lower Slaughter *cucullati* come from deep underground in a well), it can be linked to the cauldron of Diwrnach that we encountered in our earlier discussion of *Culhwch and Olwen*, and to the cauldron of regeneration we will meet when we consider *The Spoils of Annwn* and the Second Branch of the *Mabinogion*.

We cannot talk about cauldrons without mentioning the Gundestrup Cauldron, not because it is a cauldron, but because it depicts a cauldron on one of its panels. The Gundestrup Cauldron is a richly decorated silver vessel thought to date from the 1st century B.C., found in 1891 in a peat bog near the hamlet of Gundestrup, in the Aars parish in Himmerland,

Denmark. The silverworking techniques are consistent with the Thracian silver-sheet tradition, and it is thought the cauldron was made in Thrace, an area comprising what is now southeastern Bulgaria, northeastern Greece and the European part of Turkey. However, the imagery seems to be Celtic, with some possible Thracian features.

The panel depicting a cauldron is generally known as Plate E. In the lower half, a line of warriors bearing spears and shields, accompanied by carnyx players (a carnyx is a bronze war-trumpet used by Iron Age Celts) march to the left. On the left side, a large figure is immersing a man in a cauldron, possibly to restore him to life.[32] In the upper half, facing away from the cauldron, are warriors on horseback.

The most famous panel on the cauldron is Plate A. Wikipedia says that this "shows a horned male figure in a seated position. In its right hand, the figure is holding a torc (neck-ring), and with its left hand, it grips a horned serpent by the head. To the left is a stag with antlers very similar to the human figure. Other animals surround the scene, canine, feline, bovine, elephant, and a human figure riding a fish or a dolphin." The scene, says Wikipedia, has been compared to a similar seal found at Mohenjo-Daro in the Indus Valley (in what is now Pakistan), and dating from 2600 B.C.– 1900 B.C.). In theories of Celtic origin, "the figure is often identified as Cernunnos and occasionally as Mercury." Cernunnos is best known from an inscription on the Pil-

Figure 3: Image of Mercury and Rosmerta found at the Shakespeare Inn, Northgate Street, Gloucester (the Roman town of Glevum).

lar of the Boatmen, which I referred to earlier in connection with Tarvos Trigaranus. Here the antlered god is depicted alongside other Celtic deities and also Roman gods such as Jupiter, Vulcan and the divine twins Castor and Pollux. There are few representations of Cernunnos in Britain: a rare British example at Corinium portrays Cernunnos with two snakes which form his legs and rear up to eat corn or fruit by his head.[33]

Three other panels on the Gundestrup Cauldron are worth mentioning. Plate C "shows the bust of a bearded figure holding on to a broken wheel. A smaller leaping figure with a horned helmet also is holding the rim of the wheel. Under the leaping figure is a horned serpent. The group is surrounded by griffins and other creatures, some similar to those on plate B." It is unclear who the central figure is, but in Gaul many representations of a bearded god with a thunderbolt in one hand and a wheel in the other have been discovered. The Roman poet Lucan (A.D. 39–A.D. 65), in his *Pharsalia* (an epic poem on the civil war between Julius Caesar and Pompey), in writing of the Gauls, refers to "those who pacify with blood accursed/Savage Teutates, Hesus' horrid shrines,/And Taranis' altars cruel as were those/Loved by Diana, goddess of the north." Based on this, the iconography from Gaul, inscriptions to gods called Taranucno-, Taranuo-, and Taraino-, and the existence of a Welsh word *taranu*

Figure 4: Image of the genii cucullati (hooded spirits of place) with goddess, from the Corinium Museum, Cirencester.

"to thunder," it is possible that the Gaulish god with the thunderbolt and wheel is Taranis.

The Base Plate is described by Green[34] in these terms:

> The central figure is a great bull (or, more likely, a wild aurochs), apparently in its death-throes. Attacking it are a small anthropomorphic being, whose clearly demarcated breasts suggest it as female, and who wields a knife or sword, and a hunting-dog or wolf; beneath the bull are two other canids.... The bull or aurochs is itself in high relief and the head rears out in a dramatically three-dimensional manner; it has holes for a pair of detachable horns. The beast has a raised dorsal crest and a curious leaf-like pattern engraved on its neck and shoulders; its body is surrounded by the leaves of a climbing convolvulus-like plant.

Plate D is also generally interpreted as a bull-slaying scene. Three bulls are placed in a horizontal line, facing the same direction. They have massive rumps and short but thick necks. On the lower right side of each bull, a man is standing in the posture of attacking the bull with a sword. Under the feet of each bull, by the side of each man, a dog is depicted as running toward the left while a cat-like creature is running in the same direction over the back of each bull.

Other Gods and Goddesses

In Chapter 1 I referred to Mabon son of Modron as an important character in *Culhwch and Olwen*. Mabon is thought to be the Welsh version of the god Maponos ("Divine Boy" or "Divine Son"), from Gaulish *mapos* "young boy, son." Maponos, says Wikipedia, is mentioned in inscriptions from Gaul (Bourbonne-les-Bains in Haute-Marne, northeastern France, and Chamalières in central France), but is mainly attested in the north of Britain, at Brampton, near Hadrian's Wall, at Corbridge (Roman Coria), also near Hadrian's Wall in the territory of the Brigantes, at Ribchester (Bremetenacum), a Roman fort in what is now Lancashire, and at Chesterholm (Vindolanda), a Roman fort near the border with Scotland. The most interesting reference to Maponos is the one from Chamalières mentioned earlier, a magical text which calls on Maponos for help.

Modron is thought to be derived from Matrona, the goddess of the River Marne in Gaul. She has been linked to the Deae Matres or Deae Matronae, triple goddesses venerated in eastern Gaul, Germany and upper Italy. All depictions of the Matres are frontal, says Wikipedia, and "they appear almost exclusively in threes with at least one figure holding a basket

Figure 5: Three mother-goddesses from the Corinium Museum, Cirencester.

of fruit in her lap, and the women are either standing or sitting. In some depictions, the middle figure is depicted with loose hair and wearing a headband, and the other two wear head dresses. Other motifs include depictions of sacrifice — including burning incense, pigs, and bowls filled with fruit — and decorations of fruits, plants and trees." The cult seems to have spread to Britain, and Henig[35] mentions inscriptions and altars from Dover, Winchester (Venta Belgarum), York (Eboracum), and Londinium. In addition, says Henig,[36] the sculptor Sulinus set up dedications to the Matres Suleviae ("Mothers Who Govern Well") at Corinium and Aquae Sulis. As I said earlier, these triple mother-goddesses can be linked to the mother-goddess of the Dobunni and the *genii cucullati*.

It is possible that Maponos and Matrona were venerated mainly in the north of Britain. The *Welsh Triads*, a group of 13th-century texts which preserve fragments of Welsh folklore, mythology and traditional history in groups of three,[37] mention Modron (Triad 70) as the mother of Owain son of Urien, both 6th-century rulers of the northern British kingdom of Rheged.

Before I conclude this chapter, I would like to consider another divinity who will figure prominently in subsequent chapters, and that is the goddess Epona. Epona, whose name means "Great Mare" (cf. Welsh *ebol* "colt, foal"), was protector of horses, donkeys and mules. She was also, says Wikipedia, a goddess of fertility, "as shown by her attributes of a *patera* (a shallow dish used for drinking), cornucopia ('horn of plenty'), and ears of grain, and by the presence of foals in some sculptures." Henri Hubert also suggested[38] that the goddess and her horses were leaders of the soul in the after-life. The cult of Epona was widespread in the Roman Empire between the 1st and 3rd centuries A.D., and is mentioned in *The Golden Ass* by Apuleius (c. A.D. 124–c. A.D. 180), and in the *Satires* of Juvenal (c. A.D. 55–c. A.D. 138). The worship of Epona, says Green,[39] "was most popular in eastern Gaul and the German *limes* (frontier)." Green says that the "most interesting and complete British object pertaining to Epona's cult is a small bronze figurine said to be from Wiltshire [see Figure 6] depicting the goddess seated between two ponies.... Lying in Epona's lap and on a *patera* held in her right hand are huge ears of corn; on her left hand the goddess bears a yoke"[40] (see Figure 6).

This horse-goddess seems to provide one of the keys to prehistoric British religion, as we will see in Chapters 4, 5 and 6. Another key is provided by the cauldron, the triple goddesses and the *genii cucullati* of Gloucestershire, and I will be seeking to throw some light on these in the next chapter.

Chapter 3

Arthur's Voyage

The Spoils of Annwn

Taliesin and the Taliesin-Poet

The *Spoils of Annwn* is a poem attributed to Taliesin, and thought to have been composed between A.D. 800 and A.D. 1000, though, as John Koch argues,[1] some of the grammatical forms indicate that it may have been composed before A.D. 800. Most of the poems attributed to Taliesin are found in the *Book of Taliesin*, which was probably first compiled about A.D. 1350. It is generally thought that someone called Taliesin once existed, but it is highly unlikely he wrote all the poems attributed to him.

The existence of Taliesin is attested in *Historia Brittonum* (c. A.D. 830), where we read[2]:

> Then Dutigirn at that time fought bravely against the nation of the Angles. At that time, Talhaiarn Cataguen was famed for poetry, and Neirin, and Taliesin and Bluchbard, and Cian, who is called Guenith Guaut, were all famous at the same time in British poetry. The great king, Mailcun, reigned among the Britons, i.e. in the district of Guenedota, because his great-great-grandfather, Cunedda, with his twelve sons, had come before from the left-hand part, i.e. from the country which is called Manau Gustodin, one hundred and forty-six years before Mailcun reigned, and expelled the Scots with much slaughter from those countries, and they never returned again to inhabit them.

Taliesin is mentioned alongside one known poet, Neirin, that is, Aneirin, a 6th-century poet believed to have written *Y Gododdin*, which was mentioned in Chapter 1, and three who are now virtually unknown, Talhaiern Cataguen, better known as Talhaearn Tad Awen ("Talhaearn Father of the Muse"), Bluchbard and Cian. He is said by Nennius to have lived at the time of Dutigirn, who is otherwise unknown, and Mailcun, that is Maelgwn, a 6th-century king of the Welsh kingdom of Gwynedd descended from Cunedda the founder of Gwynedd.

A maximum of eleven poems in the *Book of Taliesin* have been dated to the 6th century, and many of these praise Urien of Rheged and his son Owain mab Urien, who both ruled Rheged in the late 6th century. It appears from this that he was court poet at Rheged, which included what is now Cumbria in northwest England, and possibly parts of Lancashire and southern Scotland, and may have been based at Luguvalium (Carlisle). Other early poems suggest that he may also have been court poet at Powys, which at the time was centered on the Romano-British town of Viroconium (Wroxeter in Shropshire).

It is unlikely that the historical Taliesin wrote *The Spoils of Annwn* (it is simply too different from the praise-poems he probably did write), and after I have analyzed the poem, I will consider what it tells us about the unknown author. I will analyze the poem in sections then as a whole, using the translation by Sarah Higley.[3] A warning: the language of this poem is Old Welsh, and the poem often alludes to matters that we only half understand or don't understand at all, so any translation is necessarily an interpretation. For this reason Higley's translation is likely to differ markedly from other translations, the best known of which is the 19th-century one by W.F. Skene.

Analysis of the Poem

The Spoils of Annwn

PART I

I praise the Lord, Prince of the realm, King.
His sovereignty has extended across the world's tract.
Equipped was the prison of Gweir in the Mound Fortress (*Caer Sidi*),
throughout the account(?) of Pwyll and Pryderi.
No one before him went into it,
into the heavy blue/gray chain; a faithful servant it held.
And before the spoils of Annwfyn bitterly he sang.
And until Judgment shall last our bardic invocation.
Three fullnesses of Prydwen we went into it.
Except seven none rose up from the Fortress of the Mound (*Caer Sidi*).

The first stop in this voyage to Annwn, the Welsh Otherworld, is the Mound Fortress, Caer Sidi in the original Welsh. To understand the meaning of Caer Sidi, and indeed many other names we meet on the way, we need look not just at Old Welsh but also at the language family to which

Welsh belongs, known as Indo-European. The Indo-European language family covers a huge area, from Portugal and Ireland in the West to Russia, India and Pakistan in the East, and includes languages as apparently diverse as English, German, French, Italian, Greek, Russian, Farsi (the language of Iran), Urdu (one of the languages of Pakistan) and Hindi (one of the languages of India). Our understanding of a word in one Indo-European language can often be helped if we know what words it is related to in other Indo-European languages — and we have tools to help us do that, including the *Indogermanisches Etymologisches Wörterbuch* (*Indo-European Etymological Dictionary*), first compiled by the German philologist Julius Pokorny, and available on the Indo-European Etymological Dictionary Project website.

The word *caer* means "fortress," and is thought to be from the Indo-European root *kat-* "hut, shed," which gives us Avestan (Old Persian) *kataa* "chamber," Iranian *kad* "house," Latin *casa* "hut," Latin *castrum* "fort," Old English *heathor* "enclosure, prison," Welsh *cader* "fort," Old Irish *cathir* "town."[4] Although this etymology by itself tells us very little, it does give us an early glimpse of how words get around, in this case apparently leaping from Avestan, the language of the Zoroastrian scriptures composed around 1000 B.C., to Latin, German and Celtic.

The word *sidi* is cognate with the Irish *sid* or *sidh*, which according to Koch[5] refers to "hills or mounds (often in reality containing prehistoric burials) conceived of as hollow and the residence of supernatural beings." In his *Dictionary of Continental Celtic Place-Names*, Falileyev gives the following information on *sid*[6]: "Old Irish *sid* 'tumuluus; peace,' *saidid* 'sits'; Cornish *asedhva* 'assembly'; Old Welsh in *guorsed* '(place) assembly,' Middle Welsh *sed*, Modern Welsh *sedd* 'seat' (from Indo-European root *sed-* 'sit,' Latin *sedes* 'seat,' Sanskrit *sadas* 'seat, residence, abode, dwelling, place of meeting, assembly (especially at a sacrifice),' Old English '*set*')." Sanskrit is the language of the Indian scriptures, which go back to around 1700 B.C., and of the *Rigveda*, composed between about 1700 B.C. and 1100 B.C., and among the oldest Indo-European religious texts. In the *Rigveda* the *sadas* was a ritual space belonging to the gods where the *soma* sacrifice took place[7] (soma was a stimulant drink poured into fire as an offering to the gods). While I am not suggesting that the British *sidi* was a sacred space where sacrifices took place, it is clear that the *sidi* has strong connections with the Otherworld.

Imprisoned in this Otherworld Mound Fortress is someone called Gweir. We do not know much about Gweir or Gwair, but he is mentioned in Triad 52 as one of the Three Exalted Prisoners, along with Mabon son of Modron and Llyr, who plays a large if passive role in the Second Branch of the *Mabinogion* (see Chapter 4). Gweir and Mabon son of Modron are alike in one way: Gweir is said to sing bitterly in his prison, just as Mabon, in *Culhwch and Olwen*, made "a great wailing and lamenting from the dungeon" of his prison in Gloucester. Presumably the "spoils of Annwn" before which he sings bitterly refers to the cauldron introduced in Part II.

It seems that Gweir is in Caer Sidi through the account (*ebostol*) of

Figure 6: Statuette of the horse-goddess Epona, said to be from Wiltshire. British Museum.

Pwyll and Pryderi. Pwyll is the king of Dyfed (west Wales) who, in the First Branch of the *Mabinogion*, takes over as lord of Annwn for a year and a day, and Pryderi is his son. It is unclear what the poet means here, since *ebostol* (presumably a Christian word) means "apostle" or "epistle," and neither meaning makes much sense: was Gweir in prison because of messengers (apostles) sent by Pwyll and Pryderi, or was he in prison because of formal letters (epistles) sent by Pwyll and Pryderi?

The voyage is undertaken in *Prydwen* ("Fair-Face"), and only seven returned—a theme taken up in the Second Branch of the *Mabinogion*, where only seven return from an expedition to Ireland, including Taliesin, who by then had become a figure of mythology. Interestingly, however, the seven returnees in the Second Branch did not include Arthur.

Here is the next section of the poem:

PART II

I am honored in praise. Song was heard
in the Four-Peaked Fortress (*Caer Pedryuan*), four its revolutions.

My poetry, from the cauldron it was uttered.
From the breath of nine maidens it was kindled.
The cauldron of the chief of Annwfyn: what is its fashion?
A dark ridge around its border and pearls.
It does not boil the food of a coward; it has not been destined.
The flashing sword of Lleawch has been lifted to it.
And in the hand of Lleminawc it was left.
And before the door of hell lamps burned.
And when we went with Arthur, brilliant difficulty,
except seven none rose up from the Fortress of Mead-Drunkenness
    (*Caer Vedwit*).

The next stop in this otherworldly voyage is Caer Pedryuan, with its "four revolutions"; Higley translates it as the Four-Peaked Fortress, but it can also be translated as "Four-Cornered Fortress." Since we know so little of British mythology — what we can glean from Roman Britain is necessarily seen through Roman eyes, and later medieval sources like the *Mabinogion* were influenced by centuries of Christianity — I am going far back into Indo-European prehistory to explain Caer Pedryuan.

In that ancient Indian religious text, the *Rigveda*, one of the most important gods is Varuna, king of the gods, the god of the sky, of waters and the celestial ocean, as well as god of law and of the underworld. Our knowledge of ancient Indo-European religion, however, does not come only from the *Rigveda*, for we also have the *Avesta*, the sacred texts of Zoroastrianism, the religion of pre–Islamic Persia, which were thought to have been composed between about 1000 B.C. and 500 B.C. According to Mary Boyce and Frantz Grenet,[8] Varuna lost his identity in Zoroastrianism, being invoked as Apam Napat ("Grandson of Waters"), Ahura Berezant ("High Lord") or the Baga ("God"). Interestingly, however, there is a place called *Varena* in Zoroastrianism: in the sacred book called the *Vendidad*,[9] the supreme deity Ahura Mazda is said to have created sixteen "good lands," the fourteenth of which is "four-cornered Varena, for which was born Thraetaona, who smote Azi Dahaka [Zohak]." Thraetaona, also known as Fereydun or Apam Napat, is the name of a mythical Persian king who is said to have killed the dragon Azi Dahaka or Zohak in Varena, which was said[10] to be inhabited by *Varenya daevas* ("fiends, demons").

The epithet "four-cornered" is echoed in ancient Indian descriptions of Varuna. Pettazzoni notes[11] that Varuna is given the epithet *caturanika* "four-faced," referring to the four cardinal points or four directions in which he looks, not as monarch but as sky-god; and the *Rigveda* speaks[12] of the "fearful four-edged bolt" of Mitra-Varuna, using the Sanskrit word *caturasrir* "four-cornered."

The name Varuna may be derived from the Indo-European root *wer-* "to close, cover, guard, save,"[13] which gives Old Indian *varati*, "surrounds, protects," *varutar* "protector, defender," *varutha* "protection, defense," *Vritra* "the enveloper," the Vedic demon associated with drought, Avestan *varetha* "defensive weapon," Old Irish *fertae* "burial mound," Middle Welsh *gwerthyr* "fortress," German *Wehr* "defense, protection." So it is possible that the Four-Peaked or Four-Cornered Fortress, with its "four revolutions," is not only a very ancient concept, but also one which has some connection with the heavens, in contrast to Caer Sidi, which seems much more earth-bound — though curiously "four-faced Varuna" and "four-cornered Varena" seem to have become a fortress in Britain and a burial mound in Ireland.

It soon emerges that Caer Pedryuan contains a cauldron. We have already encountered a cauldron in *Culhwch and Olwen*, and on one of the panels of the Gundestrup Cauldron, and we will also come across another cauldron in the Second Branch of the *Mabinogion*, a cauldron belonging to the main character Bran, which the Irish use to regenerate their dead warriors. It seems that this cauldron is the source of Taliesin's poetry, that it belongs to the (unnamed) chief of Annwn, that it has a dark ridge and pearls around its border, it does not boil the food of cowards, and it is kindled by the breath of nine maidens.

Let us start with the nine maidens. If the number nine sounds familiar, it is because in *Pa gur* (see Chapter 1) we are told by Arthur that Cai "slew nine witches." Surprisingly we know quite a lot about these "nine witches." Pomponius Mela,[14] describes an island called Sena (now called Ile de Sein, off the coast of Britanny). This island, he says, was famed for its oracle of a Celtic god, to whose cult nine maiden-priestesses were devoted. The priestesses were known as *Senae*, and were said to be "gifted with remarkable intelligence." It was believed that "they can raise up the waves of the sea and the winds with their songs, that they can assume the shape of any animal they choose, that they can cure complaints that to others are incurable, and that they know and predict the future."

These nine priestesses reappear in the *Life of Saint Samson*, a 6th-century saint who was born in Wales but later moved to Brittany, where he became one of the founding saints of the Breton church. In the *Life*, written between 610 and 820, Samson encounters a sorceress in a wood, pursues her and finally catches up with her. He then asks her[15]:

"Who art thou, misshapen one, and of what kind art thou?" And she, greatly trembling, said, "I am a sorceress, for indeed the women of my race and sex, as morally perverse, have to this day been transgressors in your sight, and now no one of my race is left in this wood save me only. For I have eight sisters and my mother is still living, and these are not here, but dwell in a wood more remote, and I was made over to this wilderness by my husband, and my husband is dead, and on this account I am unable to withdraw from this wood."

These nine women then reappear in Geoffrey of Monmouth's *Life of Merlin*, written after the *History of the Kings of Britain*. Here Geoffrey is describing Avalon[16]:

The island of apples which men call "The Fortunate Isle" gets its name from the fact that it produces all things of itself; the fields there have no need of the ploughs of the farmers and all cultivation is lacking except what nature provides. Of its own accord it produces grain and grapes, and apple trees grow in its woods from the close-clipped grass. The ground of its own accord produces everything instead of merely grass, and people live there a hundred years or more. There nine sisters rule by a pleasing set of laws those who come to them from our country. She who is first of them is more skilled in the healing art, and excels her sisters in the beauty of her person. Morgen is her name, and she has learned what useful properties all the herbs contain, so that she can cure sick bodies. She also knows an art by which to change her shape, and to cleave the air on new wings like Daedalus.... Thither after the battle of Camlan we took the wounded Arthur.

The nine women make a final appearance in *Peredur Son of Efrawg*, a 13th-century Welsh version of *Perceval, the Story of the Grail*, written by the 12th-century French poet Chrétien de Troyes. In this tale, which has elements not found in the French original, we read the following[17]:

Then Peredur rode forward. And above him he beheld a castle, and thitherward he went. And he struck upon the gate with his lance, and then, behold, a comely auburn-haired youth opened the gate, and he had the stature of a warrior, and the years of a boy. And when Peredur came into the hall, there was a tall and stately lady sitting in a chair, and many handmaidens around her; and the lady rejoiced at his coming. And when it was time, they went to meat. And after their repast was finished, "It were well for thee, chieftain," said she, "to go elsewhere to sleep." "Wherefore can I not sleep here?" said Peredur. "Nine sorceresses are here, my soul, of the sorceresses of Gloucester, and their father and their mother are with them; and unless we can make our escape before daybreak, we shall be slain; and already they have conquered and laid waste all the country, except this one dwelling." "Behold," said Peredur, "I will remain here to-night, and if you are in trouble, I will do you what service I can; but harm shall you not receive from me." So they went to rest. And with the break of day, Peredur heard a dreadful outcry. And he hastily arose, and went forth in his vest and his doublet, with his sword about his neck, and he saw a sorceress overtake one of the watch, who cried out violently. Peredur attacked the sorceress, and struck her upon the head with his sword, so that he flattened her helmet and her head-piece like a dish upon her head. "Thy mercy, goodly Peredur, son of Evrawc, and the mercy of Heaven." "How knowest thou, hag, that I am Peredur?" "By destiny, and the foreknowledge that I should suffer harm from thee. And thou shalt take a horse and armour of me; and with me thou shalt go to learn chivalry and the use of thy arms." Said Peredur, "Thou shalt have mercy, if thou pledge thy faith thou wilt never more injure the dominions of the Countess." And Peredur took surety of this, and with permission of the Countess, he set forth with the sorceress to the palace of the sorceresses. And there he remained for three weeks, and then he made choice of a horse and arms, and went his way.

The most intriguing of these references is in *Peredur*, where the nine sorceresses are said to come from Gloucester. It is tempting to link the nine maidens of Annwn to the mother-goddess of the Dobunni, with her bucket, tub or cauldron, and to the *cucullati*, the "hooded spirits," who almost always appear in groups of three, and the Matres or Mothers, who likewise always appear in groups of three — and the nine sorceresses of Gloucester seem to confirm this. And Pomponius Mela's allusion to the nine priestesses of Sena seems to indicate that the nine maidens represent an old tradition in British religion (as their name suggests, the Bretons originally came from Britain). This long tradition also shows that the priestesses of paganism became the witches of Christianity, except in the case of Geoffrey's *Life of Merlin*; perhaps Geoffrey was familiar with Pomponius Mela's description of Sena.

The other interesting feature of the cauldron of Annwn is that it does not boil the food of cowards, a fact which has led the cauldron to be compared with the Holy Grail. The Holy Grail was first mentioned in Chrétien's *Perceval*. In this early Arthurian tale, Perceval is a young man who, inspired by his encounters with knights, travels to King Arthur's court, where a young girl predicts greatness for him. He is taunted by Sir Kay, but receives the vermilion armor of a knight outside Arthur's castle. He then sets out for adventure, rescues and falls in love with the young princess Blanchefleur, and trains under the older knight Gornemant.

One day at a river, he sees two men in a boat fishing. Perceval is unable to cross, and one of the fishermen offers him lodging for the night. Following the directions of the fisherman, Perceval climbs to the top of a hill, where he sees a square tower and a hall. He enters the hall and is greeted by a handsome nobleman with gray hair, who apologizes for being unable to rise. A squire enters carrying a sword, and announces that the lord's niece has sent it to him — the lord gives the sword to Perceval. Another squire enters carrying a white lance, from which blood drips. Perceval refrains from asking about this lance, recalling Gornemant's earlier advice not to be too talkative. More squires bring in candelabras. Then, in the words of Chrétien[18]:

> A damsel came in with these squires, holding between her two hands a grail (*graal*). She was beautiful, gracious, splendidly garbed, and as she entered with the grail in her hands, there was such a brilliant light that the candles lost their brightness, just as the stars do when the moon or sun rises. After her came a damsel holding a carving-dish of silver. The grail which preceded her was of refined gold; and it was set with precious stones of many kinds, the richest and costliest that exist in the sea or in the earth. Without question those set in the grail surpassed all other jewels.

Perceval fails to ask who is being served by the grail. They dine at an ivory table. The grail returns, but again Perceval does not ask about it. Later that night, the nobleman excuses himself and has to be carried off to his bedroom. The next morning, Perceval discovers that the hall is deserted and everyone has left. As he rides over the drawbridge, it mysteriously rises up on its own. He then encounters a maiden weeping beneath an oak tree. She holds a dead knight, whose head has been cut off by another knight that morning. She asks where he spent the night, he describes the tower and hall, and she tells him that he stayed with the Fisher King (the name of the mysterious nobleman). She says the Fisher King was wounded in a battle by a javelin through both thighs and is still in much pain, and that fishing is the only recreation he has. She rebukes him for not asking any questions, saying that if he had asked only one question, he would have cured the king.

The Holy Grail was the dish, plate or cup used by Jesus at the Last Supper and said to possess miraculous powers. The word grail (in French *graal*) is derived from the Latin *gradalis*, meaning a dish brought to the table in different stages of a meal. For Chrétien the grail was a wide, somewhat deep dish or bowl, and Perceval learns many years later that the grail of the Fisher King contains a single consecrated host (wafer) that the King has lived on for twelve years. Like the cauldron of Annwn, the grail is jewel-encrusted, and just as the cauldron does not boil the food of cowards, the grail can only be won by those worthy of it (Perceval fails to ask any questions, and is therefore unable to cure the Fisher King).

Back in *The Spoils of Annwn* we next learn that the "flashing sword of Lleawch has been lifted to [the cauldron]," and that it was left "in the hand of Lleminawc." As Higley points out, we can compare this to the episode in *Culhwch and Olwen* in which Arthur and his men have to capture a cauldron belonging to the Irish giant Diwrnach Wyddel. They ask the giant for the cauldron, but he refuses, whereupon: "Bedwyr arose and seized hold of the cauldron, and placed it upon the back of Hygwyd, Arthur's servant, who was brother, by the mother's side, to Arthur's servant, Cachamwri. His office was always to carry Arthur's cauldron, and to place fire under it. And Llenlleawg Wyddel seized Caledvwlch, and brandished it. And they slew Diwrnach Wyddel and his company." It appears from this that Lleawch may be identified with Llenlleawg Wyddel ("Llenlleawg the Irishman"), one of the people Culhwch called on for help when he first arrived at Arthur's court, and who eventually helped Culhwch to get the giant's cauldron. As for Lleminawc, Higley links this name to Lluch Llawwynnawc, another knight of Arthur's court called on by Culhwch, which can be translated as "Lluch Windy-Hand" or "Lluch Striking-Hand"), and can be seen as another Welsh version of Lugus (compare this with the Irish epithet for Lugh, "Fierce-Striker"). As Higley notes, there does seem to be a good deal of "scribal confusion" here.

Before this section ends, we are informed for the first time that Arthur is involved in this voyage to Annwn, which is now referred to as the Fortress of Mead-Drunkenness, Caer Vedwit. The role of mead in early British societies is underlined in the poem *Y Gododdin*, which mentions Arthur in passing (see Chapter 1). Mead is mentioned forty-three times; here are some examples.[19] Note that Catraeth is the scene of the battle where so many warriors were killed:

> Men went to Catraeth, keen their war-band.
> Pale mead their portion, it was poison.
> Men went to Catraeth at dawn:
> Their high spirits lessened their life-spans.
> They drank mead, gold and sweet, ensnaring;
> For a year the minstrels were merry.
> Men launched the assault, nourished as one
> A year over mead, grand their design.
> How sad their tale, insatiable longing,
> Bitter their home, no child to cherish it.
> Because of wine-feast and mead-feast they charged,
> Men famed in fighting, heedless of life.
> Bright ranks around cups, they joined to feast.
> Wine and mead and bragget, these were theirs.

The attitude towards mead, "gold and sweet, ensnaring" and ultimately "poison," is highly ambivalent. However, the fact that one of the
locations in the Otherworld is associated with mead suggests that more is
involved. In Irish mythology there is a queen called Medb, whose name
is related to *mead* and means "intoxicating." She was queen of Connacht
in the Ulster Cycle of Irish mythology, whose husband was Aillil mac
Mata, although she had several husbands before him who were also kings
of Connacht. She was probably originally a sovereignty goddess, whom a
king would ritually marry as part of his inauguration. We will return to
the theme of the sovereignty goddess in Chapter 4 when we look at the
First Branch of the *Mabinogion*.

One last point to make is that before the Fortress of Mead-Drunkenness is mentioned, the poet refers the "doors of hell," in Welsh *porth
uffern*, apparently based on two Latin words, *porta* "gate" and *infernus*
"hell."

Part III

I am honored in praise; song is heard
in the Fortress of Four-Peaks, isle of the strong door.
Flowing water and jet are mingled.
Sparkling wine their liquor before their retinue.
Three fullnesses of Prydwen we went on the sea.
Except seven none rose up from the Fortress of Hardness (*Caer Rigor*).

We now return in Part III to the Fortress of the Four-Peaks, which
is apparently an island. In another poem attributed to Taliesin, *Song Before
the Sons of Llyr*,[20] the Otherworld is also seen in terms of an island:

Complete is my chair in Caer Siddi,
No one will be afflicted with disease or old age that may be in it....
And around its borders are the streams of the ocean.
And the fruitful fountain is above it,
The liquor is sweeter than white wine.

In the Second Branch of the *Mabinogion*, after the Welsh have
defeated the Irish, the seven survivors, together with Bran's head, spend
eighty years on an otherworldly island, Gwales. Before they go, Bran warns
them[21]: "You will be at Gwales in Penfro eighty years. Until you open the
door facing Aber Henvelen on the side facing Cornwall, you will be able
to abide there, along with the head with you uncorrupted. But when you
open that door, you will not be able to remain there." In the end, of course,
one of the seven opens the door and "when he looked, suddenly everything

they had ever lost — loved ones and companions, and all the bad things that had ever happened to them; and most of all the loss of their king — became as clear as if it had been rushing in towards them." The "strong door," in Welsh *pybyrdor*, this time with the normal Welsh word *dor*, seems to be the door between the Otherworld and the world of the living — strong because in this case it prevents the dead from regretting all that they have left behind in the world of the living.

In line 25 the poet tells us that "Flowing water and jet are mingled," presumably in or around the isle of the strong door. Jet is a form of lignite used in jewelry. Jet beads have often been found in Bronze Age barrows, says the Discover Yorkshire Coast website, and it is thought that the stone "might have been worn to ward off evil spirits. The Romans also had great liking for jet and jet objects are often found on Roman sites, these including hair pins, bracelets, medallions and finger rings; jet rings were found in excavations at Huntcliff and Normanby around 1920" (both these sites are in Yorkshire). As Higley points out, the mingling of water and jet may refer to a passage from Isidore of Seville (c. 560–636), the Archbishop of Seville said to be the "last scholar of the ancient world." In his *Etymologiae* (*Etymologies*) he writes[22]: "[Jet] is black, flat, smooth, and burns when brought near to fire. Dishes cut out of it are not destructible. If burned it puts serpents to flight, betrays those who are possessed by demons, and reveals virginity. It is wonderful that it is set on fire by water and extinguished with oil."

Part III ends with a reference to the fourth fortress to be mentioned, the Fortress of Hardness (*Caer Rigor*). This is sometimes translated as the Fortress of Kings or Kingly Castle, because in Old Irish the word *ri* (genitive *rig*) means "king" (compare Gaulish *rix*, latin *rex* and Old Indian *raj-*). The word comes from the Indo-European root *reg-*, and Pokorny[23] lists as derived from this root not only *rigor* and *rex*, but also Old Irish *reg-*, *rig-* "to stretch out (e.g. the hand)," *at-reig* "uplifts oneself," *eirge* "raising up"; Middle Welsh *dy-re* "stands up," *rhein* "stiff, elongated"; Old Welsh *arcib-renou* "buried," and Middle Welsh *ar-gyu-rein* "to bury." So the word may be borrowed from Latin, or may be an old Celtic word. As to what Caer Rigor means, we will consider that when we try to interpret the poem.

PART IV

I merit not the Lord's little men of letters.
Beyond the Glass Fortress (*Caer Wydyr*) they did not see
    the valor of Arthur.

Six thousand men stood upon the wall.
It was difficult to speak with their sentinel.
Three fullnesses of Prydwen went with Arthur.
Except seven none rose up from the Fortress of Guts (Hindrance?)
(*Caer Golud*).

The Glass Fortress, or Caer Wydyr, has sometimes been compared to Glastonbury in Somerset. The reason for this can be found in two works by the 12th-century Norman-Welsh priest and writer Giraldus Cambrensis, *De principis instructione* (*On the instruction of a prince*) and *Speculum Ecclesiae* (*Mirror of the Church*). Here is the relevant passage from *De principis instructione*[24]:

> What is now known as Glastonbury used, in ancient times, to he called the Isle of Avalon. It is virtually an island, for it is completely surrounded by marshlands. In Welsh it is called "Ynys Avallon," which means the Island of Apples and this fruit used to grow there in great abundance. After the Battle of Camlann, a noblewoman called Morgan, who was the ruler and patroness of these parts as well as being a close blood-relation of King Arthur, carried him off to the island, now known as Glastonbury, so that his wounds could be cared for. Years ago the district had also been called "Ynys Gutrin" in Welsh, that is the Island of Glass.

Here is the relevant passage from *Speculum Ecclesiae*[25]:

> After the Battle of Camlann ... the body of Arthur, who had been mortally wounded, was carried off by a certain noble matron, called Morgan, who was his cousin, to the Isle of Avalon, which is now known as Glastonbury.... It is called Avalon, either from the Welsh word "aval," which means apple, because appletrees and apples are very common there, or from the name of a certain Vallo who used to rule over the area long ago. In remote times, the place used to be called "Ynys Gutrin" in the Welsh language, that is the Island of Glass, no doubt from the glassy colour of the river which flows round it in the marshland.

This is obviously inspired by the tale in Geoffrey of Monmouth's *Life of Merlin*, except that Avalon is now equated with Glastonbury, or rather Glastonbury Tor, which in the past was surrounded by marshes, and resembled an island.

Something similar to the Glass Fortress is also mentioned in the *Historia Brittonum*.[26] Nennius writes that as the Milesians (the final inhabitants of Ireland, according to Irish mythology) were voyaging towards Ireland, "there appeared to them, in the middle of the sea, a tower of glass, the summit of which seemed covered with men, to whom they often spoke, but received no answer." This is reminiscent of the scene in the Second

Branch of the *Mabinogion*, where the dead Irish warriors are brought back to life by Bran's cauldron but cannot speak.

At the end of Part IV we move on to another fortress — or is it the same fortress with different names? — the Fortress of Guts or Hindrance. Higley notes that either interpretation is possible, and points out that other translators have seen it differently, with Loomis opting for "Fortress in the Middle of the Earth," and Koch choosing "Concealed Fort." In modern Welsh *golud* means "wealth, riches"; the Anglo-Saxon monk and historian, Bede, refers to an *urbs Coludi*, a 6th-century fort near St. Abbs, Berwickshire, where St. Aebbe established a monastery.

PART V

I do not merit little men, slack their shield straps.
They do not know which day who was created (or: created whom?);
what hour of midday (?) Cwy was born.
Who made him who did not go (to the) meadows of Defwy?
They do not know the brindled ox, thick his headband.
Seven score links on his collar.
And when we went with Arthur, dolorous visit,
except seven none rose up from the fortress of God's Peak
    (*Caer Vandwy*).

At this point the poem becomes especially challenging, both difficult to translate and with allusions to characters and places whose meaning is lost (e.g. Cwy and the meadows of Defwy). Two elements do stand out: the "brindled ox" and the fortress of God's Peak, or Caer Vandwy. The brindled ox may be related to "the two dun oxen of Gwlwlyd" that Culhwch must get as one of the tasks he has to complete in order to win the hand of Olwen; or to the "yellow and the brindled bull" that Culhwch must obtain; or to "the two horned oxen, one of which is beyond, and the other this side of the peaked mountain, yoked together in the same plough" that he is required to get. The brindled ox may also be related to Tarvos Trigaranus, whose statue was found at the Roman temple at Maiden Castle hillfort (see Chapter 2), and to the bulls depicted on two of the panels of the Gundestrup Cauldron.

The bulls depicted on the Gundestrup Cauldron were either about to be sacrificed or had just been sacrificed. Pliny tells us that the druids sacrificed bulls, and such a ceremony is described in *The Sick-Bed (Wasting Sickness) of Cuchulain*, a 10th/11th-century Irish text that is part of the Ulster Cycle of Irish mythology[27]: "A white bull was killed, and one man would eat his fill of the meat and of the broth, and in his sleep after that meal, a charm of truth would be said over him by four Druids. And whoever he would see in his sleep would be king." The brindled ox is said to have seven-score links on his collar. In a poem attributed to Taliesin, *Angar Kyfyndawt* (*Hostile Confederacy*), the poet says: "Seven score Ogyrven/Are in the Awen."[28] The Welsh word *awen* means "inspiration," and derives from the Indo-European *-uel*, meaning "to blow," and has the same root as the Welsh word *awel* meaning "breeze." The meaning of *ogyrven* is unclear: in another poem attributed to Taliesin, "The Chair of the Sovereign," the poet says of *awen* and *ogyrven*[29]:

> High (is) truth when it shines,
> Higher when it speaks.
> High when came from the cauldron
> The three awens of Gogyrwen (= Ogyrven).

All that is clear is that the "little men of letters" do not know the brindled ox, suggesting that the brindled ox has something to do with poetic inspiration.

The next fortress encountered in this otherworldly voyage is the fortress of God's Peak, or Caer Vandwy. This is not the only reference to Caer Vandwy in early Welsh literature: in *The Dialogue of Gwyddno Garanhir and Gwynn ap Nudd* from *The Black Book of Carmarthen*, the poet says (speaking here in the voice of Gwynn)[30]:

> To my sadness
> I saw a conflict before Caer Vandwy.
> Before Caer Vandwy a host I saw,
> Shields were shattered and ribs broken
> Renowned and splendid was he who made the assault.

Gwynn ap Nudd ("Gwynn son of Nodens") first appears in *Culhwch and Olwen*, where he abducted a maiden called Creiddylad, daughter of Llud Llaw Eraint ("Nodens of the Silver Hand") after she eloped with Gwythr ap Greidawl, Gwyn's longtime rival. Gwyn and Gwythr are condemned to fight, every May Day until Doomsday, a fight which represents the contest between summer and winter. If Gwyn is associated with Caer Vandwy, then Caer Vandwy may also be associated with the contest between summer and winter, between life and death.

Part VI

> I do not merit little men, slack their will.
> They do not know which day the chief was created,
> what hour of the midday the owner was born,

what animal they keep, silver its head.
When we went with Arthur, sorrowful strife,
except seven none rose up from the Fortress of Enclosedness
  (*Caer Ochren*).

Part VI seems to consist mainly of complaints about the "little men," particularly about their lack of knowledge. Line 43 parallels line 35, line 44 is similar to line 36, line 45 is almost identical to line 37, so line 46 may perhaps be linked to lines 39–40, suggesting that the animal with the silver head is in fact the brindled ox with the thick headband. This section ends with yet another fortress, Caer Ochren, which Higley translates as "Fortress of Enclosedness." It has been linked to Welsh *ochr* "slope (mountain side), hill." It also seems that in Roman times Lizard Point in Cornwall was called "Ocrinum Promontorium," and Greek *okrin* is "a jagged point or prominence" (see also Latin *ocris* "a broken, rugged, stony mountain").

PART VII

Monks howl like a choir of dogs
from an encounter with lords who know:
is there one course of wind? is there one course of water?
is there one spark of fire of fierce tumult?

PART VIII

Monks pack together like young wolves
from an encounter with lords who know.
They do not know when midnight and dawn divide.
Nor wind, what its course, what its onrush,
what place it ravages, what region it strikes.
The grave of the saint is hidden (or: lost, vanishing, in the
    Otherworld), both grave and ground (or: champion).
I praise the Lord, great prince,
that I be not sad; Christ endows me.

It now appears that the "little men" of Parts IV–VI are in fact monks, who are ignorant of some very basic facts of Celtic lore. In line 55 they are said to "not know when midnight and dawn divide," which sounds like a reference to the way the Gauls computed time, as explained by Julius Caesar (see Chapter 1). Line 58, says Higley, is very difficult to translate, and could mean:

"The grave of the saint is vanishing, both grave and ground."
"The grave of the saint is hidden, both grave and champion."
"How many saints in the Otherworld, and how many on earth?"

"How many saints lost, and how many altars?" or:
"How many saints in the void, and how many on earth?"

Whatever the line means, says Higley, "*diuant* is a gloomy concept, and the sense expressed here is of sadness and loss, which is confirmed by the last line of the poem ('that I be not sad')." It seems that the poet is lamenting the passing of those who know the old religion (the knowledge of the Druid, the world view of Celtic religion), and the loss not only of their material remains, but also of their spiritual legacy. It recalls Chinua Achebe's 1958 novel *Things Fall Apart*, which is set during the coming of the white man to Nigeria in the 19th century. Although on the face of it the setting of this novel could not be more different from the setting of *The Spoils of Annwn*, at a deeper level the protagonists of the two are living through a similar experience. In *Things Fall Apart* Nwoye, the son of the main character, Okonkwo, converts to Christianity, and Okonkwo, who still follows the traditional religion, has a sudden terrible thought[31]:

> Suppose when he died all his male children decided to follow Nwoye's steps and abandon their ancestors? Okonkwo felt a cold shudder run through him at the terrible prospects, like the prospect of annihilation. He saw himself and his fathers crowding round their ancestral shrine waiting in vain for worship and sacrifice and finding nothing but ashes of bygone days, and his children the while praying to the white man's god.

Interpretation of the Poem

The Spoils of Annwn is often interpreted as a military expedition, and there are certainly links between the poem and Bran's expedition to Ireland in the Second Branch of the *Mabinogion* (seven survivors, cauldron, strong door, uncommunicative sentinel). However, a good work of art can be interpreted on more than one level, and I believe that *The Spoils of Annwn* is more about a symbolic voyage than a real one. This idea is certainly not a new one. The Scottish journalist, folklorist and scholar of the occult, Lewis Spence, in *The Mysteries of Britain*, first published in 1905, says[32]: "The poem is on the same lines as 'The Harrying of Hell,' the descent into the gulf, to cow its evil denizens and carry away its secret and treasures. It is, indeed, part of the ritual of the candidate for adeptship into the British mysteries."

Let us assume for the sake of argument that *The Spoils of Annwn* is a symbolic voyage, an initiation — real or metaphorical — into Druid knowledge or the mysteries of British religion. The first stop on this symbolic voyage is Caer Sidi, the Mound-Fortress. This was interpreted as a burial mound, but as *Song Before the Sons of Llyr* suggests, Caer Sidi is more than this, since "around its borders are the streams of the ocean./And the fruitful fountain is above it," suggesting its location is in the sea or even in the heavens. The Welsh word *sidydd* means "zodiac," so it is not surprising that Caer Sidi is also seen as a heavenly abode. The Welsh word is similar to the Latin *sidus* "stars, constellation," which Pokorny[33] derives from the Indo-European root *sueid-* "to shine," which also gives Avestan *x^waena* "glowing," Lithuanian *svidus* "shining, bright," *svidu* "gleam." For this reason, it is not clear whether the Welsh word was borrowed from Latin or developed independently, and whether the Taliesin-poet was thinking of the zodiac when he referred to Caer Sidi in *The Spoils of Annwn*.

However, this link is arguably being made by the author of *Song Before the Sons of Llyr*, and it may be reinforced by the two lines that precede the reference to Caer Sidi:

> In the festivals of the Distributor, who bestowed gifts upon me.
> The chief astrologers received wonderful gifts.

A few lines before, the poet said:

> I liberated my lord in the presence of the distributor.
> Elphin, the sovereign of greatly aspiring ones.

We saw earlier that Varuna, the sky-god in the *Rigveda*, was sometimes called in Old Persian texts Baga, which signifies God but literally means "The Distributor."[34] If the Distributor of the Taliesin-poet is the sky-god, then Caer Sidi is surely a celestial dwelling-place.

If Caer Sidi is both an earthly and celestial abode, what does this tell us about the symbolic voyage described in *The Spoils of Annwn*? We saw in Chapter 1 that Hippolytus of Rome linked the Druids to Pythagoras, so perhaps this question can be answered by looking at the philosophy of Pythagoras and the Pythagoreans. Pythagoras himself wrote nothing, so everything we know about his philosophy comes from Pythagoreans like Philolaus, and later philosophers like Aristotle.

According to the *Stanford Encyclopedia of Philosophy*, Philolaus (c. 470 B.C.–c. 385 B.C.) believed that nature "was fitted together" out of two opposites which he calls *limiters and unlimiteds*. The first thing "fitted together," he says, is called "the hearth," the central fire around which all heavenly bodies, including the earth, orbit. What he means by "fitted together" is explained in Fragment 7[35]:

... since these beginnings [i.e. limiters and unlimiteds] preexisted and were neither alike nor even related, it would not have been possible for them to be ordered, if a harmony had not come upon them.... Like things and related things did not in addition require any harmony, but things that are unlike and not even related ... it is necessary that such things be bonded together by a harmony, if they are going to be held in an order.

Aristotle, in his *Metaphysics*, after presenting his account of the philosophy of "the so-called" Pythagoreans, which has strong connections to the philosophy of Philolaus, turns to "others of this same group" and assigns to them what is commonly known as the *table of opposites*. These Pythagoreans presented the principles of reality as consisting of ten pairs of opposites[36]:

limit	unlimited
odd	even
unity	plurality
right	left
male	female
rest	motion
straight	crooked
light	darkness
good	bad
square	oblong

Pythagoreanism is often linked to Orphism, the mystery religion associated with Orpheus (see Chapter 2 for a discussion of two Orpheus mosaics in Britain). As Orphism was a mystery religion, very little is known about its doctrine, but some texts do survive. One of these is the Petelia tablet, discovered in lower Italy near Sybaris. The poem was written on thin gold leaf, rolled up and placed in a cylinder hanging from a gold chain. It was presumably hung around the neck of a dead person as an amulet. The tablet reads[37]:

Thou shalt find out to the left of the House of Hades a Wellspring
And by the side thereof standing a white cypress.
To this Wellspring approach not near.
But thou shalt find another by the lake of Memory,
Cold water flowing forth, and there are guardians before it.
Say "I am a child of the Earth and Starry Heaven:
But my race is of heaven alone. This ye know yourselves.
And lo, I am parched with thirst and I perish. Give me quickly
   the cold water flowing forth from the lake of memory."
And of themselves they will give thee to drink from the holy Well spring.
And thereafter among the other Heroes thou shalt have lordship.

It seems likely, therefore, that if Caer Sidi is both of the earth and of the heavens, it embodies one or more of the opposites proposed by the Pythagoreans, and represents the possibility of the kind of rebirth — symbolic or real — hinted at in the Petelia tablet.

Some clue as to the nature of Caer Sidi is given by the plight of Gweir, the man held prisoner there. Koch suggests[38] that Gweir may be a variant of Gwri, the name given to the infant Pryderi in the First Branch of the *Mabinogion*. The Canadian psychoanalyst Dan Merkur, following a suggestion made by W.J. Gruffydd,[39] believes that Gweir's imprisonment is equivalent of that of Pryderi in the Third Branch of the *Mabinogion*, in which Pryderi enters an enchanted *caer*, touches a golden bowl and becomes stuck to it (see Chapter 4). Merkur interprets the imprisonment thus[40]:

> The statement in "The Spoils of the Otherworld" that Gweir sang sadly in front of the spoils or booty of the otherworld suggests that like Pryderi, Gweir was imprisoned in the presence — indeed, imprisoned by — the very object that he sought to carry off.... The meaning of the motif is implicit. The cauldron or [bowl] imprisoned in that a person could not let go of it once it had been touched.... The cauldron or [bowl] implicitly contained a potable and/or edible substance that was addictive.

Merkur's suggestion that the imprisonment of Gweir is a psychological one, arising from an addiction to a psychedelic substance, is an intriguing one. Certainly mead is mentioned later in the poem, and we know that one possible interpretation of the name Belenus (a Celtic god especially popular in Aquileia, on the Adriatic coast) is the "Henbane (God),"[41] implying that this hallucinogenic substance was used among the Celts. The use of mead or henbane suggests that Caer Sidi could well be a place where hell and heaven could be experienced.

The second stage of the symbolic voyage is Caer Pedryuan, the Four-Peaked or Four-Cornered Fortress. The Four-Cornered Fortress, we saw earlier, represents the heavens and as such may be the other "face" of Caer Sidi. What it means in the poem, however, can only be defined by what is found there, namely the cauldron. The cauldron is kindled by the breath of nine maidens, those figures who keep emerging from the mist for over a thousand years of Celtic history, in Britanny, Wales, the Fortunate Isle and Gloucestershire. But what is their connection with fire? I may be stretching a point here, but the answer may lie with the Irish saint Brigit, who has the same name as the Irish goddess Brigit ("Exalted One"), whose British counterpart is Brigantia, the goddess of the Brigantes of northern Britain. Giraldus Cambrensis tells us[42] that at Kildare there is a perpetual fire tended by nineteen nuns, who take it in turns to watch the fire for nineteen nights, with Brigit taking her turn every twentieth night. The fire, says Giraldus, is surrounded by a hedge, made of stakes and brushwood, and forming a circle, within which no male can enter. It is only lawful for women to blow the fire, fanning it or using bellows only, and not with their breath (unlike the nine maidens in the Four-Cornered Fortress).

Now Brigit was the goddess of poetry and prophecy, and Brigantia was equated with Minerva, goddess of poetry, wisdom, crafts and magic, so this would strengthen the argument that we are dealing here with a cauldron of inspiration. It is said, however, that the cauldron does not boil the food of a coward, and we can infer from this that a poet must make a dangerous symbolic voyage into the depths of the Otherworld and eat (or drink) from the cauldron of regeneration before he can draw on the cauldron of inspiration. If the Four-Cornered Fortress is the high point of the symbolic voyage, it can only be reached by those brave enough to descend to the depths.

Until now the poet has in a way been mapping out the symbolic voyage he is about to make, but the voyage proper begins with the next stop, Caer Vedwit, the Fortress of Mead-Drunkenness. This at first brings euphoria and possibly a trance state as we are transported back to the Four-Cornered Fortress, the isle of the "strong door" (the gateway to higher knowledge), and the uniting of opposites in the mingling of water and jet. But not long after comes the next stage, Caer Rigor, the Fortress of Hardness — *rigor* may be translated as "hardness," but also as "the stiffness produced by cold," perhaps the stiffness and coldness of a trance state.

This seems to mark a transition from one stage of the symbolic voyage to another, since it is at this point that the poet begins complaining about the "little men." It is now that the poet reaches Caer Wydyr, the Glass Fortress, where communication becomes difficult, either because the poet is in a trance state, or because he is symbolically like a small child who cannot talk. This is perhaps reinforced by the next stage, Caer Golud, if it means Fortress of Hindrance.

By now the poet's complaints about the little men have intensified, as if they are preventing him from completing his symbolic voyage. However, he does reach the last two stages, Caer Vandwy, the Fortress of God's Peak, and Caer Ochren, the Fortress of Enclosedness or Fortress of the Sloping Hill. It is impossible to know whether the poet has completed the symbolic voyage, but judging from Parts VII and VIII, where monks "howl like a choir of dogs" or "pack together like young wolves," and the poet expresses his sadness and loss, it seems highly unlikely. After all, Caer Vandwy and Caer Ochren both sound like points in an actual or symbolic landscape which are difficult to reach (like the Fortress of Hindrance, perhaps) and, once reached, lead on to some higher realm.

In summary, *The Spoils of Annwn* may on one level be the story of a military expedition, but on another level it is the account of a symbolic voyage in search of a metaphorical rebirth through a bringing together of the dark forces of Caer Sidi, the Mound-Fortress, and the forces of light represented by Caer Pedryuan, the Four-Cornered Fortress. The voyage appears to fail, however, just as it failed for Gweir, now imprisoned in the Otherworld. It fails because the traditions and oral poetry of a culture whose ultimate prize is a mystical cauldron are being drowned out by "little men" who no longer appreciate the beauty of the cauldron and all that it represents, who have all but forgotten the knowledge accumulated over centuries and handed down from father to son. *The Spoils of Annwn* is probably the closest we will ever get to a Druid text, a fleeting glimpse into a vast and ancient tradition gone beyond recall.

And what of Arthur? In the poem he plays no obvious role, implying that he is a kind of spirit-guide. We will be returning to Arthur later in the book, when we try to determine how a warrior and king can also initiate the Taliesin-poet and his companions into the mysteries of the Otherworld.

Some Notes on the Author of *The Spoils of Annwn*

Was the author of *The Spoils of Annwn* a Druid? We will probably never know, but this enigmatic poem does give us some clues about its author. The most important clue is that the poem is plainly not a Christian poem, although the author pays homage to "the Lord" at the beginning and end of the poem, and refers to Christ in the last line. We can infer from this that the poem was composed in a society where the old British religion still existed, but was gradually being replaced by the new Christian religion.

Christianity came to Britain slowly over a period of several hundred years. The martyrdom of St. Alban, which occurred between about A.D. 200 and A.D. 300, suggests that Christianity was established in Britain well before it became the official religion of Rome under the Emperor

Constantine. We know little of Christianity in Britain after the withdrawal of Roman forces, but the fact that the British cleric Gildas wrote *De excidio et conquestu Britanniae* (*On the ruin and conquest of Britain*) in the early 6th century, castigating the sinfulness of its rulers, suggests that there was a sizeable Christian community in Britain at the time.

Another important clue is the reference to the cauldron kindled by the breath of nine maidens. If I am right, this cauldron and the nine maidens can be associated with Gloucestershire, with the *genii cucullati* and the triple mother-goddesses, divine figures before Christianity transformed them into sorceresses. Gloucestershire was also an important focus of the underworld cult which seems to have been observed in large parts of Southern England, from Gloucestershire to Dorset. According to the *Anglo-Saxon Chronicle*, three towns in the territory of the Dobunni, Corinium (Cirencester), Glevum (Gloucester) and Aquae Sulis (Bath), fell to the Saxons in 577, and Gloucestershire was incorporated into the kingdom of the Hwicce by 600. Interestingly, the Anglo-Saxon monk Bede, in his *Historia ecclesiastica gentis Anglorum* (*Ecclesiastical History of the English People*), completed in about 731, does not tell us how the Hwicce converted to Christianity, and we can only surmise that the Dobunni/Hwicce remained Christian from Roman times (we saw in Chapter 2 that the Roman temple at Uley became a church, and Dorothy Watts[43] demonstrates that there were probably also very early churches in Woodchester Roman villa, Chedworth Roman villa, and possibly on the site of St. Mary de Lode, Gloucester).

So it is unlikely that the Taliesin-poet came from Gloucestershire. By around 650, the only parts of England that remained securely in British hands were Devon and Cornwall, in the kingdom of Dumnonia, and west Herefordshire, in the kingdom of Ergyng. The Taliesin-poet could therefore have lived in Ergyng, which was close to Gloucestershire and centered on the Roman ironworking settlement of Ariconium, but it is more likely that he lived in Gwent, also close to Gloucestershire and centered on Venta Silurum (Caerwent) or perhaps Caerleon (Isca Augusta), a Roman legionary fortress and settlement. Gwent is thought to have been Christianized by Cadoc, who flourished in the 6th century, and Dubricius, who died in 612. However, Britain only became part of the wider Christian community when Pope Gregory sent Augustine to England in 597 to convert the pagan king Aethelberht of the Kingdom of Kent to Christianity. Augustine became the first Archbishop of Canterbury, but despite a decree from the Pope, was unable to extend his authority to the bishops of Wales and Dumnonia.

I see the Taliesin-poet as the descendant of people from Gloucester-shire, perhaps even of a Druid priest (the Romans suppressed the Druids, but they probably survived as an underground movement, and made a comeback when Roman power in Britain declined and paganism was restored in the late 4th century). He lived perhaps in Gwent around A.D. 700, but grew up listening to stories of the nine maidens of Gloucestershire and their magic cauldron, and of heroic exploits in the underworld. His family may have been Christians, and he himself may nominally have been a Christian, but his heart was with the old religion and the mysteries of that land called Annwn.

Chapter 4

Magic Mounds, Sea People and Shape-Shifters

The Wonderful World of the Mabinogion

Introduction

The tales that make up the *Mabinogion* (more correctly, *Mabinogi*) are thought to have been composed between 1060 and 1200. Here I will be focusing on the Four Branches of the *Mabinogion*, which are:

First Branch: *Pwyll, Prince of Dyfed*
Second Branch: *Branwen, Daughter of Llyr*
Third Branch: *Manawydan, Son of Llyr*
Fourth Branch: *Math, Son of Mathonwy*

The word *mabinogion*, or rather, *mabinogi*, originally meant "the (collective) material pertaining to the god Maponos."[1] It traditionally includes not only the Four Branches, but also the so-called native tales (derived from Welsh tradition and legend), one of which, *Culhwch and Olwen*, we are already familiar with, and another of which, *Lludd and Llefelys*, we will examine later in the book. Finally in the *Mabinogion* are three romances, Welsh versions of Arthurian tales — one of these is *Peredur, Son of Efrawg*, which features the nine sorceresses of Gloucester.

Only one character appears in all four branches, and that is Pryderi, son of Pwyll; Pryderi's mother Rhiannon appears in two branches (the First and Third), and Pryderi's later companion Manawydan also appears in two branches (the Second and Third). Otherwise the Four Branches appear to be separate, which obviously presents the analyst with a problem. So to simplify discussion of the *Mabinogion*, I am going to approach it as the story of three sets of characters, the children of Llyr and the children of Don, whose names are self-explanatory, and the Mound-People, whose name is less transparent. I will look at each Branch in turn and in order, drawing on the translation and notes of Will Parker.

The Mound-People (1):
Pwyll, Pryderi and Rhiannon

The First Branch is called *Pwyll, Prince of Dyfed*, and this raises two immediate points: Pwyll, unlike most Welsh heroes, apparently has no father or mother, and he has an unusual name. Pwyll means "mind, spirit, reason," and Matasovic, in *An Etymological Lexicon of Proto-Celtic*, links *pwyll* to Old Irish *ciall* and ultimately to the Indo-European root *kʷeys-* "perceive,"[2] which also gives Old Indian *cayati* "observe," *citi* "understanding," and Old Greek *tereo* "observe." As the First Branch opens, Pwyll, ruler of the seven *cantrefs* (administrative divisions) of Dyfed, is out hunting with his dogs and sees another pack of dogs bring down a stag — dogs that were "dazzling bright white and with red ears."[3] Pwyll drives away these strange dogs and lets his dogs feed on the stag. The owner of the strange dogs turns up and berates Pwyll for his discourtesy. This man, it emerges, is Arawn, king of Annwn, the Otherworld, and to make amends to Arawn, Pwyll agrees to take Arawn's place for a year and a day then fight Arawn's enemy Hafgan ("Summer-Bright"). After this he assumes the title of Pwyll Pen Annwn "Pwyll Head of Annwn."

It might appear from this that we are in the same mythical territory as *The Spoils of Annwn*, but in fact this Annwn is a harmless place, rendered safe by centuries of Christianity. However, potentially more dangerous are the otherworldly events that follow Pwyll's sojourn in Annwn. Pwyll is in Arberth, a "chief court of his," when after the first course of a feast, he goes for a walk and makes for "the top of a mound which was above the court and was called Gorsedd Arberth." Arberth is modern Narberth in Pembrokeshire — Koch says[4] that the name is "probably derived from Celtic *are-kʷert-*, referring to 'what stands before a dyke' or 'hedge,' though a connection with *arberth* 'sacrifice' is not impossible." A *gorsedd* is the later Welsh equivalent of the *sidi* of *The Spoils of Annwn*, and therefore a place combining the darkness of the burial-mound and the dazzling brightness of the heavenly abode. One of Pwyll's court knows this because he says to Pwyll[5]: "Lord, ... it is a peculiarity of the mound that whatever high-born man might sit upon it, he will not go away without one of two things: either wounds or blows, or his witnessing a marvel."

As Pwyll and his court were sitting on the *gorsedd*, they could see "a woman on a large stately pale-white horse, a garment of shining gold brocaded silk about her, making her way along the track which went past the mound."[6] Pwyll sent one of his men to find out who this woman was. The horse was proceeding at an "even, leisurely pace," so the man "went after her as fast as he was able to on foot, but the greater was his speed, the further away from him she became."[7] The man then fetched a horse and pursued her, with the same result. The next day Pwyll pursued her on horseback, and the same thing happened until he spoke to her, whereupon she stopped and conversed with him. It turned out that her name was Rhiannon ("Divine Queen"), and she was promised to another man, but wanted Pwyll to rescue her from this man in a year's time, at the court of her father.

As most commentators on the *Mabinogion* agree, Rhiannon is the equivalent of the Celtic horse-goddess Epona (see Chapter 2), and a sovereignty goddess, that is, a goddess whom the king must ritually marry in order to assume the kingship (like the goddess of mead Medb mentioned in Chapter 3). As we will see in Chapter 6, she can also be linked to the rider-god known as the Thracian Horseman, whose horse also proceeds at a walking pace. After the year laid down by Rhiannon, Pwyll goes to the court of Rhiannon's father, and a feast is prepared for him. As they start their after-dinner drinking, a young man approaches Pwyll and says he has a request, and Pwyll tells him he will grant him any request he can. The young man then tells Pwyll he is about to sleep with the woman he loves, and asks for Rhiannon, along with the "provisions and victuals which are here." Telling Pwyll that "there was never a man so slow with his wits as you were [just] then," Rhiannon gives him a bag, and says she will arrange to meet the young man Gwawl in a year's time to sleep with him, when Pwyll will also be there with the bag. After the year has passed, Pwyll goes to the court wearing "dull rags" and "big rag-boots," and during the after-dinner drinking, he approaches Gwawl and begs him to fill his little bag with food. But Rhiannon's bag is a magic bag, so "however much they threw in, it was no more full than before." Pwyll then advises Gwawl to press his feet down on the food in the bag and say, "Enough has been placed herein"—then immediately turns the bag so that Gwawl is head over heels in the bag, closes the bag and ties it up. Not long after this, Pwyll sleeps with the sovereignty-goddess Rhiannon.

The magic bag also links Rhiannon to Epona, who was a goddess of fertility, often shown with a cornucopia. Rhiannon's link to Epona is reinforced in the third and last part of the tale. Here Rhiannon gives birth to a boy, and on the night of his birth, some women are assigned to keep watch over him. They fall asleep, and when they awake next morning, the little boy has disappeared. The women then kill a puppy and smear the blood on Rhiannon, accusing her of killing the baby. Rhiannon is then punished in the following way[8]: "There was a mounting-block by the gate. She had to sit beside it every day telling anyone coming by the whole story (of those she supposed did not know it) and offering whichever guest and stranger would allow themselves to carried, to be carried on her back to the court." While Rhiannon is serving out her punishment as a horse, her baby boy is discovered in strange circumstances. One night a certain lord, Teyrnon (="Great Lord") Twryf Liant, ruler of Gwent, is watching over his prize mare, who has just given birth to a foal inside his house. There is a commotion, and Teyrnon goes outside to investigate, and when he returns he sees a small child in swaddling clothes wrapped in a sheet of brocaded silk. Teyrnon and his wife name this child Gwri Golden-Hair. Eventually they realize that this boy must be the lost child of Pwyll and Rhiannon, and return him to his rightful parents, who rename him Pryderi, usually interpreted as meaning "care, anxiety." The tale ends with Pryderi growing up, becoming the ruler of Dyfed after the death of Pwyll, then conquering the three *cantrefs* of Ystrad Tywi (now Carmarthenshire in southwest Wales) and the four *cantrefs* of Ceredigion (now Cardiganshire in mid-west Wales). After this he marries Cigfa, granddaughter of Gloyw Wallt, the mythical founder of Gloucester (Caer Gloui, in *Historia Brittonum*).

Pryderi is clearly linked to horses, like his mother Rhiannon, and is also linked to Mabon (Maponos), who was stolen from his mother when he was three nights old. His infant name of Gwri also identifies him with Gweir, the prisoner of *The Spoils of Annwn*, and his wife Cigfa permits us to associate him with Gloucester. Pryderi, like Pwyll, is an unusual name, and while it is conventionally translated as "care, anxiety" (Welsh *pryder*), the Welsh academic Ifor Williams[9] links it to an Old Breton word *pritiri* "loss," which is even more appropriate in the circumstances. An even more radical interpretation is given by the Czech folklorist Joseph Baudis,[10] who sees Pryderi as derived from the IE root *qrt*, which appears in Irish *cruth*, Welsh *pryd* "form, aspect," the Old Welsh name of Britain *Prydain*, and the Irish name of the Picts, *Cruithne*. This is an intriguing suggestion which we will return to later in the book.

The Children of the Sea: Bran, Branwen and Manawydan

Analysis

The Second Branch of the *Mabinogion, Branwen, Daughter of Llyr*, focuses on the exploits of the children of Llyr, Bran, also known as Bran the Blessed, his sister Branwen, his brother Manawydan, and his two half brothers from his mother's side, Nisien and Efnisien. The mother of all five is Penarddun, daughter of Beli, also known as Beli Mawr; the father of Nisien and Efnisien is Euroswydd. As the story opens, Bran is "the crowned king of this Island, and exalted with the crown of London."[11] According to Matasovic,[12] the name Llyr is from Proto-Celtic *liro-* "sea ocean," Old Irish *ler*, Middle Welsh *lirou* "seas, oceans," meaning that his offspring are the Children of the Sea. Just what this means will become clear in the course of this chapter.

Before I say anything more about Llyr's children, I need to outline the story of the Second Branch. One day Bran and his followers were sitting above the ocean at Harlech (northwest Wales), when they saw a fleet of ships approaching. Matholwch, king of Ireland, wished to marry Bran's sister Branwen, and landed to discuss the matter with Bran. There was great feast at Abberfraw (on Anglesey, and once the capital of Gwynedd), and Matholwch slept with Branwen there. The next morning Efnisien, a "quarrelsome man," noticed Matholwch's horses and asked who they belonged to. When he discovered that they belonged to Matholwch, and that Matholwch had just slept with his sister, he was angered that his sister had been given away to Matholwch without his consent, and muti-lated Matholwch's horses, the symbol of his royal authority according to the First Branch. On hearing the news, Matholwch left the court. When Bran discovered what had happened, he offered to replace the horses that had been mutilated, and also gave him a silver rod as thick as his finger. Matholwch returned, but when he and Bran were dining together, Math-olwch seemed out of sorts — so, thinking the compensation he had given him was insufficient, Bran also offered Matholwch the cauldron of regen-eration that plays such an important part in *The Spoils of Annwn*.

Matholwch then cheers up, and the two exchange stories about the origin of the cauldron. Bran says he got it from an Irishman called Llasar Llaes Gyfewid and his wife Cymidei Kymeinvoll, who had escaped from the Iron House in Ireland. Matholwch then tells Bran about the history of these two individuals. One day while hunting he was on top of a tumulus (*gorsedd*) above a lake in Ireland called the Lake of the Cauldron. A large, monstrous man emerged from the lake with a cauldron on his back, accom-panied by an even bigger woman. Matholwch took them in, but they insulted and injured people, and made themselves generally hated. How-ever, the two, plus their children (they reproduced warriors every three months!) would not go of their own free will, nor could they be forced to go. So Matholwch and his people decided to forge a solid iron chamber, surround it with charcoal, and fire it until it was red hot. The man and woman escaped and presumably fled to Wales with their cauldron. This is a fascinating story, and the use of an Iron House to imprison the two monstrous creatures reminds us that according to Pliny, the Druids of Gaul gathered selago "without the use of iron," suggesting that iron may have been considered impure. If the Druids shunned the use of iron, it is only a short step to imagining that they feared it and envisaged it as capable of being used in the building of a place where they could be imprisoned. Interestingly, Oosten suggests[13] that the Iron House is an inverted cauldron which kills warriors instead of regenerating them.

After this, Matholwch returned to Ireland with Branwen, who bore him a son. Eventually people started talking about the humiliation that Matholwch suffered at the hands of Efnisien, and mocked Matholwch. In reaction, Matholwch drove Branwen from his bed, and made her work as a baker in the court. Branwen then raised a starling, tied a letter around the bird's wing, and sent it off to Bran. Once the message was delivered, Bran decided to attack Ireland — the ocean was not extensive then, so he "went by wading," carrying the "string-minstrels" on his back (Bran, it should be said, is a giant). The Irish decided to make peace with Bran, and offered to give the sovereignty of Ireland to Gwern, Branwen's son, and to build Bran a house large enough to contain him. The house was built, but the Irish laid a trap, hanging a "crane skin-bag" on each of the hundred columns of the house with an armed fighting man in each. Efnisien came ahead of the others, and asked what was in the bags. When he was told "Flour," he felt in each bag and crushed the head of each hidden man.

Then Bran with his entourage arrived and sat down with the Irish to conclude the peace deal. Bran and Manawydan then spoke to their nephew Gwern; Gwern went up to Efnisien to speak to him, and Efnisien threw him into the fire. Branwen tried to go after him, but Bran restrained her; the Irish lit the fire under the cauldron of regeneration, and started regenerating their dead warriors. Efnisien then crawled among the Irish corpses, was thrown into the cauldron, and stretched himself out until the cauldron broke into four pieces.

In the end, the British were victorious but, as we saw in Chapter 3, only seven survived, including Manawydan, Pryderi and Taliesin. Bran, wounded in his foot with a poisoned spear, ordered the survivors to cut off his head and bury it in the White Hill in London. But, he said, they would take a long time to get to London: they would spend seven years feasting in Harlech, with the "birds of Rhiannon" singing to them; and they would spend eighty years at Gwales in Penfro (thought to be Grassholm off the southwest coast of Pembrokeshire). In the meantime, he said, the head would remain uncorrupted and "be as good company to you as it was at its best when it was ever on me." Once arrived on the coast of Wales, they discovered that Casswallawn son of Beli had overrun the Island of Britain and become crowned king in London. They made for Harlech and feasted there for seven years; as soon as they began to eat and drink, "there came three birds, which began to sing a kind of song to them; and when they heard that song, every other [tune] seemed unlovely beside it"— these were presumably the mysterious birds of Rhiannon. After their allotted seven years they headed for Gwales, where "Of all the grief that they had witnessed or experienced themselves— there was no longer any memory." Eventually, of course, one of the seven survivors opened the door to Cornwall which was supposed to remain closed, and they were forced to leave Gwales and head for London, where Bran's head was buried.

Commentary

Who are the children of Llyr? The answer to this question may lie not in the mythological elements of the tale (the cauldron of regeneration, the Iron House, the sojourn in the otherworldly Gwales), but in the names of the children and their relatives. The name Bran means "crow" or "raven" in Welsh, which reminds us that Lugdunum, the city of Lugus, was associated with ravens, and that ravens were found buried in the shaft at Jordan Hill temple in Dorset (see Chapter 2). However, Koch[14] believes that Bran's name also has a historical basis.

In 280–279 B.C., an army of Celts, coming from Pannonia (an area around the Danube), invaded Macedonia (northeast Greece). One division of the army, led by Bolgios, inflicted heavy losses on the Macedonians and killed their king; another contingent, led by Brennus, urged an attack on Greece. The Greeks sent their cavalry and light infantry to meet Brennus's forces at the river Spercheios; the Greeks broke down the bridges, but Brennus and his army crossed further downriver, where the river formed a marshy lake. Eventually Brennus defeated the Greeks at Thermopylae, and marched on to Delphi, home of the famous oracle. There, according to the Pausanias,[15] the forces of Brennus were defeated, and Brennus, wounded by a spear or javelin, took his own life. However, Diodorus Siculus[16] has a slightly different version: "In the mighty battle fought [at Delphi] he lost tens of thousands of his comrades-in-arms, and Brennus himself was three times wounded. Weighed down and near to death, he assembled his host there and spoke to the Gauls. He advised them to kill him and all the wounded, to burn their waggons, and to return home unburdened."

Pausanias makes it clear that Brennus and his forces were defeated at Delphi, but apparently rumors circulated that the Celts had managed to sack Delphi and loot it. Strabo, in his *Geography*, written over two centuries later, reports[17] that treasures said to have been looted from Delphi were found in Tolosa (Toulouse) by the Roman statesman and general Caepio in 105 B.C., though to his cost, for "it was on account of having laid hands on them that Caepio ended his life in misfortunes — for he was cast out by his native land as a temple-robber, and he left behind as his heirs female children only, who, as it turned out, became prostitutes, as Timagenes has said, and therefore perished in disgrace." Strabo further says that the treasure found in Tolosa amounted to about fifteen thousand talents (a talent is about 70 lbs), "part of it in sacred lakes," mostly gold and silver bullion. However, he says, treasure was commonplace in Gaul, especially in lakes — but he adds that the temple of Tolosa was "hallowed," since it "was very much revered by the inhabitants of the surrounding country, and on this account the treasures there were excessive, for numerous people had dedicated them and no one dared to lay hands on them."

On the basis of the similarities between the Brennos and Bran stories (both crossed water to engage the enemy, both were wounded by a missile, both begged their men to kill them, and the treasures looted from Delphi were ritually buried in lakes just as Bran's head was ritually buried in London), Koch believes that Bran is in one sense Brennos, and that the story was transmitted orally across the Celtic world until it assumed its present form in *Branwen, Daughter of Llyr*.

Manawydan's name is cognate with that of the Irish god Manannan mac Lir, the god of the sea, but Manawydan seems to have no connection with the sea, or with the Isle of Man, from which his name is said to be derived. Koch proposes[18] that Manawydan's name is derived from Mandubracius, the king of the Trinovantes who was deposed by Cassivellaunus and restored to power by Julius Caesar (see Chapter 2). This proposal is given some support by the fact that when Bran and the seven survivors return to Wales, they discover that Bran has been deposed by Casswallawn son of Beli.

Beli is also the father of Penarddun, the mother of Bran and Manawyddan. Beli or Beli Mawr, says Koch,[19] is a legendary Welsh ancestor at or near the prehistoric opening of several royal pedigrees. In the *Lludd and Llefelys* he is said to be the father of Lludd and Caswallon or Casswallawn. The belief that he was father of Cassivellaunus probably arose from a phrase in the *Historia Brittonum*,[20] where the British king who fought against Caesar is called *Bellinus filius Minocanni* ("Belinus the son of Minocannus"), a textual garbling of *Adminius Cynobellini Britannorum regis filius* ("Adminius son of Cunobelinus king of the Britains"). Koch believes that the name Beli actually derives from Bolgios or Belgius, the name of the chieftain who fought alongside Brennus in the campaign against the Macedonians and Greeks. Later Bolgios or Belgios may have become identified with the Belgae of northern Gaul, and been seen as an ancestor-figure.

As to why Bran and Manawydan are "children of the sea," this may have something to do with British prehistory. Nobody knows for certain when Celts first settled in Britain (see Chapter 5 for further discussion), but it is likely to have happened during the period 450 B.C.–200 B.C., which saw a large-scale migration of people called Celts (it was during this migration period that Brennus and Bolgios attacked Macedonia and Greece). Later, after about 100 B.C., Belgae from northern Gaul also settled in parts of southeast England — and from the perspective of those settled there, these Belgae would have come from the sea. It may be significant that in Triads 8 and 52, Llyr is referred to as "Llyr Half-Speech," implying that the "sea-people" spoke a dialect that was only half-understood. Curiously, East Walloon (Walloon is the French dialect of Belgium) and Coastal Dutch (Dutch is the other national language of Belgium) share some phonological (sound) features with Welsh,[21] suggesting a "particularly close link between the language of Belgic Gaul and British (the language that became Breton and Welsh)."

The Mound-People (2): Pryderi, Rhiannon, Manawydan

The Third Branch of the *Mabinogion, Manawydan, Son of Llyr*, follows on from the Second Branch, with Manawydan and Pryderi burying Bran's head in the White Hill in London. Manawydan does not wish to live with his cousin Casswallawn who is now king of Britain, so Pryderi offers him the seven *cantrefs* of Dyfed, along with marriage to his mother Rhiannon. The two then return to Dyfed, and Manawydan assumes the

rulership of the seven *cantrefs* of Dyfed, and marries the willing Rhiannon.

One evening Pryderi and his wife Cigfa and Manawydan and his wife
Rhiannon were feasting at Arberth when they decided to take a stroll on
the *gorsedd*. As one of Pwyll's courtiers said in the First Branch, if a high-
born man sat on the *gorsedd*, he would not leave without "wounds or
blows" or "his witnessing a marvel," and this is indeed what happened as
they were sitting there[22]:

> Suddenly there was a clap of thunder and, with such a great clap of thun-
> der, a fall of mist so that no-one could see anyone else. After the mist,
> everywhere [was filled] with bright light. And when they looked where
> before they would have once seen flocks and herds and dwellings, they
> could see nothing at all: neither house, nor animal, nor smoke, nor fire,
> nor man, nor dwellings; [nothing] except the empty buildings of the
> court, deserted, uninhabited, without man or beast within them, their
> own companions lost, without them knowing anything about them; [no-
> one left] except the four of them.

So the four of them wandered the countryside, but found nothing, and
for a year lived off hunted meat, fish and wild swarms. Tiring of this, they
made for England and took up saddle-making; Manawydan "began to
fashion pommels, and they were coloured in the way he had seen Llassar
Llaes Gyfnewid do with blue azure" (Llassar is the escapee from the Iron
House in the Second Branch who gave Bran the cauldron of regeneration).
Manawydan's saddles and pommels were so good that the other saddlers
decided to kill him and Pryderi. Hearing about this, the four left for
another town, and started making shields, but the same thing happened;
so they moved on and became shoemakers, with the same results; fed up
by this time, they then moved back to Dyfed. They made for Arberth and
once more lived by foraging and hunting.

One morning Manawydan and Pryderi were hunting, when their dogs
ran ahead into a small copse, then withdrew again swiftly, all bristling and
fearful. Manawydan and Pryderi approached the copse and saw a "shining
white boar," which left the copse. They went after the boar, which led
them to a "great, towering *caer*" which they had never seen before. The
dogs and boar entered the *caer*, and Pryderi followed them, despite the
warnings of Manawydan. When he went inside the *caer*, all he could see
was[23]

> a fountain with marble stonework around it. Beside the fountain [was] a
> golden bowl, attached by four chains, which was above [the] marble

slab — with the chains reaching up into the air, and he could not see the end of them.

He was inspired at the beauty of the gold, and [at] how good the workmanship of the bowl [was]. He came up to where the bowl was, and laid hold of it. As soon as he had laid hold of the bowl, his hands stuck to the bowl, and his two feet to the slab on which he was standing. The power of speech was taken from him so he could not utter a single word. And thus he stood [unable to move].

Manawydan then told Rhiannon what had happened. Rhiannon went inside the *caer* and got stuck to the bowl like Pryderi, after which there was a peal of thunder, a mist fell, and the *caer* disappeared along with Pryderi and Rhiannon.

Manawydan and Cigfa then went back to England, where Manawydan once more became a shoemaker, with the same results as before. The two then returned to Dyfed, and this time Manawydan took with him a bushel of wheat. He planted three fields of wheat, which grew exceptionally well, but as he was about to harvest two of the fields, he found them stripped bare. He kept watch on the third field, and discovered the culprits were mice. He managed to catch one of the mice, larger and slower than the rest, and was about to hang it, when a bishop approached and offered Manawydan large sums of money to release the mouse. It turns out that the bishop is Llwyd Cil Coed, who "put magic" on the seven *cantrefs* of Dyfed to avenge Gwawl (Rhiannon's suitor who was humiliated by Pwyll and Rhiannon), and the mouse is the bishop's wife. Manawydan releases the mouse, the enchantment is lifted, and Pryderi and Rhiannon return.

As in the First Branch, the focus of the action is the *gorsedd* or mound, where the magic is first put on the seven *cantrefs* of Dyfed. The central episode in this chain of magic is the episode where Pryderi and Rhiannon get stuck to the golden bowl in the mysterious *caer*— an episode we have commented on in Chapter 3 as being similar to the imprisonment of Gweir in Annwn. The man responsible for the magic is Llwyd Cil Coed: Parker says his name means "The Grey One of the Wooded Cell," and is thought to be a corruption of the Irish *Líath Mac Celtchair*, who is mentioned in the Irish *Metrical Dindshenchas* 63[24] (*dindshenchas* means "tradition or lore of places"). Liath is the son of Celtchar or Celtchair, who lives in Dun Lethglaise, also known as the Mound of Down. He was in love with Bri, the daughter of Midir, who was one of the sons of the great god of Irish mythology, the Dagda, and lived in the *sidh* of Bri Leith. Midir refused to let his daughter see Liath, and she died of a broken heart. If Llwyd is related to Liath, then he is also one of the Mound-People.

It is significant that Pryderi and Rhiannon are largely victims in the Third Branch, and it is Manawydan, the Child of the Sea, who is the man of action — he is best at all the jobs they do when they are in England, and it is he who finally frees Dyfed from its enchantment, and rescues Pryderi and Rhiannon from their imprisonment.

The Children of the Earth: Gwydion and Arianrhod

Analysis

The Fourth Branch of the *Mabinogion, Math, Son of Mathonwy*, concerns the children of Don, Arianrhod, Gwydion and Gilfaethwy, together with their uncle — Don's brother — Math son of Mathonwy, and Arianrhod's son Lleu. At the time, Math was lord of Gwynedd (north Wales), and Pryderi was lord of the twenty-one *cantrefs* in the south (Dyfed, Ceredigion. Ystrad Tywi, mentioned in the Third Branch, plus Morganog, now Glamorganshire).

Any discussion of the Fourth Branch must start with Don. Don is often compared to the Irish Danu, mother of the Irish gods, the Tuatha De Danann ("Peoples of Danu"), whose name is sometimes linked to the Indo-European root *ad(u)-* "water current."[25] However, in his discussion of Don, Koch[26] follows Carey[27] in his interpretation of the Fourth Branch as a creation myth. This, says Koch, suggests a different etymology for the name *Don*, namely that it is cognate with Old Irish genitive, dative and accusative singular *don* "place, ground, earth," and with Greek *khthon* "earth." Before I look at the names of the other characters, I need to summarize the story.

Math, it seems, had a strange disability: he could not live except when he had his feet in the lap of a maiden, unless he had to go to war. His footholder at the time was Goewin, and Gilfaethwy fell in love with her, but could do nothing as long as Math was around. Gwydion asked him what the matter was, but Gilfaethwy was afraid to say anything, because of Math's "ability: whatever whisper, however small, that there might be between people, once the wind has met it, he will know it."[28] But Gwydion guessed what the problem was, and said he would arrange a war so that Gilfaethwy could be alone with Goewin. Gwydion approached Math and told him that Pryderi had a new kind of animal, called a pig, sent to him by Arawn, lord of Annwn, and that he, Gwydion, would get hold of the pigs for Math. He and Gilfaethwy then went to Pryderi's court disguised as bards, and Gwydion, who was the best storyteller in the world, delighted the court with entertaining recitals and storytelling. Gwydion then asked Pryderi for the pigs, but Pryderi said he could not give them to Gwydion until they had bred twice their number. Thinking Pryderi might be willing to exchange the pigs, Gwydion then used his magic to create twelve greyhounds, twelve steeds and twelve golden shields. Pryderi agreed to give Gwydion the pigs in exchange for these items, and Gwydion and Gilfaethwy hurried away with the pigs, for, said Gwydion, the magic would not last from one day to the next.

As expected, Pryderi then went to war with Gwynedd, and Math set out with his army, leaving Gilfaethwy alone with Goewin, who was "put to sleep with Gilfaethwy" in Math's bed, and "slept with against her will." Meanwhile, the battle between the armies of Math and Pryderi was joined, and there was great slaughter on both sides. Finally it was agreed that since Gwydion had caused all the trouble, the matter should be decided by single combat between Gwydion and Pryderi, and as the tale says, through "strength and valour and aggression and magic and enchantment Gwydion prevailed, and Pryderi was killed."[29] When Math returned to court and discovered that Goewin had been raped by Gilfaethwy with Gwydion's help, he punished Gwydion and Gilfaethwy in a rather unusual way[30]:

> "Since you have been in league together, I will make you fare together and be mated. You will have the same nature as the beasts whose shapes you are in; and during this time, they will have offspring — so you will have them too. A year from today, come to me here."
>
> After a year to the day, lo! he could hear an uproar below the wall of the chamber, with the dogs of the court barking on top of that uproar.
>
> "[Go and] see what's outside," said he.
>
> "Lord," someone said, "I have looked. There is a stag and a hind and a fawn with them."
>
> At that, he arose and came outside. When he came, what he could see was the three creatures. The three creatures were a stag, a hind and sturdy fawn.

The same punishment was then repeated, with the hind becoming a wild boar, and the stag a sow; after a year, these two returned with their offspring, and were again transformed, with the wild boar becoming a she-wolf, and the sow a wolf. A year later, they returned with their offspring, and were changed back into their human form.

Since Math no longer had a footholder, Gwydion suggested his sister Arianrhod, daughter of Math's sister Don. First Math had to be sure Arianrhod was a virgin, so he asked her to step over his magic wand. As she did so, she gave birth to a large boy with curly yellow hair, and shortly after that "a little something dropped from her"—Gwydion picked it up and wrapped a sheet of brocaded silk around it and hid it in a small chest at the foot of his bed. The boy was baptized Dylan and immediately made for the sea. Not long after, Gwydion heard a cry from the chest, opened it, and saw a little boy. He took the boy to a wet nurse, and the boy grew rapidly, much as Pryderi did in the First Branch.

Gwydion virtually became the boy's father, and one day he took the boy to see Arianrhod at her home, Caer Arianrhod, a rocky island off the coast of Gwynedd and opposite the hillfort of Dinas Dinlle ("City of Lleu's Fortress"). Arianrhod welcomed them, but on discovering that the boy was hers, became upset and, learning that he had no name, swore an oath on him, that he would not get a name unless he got it from her. To overcome this curse, Gwydion conjured up a ship, disguised himself and the boy as shoemakers, and sailed to Caer Arianrhod. When Arianrhod saw the shoemakers, she ordered some shoes, but Gwydion deliberately made them too large. When Arianrhod came to complain, the boy was stitching[31]:

> Suddenly, there was a wren alighting on the deck of the boat. The boy took aim and hit it between the sinew and the bone of its leg. She laughed.
> "God knows," said she, "the fair one strikes it with a skillful hand!"
> "Aye," he replied, "and the wrath of God upon you! He has obtained a name, and the name is good enough. 'Lleu Skillful Hand' he will be from now on."

When Arianrhod realized who they were, she swore another oath on the boy—that he would never take arms unless she armed him herself. To overcome this oath, Gwydion disguised himself and Lleu as bards, and went to Caer Arianrhod. They spent the night there, and in the morning Gwydion used his magic to make everyone believe there was an army approaching Caer Arianrhod. Arianrhod then provided Lleu with all the arms he needed, and Gwydion dispersed his enchanted army. Angry at this, Arianrhod swore a destiny on him—that he would never get a wife "from any race that is in the world today."

To overcome this destiny, Math and Gwydion decided to "conjure a wife for him out of flowers, using our magic and enchantment."[32] So "they took the flowers of the oak, the flowers of the broom, and the flowers of the meadowsweet—and from those they called forth the fairest and most beautiful woman anyone had ever seen. She was baptised with the baptism they practised [back] then, and [the name of] 'Blodeuedd' was put upon her." Lleu and Blodeuedd were married, and while Lleu was visiting Math, Blodeuedd met and fell in love with a passing lord called Gronw. They decided to kill Lleu, and not long afterward Blodeuedd asked Lleu about how he might be killed, on the pretense of being worried about him. It turned out he could only be killed by a spear made under certain conditions, in a bath by the side of a river, while Lleu had one foot on the bath and one foot on the back of a buck (young male deer). Blodeuedd said she didn't understand, and asked him to demonstrate. So the bath was set up by the river, and goats were brought (a misunderstanding on the part of Blodeuedd). Llleu demonstrated what he meant, and Gronw threw the specially made spear at Lleu, who "took flight in the form of an eagle, and gave a terrible scream."

On hearing the news, Gwydion set out to find Lleu. One day he followed a sow, until she stopped to graze. He went under a tree and saw that the sow was grazing on rotting flesh and maggots. He looked up into the top of the tree.[33]

> When he looked up, he could see an eagle in the top of the tree. When the eagle shook himself, worms and rotting flesh fell from him, and those the sow was devouring. It occurred to him that the eagle was Lleu, and he sung an englyn:
>
> > "An oak grows between two pools,
> > Dark-black branches sky and glen
> > If I do not tell a lie
> > From the flowers of Lleu this has come!"
>
> The eagle let himself down until he was in the middle of the tree. [Then] Gwydion sang another englyn:
>
> > "An oak grows upon a high plain
> > Rain neither wets it, nor drips upon it
> > Nine-score strikes has it endured
> > In its top, Lleu Skillful-Hand."
>
> And then he let himself down until he was on the lowest branch of the tree. Then [Gwydion] sang an englyn:
>
> > "Grows an oak upon a steep
> > The sanctuary of fair lord
> > Unless I speak falsely:
> > Lleu will come down into my lap."
>
> And he fell onto Gwydion's knee; and then Gwydion struck him with a magic wand, until he was [back] in his own form. However, no-one had ever seen a man in a sorrier state. He was nothing but skin and bones.

Afterwards, Lleu was restored to health, Gwydion changed Blodeuedd into an owl, and Lleu threw a spear at Gronw, as Gronw had done to him, breaking Gronw's back and killing him.

Commentary

The first general point to make about the Fourth Branch is that Gwydion kills Pryderi in single combat early on in the tale, suggesting that the Children of the Earth have in some sense replaced the Mound-People. The second general point is that the Children of the Sea are apparently nowhere to be seen, with two possible qualifications: in Triad 35, Arianrhod is said to be the daughter of Beli Mawr; and in the course of the Fourth Branch, Lleu is referred to as one of the Three Golden Shoe-makers, named in Triad 67 as Casswallawn, Manawydan and Lleu.

As for the main characters, much can be learned by looking at their names. The name Math was first studied by the French historian and philologist Henri d'Arbois de Jubainville. He says[34] that the word *math* can be recognized in the term *math-ghamhuin* "bearcub" (literally "calf of bear"), used in the Irish translation of the Bible to render the Hebrew *dob* "bear." The word *matus* "bear" appears as the first term in the Gallic men's names *Matu-genos* "Son of the Bear," that is, son of the Bear-God, and *Matu-murus* "Great like a Bear," that is, as great as the Bear-God. The Gallic god *Matunus* is also derived from this root, and a variant of this, *Matunnos*, provided the second element of the Gallo-Roman name of Langres, *Ande-matunnum* ("Great Bear"), fortress of the divinized great bear. There is also an Irish proper name *Mac-Mathghamhna*, which today is written as Mac-Mahon, and means "son of the bearcub." To this list we may add, says Boekhoorn,[35] Math son of Mathonwy, *Math mac Úmóir in druí*, the druid of the Tuatha De Danann according to the *Book of Invasions*, and *Matgen* ("Son of the Bear"), the *corrguine*, or "sorcerer," of the Tuatha. It is not clear in what sense Math is a bear, but he can certainly be seen as a Druid and sorcerer — in fact, in Triad 28, Math is said to have taught one of the "Three Great Enchantments of the Island of Britain" to Gwydion son of Don.

Turning now to Gwydion, Koch[36] notes that in the genealogy of Brycheiniog (a kingdom in southeast Wales) contained in the Harleian 3859 manuscript, we find the Old Welsh name *Lou Hen map Guidgen*. If this can be interpreted as "Lleu the Old, son of Gwydion," then it means (1) Gwydion is actually the father of Lleu — which would certainly explain

Arianrhod's violent reaction toward Lleu and Gwydion — and (2) the name Gwydion is derived from *Widu-genos* "Son of a Tree." As for Arianrhod, her name is usually translated as "Silver Wheel," and she is seen in terms of the moon, especially since the name Lleu is associated with light (see Welsh *lleuad* "moon"[37]). The eminent Welsh scholar John Rhys (1840–1915) said that Caer Arianrhod is also used in Welsh to denote the constellation Corona Borealis.[38] Lleu is usually identified with the god Lugus[39]: his epithet "Skillful-Hand" is similar to that of the Irish Lugh, who is called *Lamhfhada* "Long-Arm" or "Long-Hand"; he was celebrated as a shoemaker, and as we saw earlier, there is a dedication in Roman Iberia to Lugus from the shoemakers' guild; and the second element of Dinas Dinlle, the Welsh hillfort referred to earlier, is exactly the same as Lugdunum, but in reverse order. The association between Lleu and Lugus may seem rather tenuous, but I hope to reinforce it in later chapters.

It was said earlier that *Math, Son of Mathonwy* is a creation myth, and this is supported by the fact that Lleu may be the child of a brother-sister relationship. Elizabeth Archibald[40] notes that in the Greek creation myth Cronus married his sister Rhea, and was subsequently deposed by their son Zeus, and in Egyptian myth the brothers Osiris and Set married their sisters Isis and Nephthys, since the "first stages of creation permit, indeed necessitate incest." Fee and Leeming tell us[41] that in Norse mythology Njordr's sister was said to have borne him his children Freyr and Freya, and "no discernable shame seems attached to this union."

If *Math, Son of Mathonwy* is a creation myth, then Gwydion and Math are the creative forces of the tale. They are both Druids — when they made Blodeuedd, one of the ingredients was "flowers of the oak," and when Gwydion found the eagle Lleu, he was perched on an oak tree. Math has a magic wand, and both Math and Gwydion can perform magic. The ancient Greek and Roman writers said that the Druids studied astronomy, and perhaps the Welsh knew this, because, as Rhys points out, not only is Caer Arianrhod the Corona Borealis, but *Llys Don* ("Don's Court") is the constellation Cassiopeia, and Caer Gwydion is the Milky Way. Classical writers also affirmed that the Druids believed in reincarnation, and certainly a good deal of shape-shifting occurs in this tale, with Math changing Gwydion and Gilfaethwy into a variety of animals, and Lleu taking the shape of an eagle. This reincarnation or shape-shifting is most noticeable is some of the poems attributed to Taliesin. In *Angar Kyfyndawt* (*Cruel Bondage* or *Hostile Alliance*), as translated by Sarah Higley, the poet says[42]:

> I was a blue salmon,
> I was a dog, I was a stag,
> I was a buck on the mountain,
> I was a trunk, I was a spade (?)
> I was a drinking horn in the hand,
> I was a peg in forceps
> for a year and a half
> I was a speckled white rooster
> among chickens in Edinburgh.
> I was a steed in a herd,
> I was a fierce bull,
> I was a miller's billygoat,
> like the nourisher (?)
> I was a scaly grain,
> it grew on a hill,
> I will be reaped, I will be placed
> into the chimney I will be driven,
> I will be torn from the hand,
> by my bagfulls,
> a red-clawed hen received me,
> combed foe.
> I rested nine nights in her womb as a lad.

The next poem in *The Book of Taliesin, Kat Godeu* (*The Battle of the Trees*), continues in a similar vein[43]:

> I have been in a multitude of shapes,
> Before I assumed a consistent form.
> I have been a sword, narrow, variegated ...
> I have been the dullest of stars.
> I have been a word among letters,
> I have been a book in the origin.
> I have been the light of lanterns,
> A year and a half.
> I have been a continuing bridge,
> Over three score Abers.
> I have been a course, I have been an eagle.
> I have been a coracle in the seas:
> I have been compliant in the banquet.
> I have been a drop in a shower;
> I have been a sword in the grasp of the hand
> I have been a shield in battle.

It is hard to know what to make of these transformations: some sound like possible reincarnations, some sound like shape-shifts, and some sound like poetic identification with nature (and culture) in all its facets.

The Battle of the Trees is a difficult poem. In her notes to the poem, Mary Jones points out[44] that the theme of a battle of the trees can be seen in the Irish story *The Second Battle of Magh Tuiredh*, between the Tuatha De Danann and the Fomorians (the pre–Celtic gods of Ireland), in which Lugh said:

> "And ye, O Be-cuile and O Dianann," said Lugh to his two witches, "what power can ye wield in the battle?"
>
> "Not hard to tell," said they. "We will enchant the trees and the stones and the sods of the earth, so that they shall become a host under arms against them, and shall rout them in flight with horror and trembling."

Whatever the battle may be, later in the poem the narrator tells us:

> I was enchanted by Math,
> Before I became immortal,
> I was enchanted by Gwydyon
> The great purifier of the Brython ...
> I was enchanted by the sage
> Of sages, in the primitive world.
> When I had a being.

He then goes on to say:

> I travelled in the earth,
> Before I was a proficient in learning.
> I travelled, I made a circuit,
> I slept in a hundred islands
> A hundred Caers I have dwelt in.
> Ye intelligent Druids,
> Declare to Arthur,
> What is there more early
> Than I that they sing of.

The Taliesin-poet's reference to the "primitive world" does suggest that he is talking about reincarnation, and evokes the Irish story of Tuan mac Cairill,[45] which first appeared in the 12th-century *Book of the Dun Cow*. This describes how a man who first came to Ireland as part of the first settlement after the biblical flood lived on though all the subsequent phases of its legendary history by passing through the shapes of a stag, a boar, a cormorant and a salmon; with each metamorphosis his youth was renewed. The fact that the poem also refers to Math and Gwydion, to Druids and to Arthur (possibly the Arthur of *The Spoils of Annwn*), seems to reinforce the link between the Children of Don and Druidism.

Conclusion

As I said at the beginning of this chapter, the *Mabinogion* concerns three sets of characters, the Mound-People, the Children of the Sea (Llyr) and the Children of the Earth (Don). We saw that from a historical perspective, the Children of the Sea seemed to be linked to figures from early history, like Brennus, Mandubracius, Bolgios and Cassivellaunus. The other two sets of characters seem largely ahistorical, though the Mound-People seem to be associated with the horse-goddess Epona, and the Children of the Earth seem to be connected with Druidism. In the following chapter I will try to put a face to the Mound-People and the Children of the Earth by going back deep into the prehistory of southern England.

Chapter 5

Mounds, Mounds, Mounds

Rubbish Heaps, Hillforts and the
Prehistory of Southern England

Prelude

If we want to find the origins of the Mound-People and the Children of the Earth, one very good place to start looking is southern England, or rather an area of southern England to the southwest of London stretching from the Marlborough Downs and Kennet Valley in the northern part of Wiltshire through the Vale of Pewsey to Salisbury Plain in the south of Wiltshire, and east into what is now the western part of Hampshire. This is a good place to look for ancestors because the ancestors certainly left their mark there, with West Kennet Long Barrow, Avebury Stone Circle, Silbury Hill and, of course, the most impressive mark of all, Stonehenge. I'll be focusing on three of these — West Kennet Long Barrow, which is certainly a burial-mound or *sidi*; Silbury Hill, which legend says is the last resting-place of King Sil; and Stonehenge, which Geoffrey of Monmouth[1] called the Giants' Dance, and which he said had been erected to commemorate the 460 British treacherously slain by the Saxon king Hengist.

West Kennet Long Barrow is a Neolithic tomb or barrow, situated on a prominent chalk ridge near Silbury Hill, and one-and-a-half miles south of Avebury (see Map 4). According to Wikipedia, archeologists "classify it as a chambered long barrow, and one of the Severn-Cotswold tombs" (other examples are Hetty Pegler's Tump, near Uley, Gloucestershire, site of the much later Roman temple, and Wayland's Smithy in Oxfordshire). It has "two pairs of opposing transept chambers and a single terminal chamber used for burial. The stone burial chambers are located at one end of one of the longest barrows in Britain at 330 feet: in total it is estimated that 15,700 man hours were expended in its construction. The entrance consists of a concave forecourt with a facade made from large slabs of sarsen stones which were placed to seal entry." Construction of the barrow began around 3600 B.C., and it was in use until around 2500 B.C.

Julian Thomas says[2] that

> initial burial deposits included both articulated bodies and clean bones, and it seems skeletal parts were taken out of the chambers as well as placed in them. Seemingly the chambers were entered and used over a long period, with their contents being repeatedly reorganized. If the deposition, removal and repositioning of human remains were not casual activities, then the spatial configuration of the chambers would have limited the numbers of people who could have been present and witnessed these events. So even if access to the tomb were not generally limited, then this kind of ritual activity would have generated a form of socially restricted knowledge.

In terms of the deposition of bones, the westernmost chamber was dominated by the bodies of adult males, while there were many young persons in the southeast transept.

At some time during the centuries that followed, says Thomas, a "series of secondary deposits were introduced into the chambers, consisting of alternating layers of clean chalk and burnt material with a higher organic content.... The dark, organic layers in particular contained large quantities of broken pottery, stone tools and waste, and human and animal bones. Piggott, the excavator, noted the diversity of the cultural material in the secondary deposits, and the presence of Grooved ware and Beaker pottery at the base of the sequence." The excavator Piggott argued, says Thomas,[3] that "the material must have accumulated over a lengthy period, before being placed in the tomb." This meant that the artefacts must have originally been placed in some "offering-house" which "would receive ritual or votive offerings including pottery, and contain the debris of ritual meals including animal bones and the ashes of the hearth." Thomas goes on to say[4] that the artefacts were treated in the same way as the dead bodies: just as the bodies were brought into the chambers whole, "allowed to rot, parts of them removed, and the remaining elements reorganized in various ways," so the pottery vessels in the secondary deposits "had been broken and the parts scattered."

Around 2500 B.C., the passage and chamber were filled to the roof by Beaker people (of whom more later) with earth and stones containing the secondary deposits excavated by Piggott. Barry Cunliffe notes[5] that the culture of the Beaker people took over only gradually in the Kennet

Valley area, "after a prolonged struggle with older entrenched orthodoxies" represented by monuments like West Kennet Long Barrow. The first Beaker culture burials occurred well away from existing ritual centers, as if these were "reflections of incompatible systems of belief and social practice." Only the later forms of the Beaker culture occur at such ceremonial sites, and their growing power is demonstrated at West Kennet Long Barrow, which was blocked with massive stones as if to emphasize the final assumption of symbolic authority by beaker users.

Silbury Hill lies on the valley floor of the River Kennet, at a point where the capacity of the stream is increased by contributions from a small tributary together with water from a spring where the stream changes its course. The underlying rock is Cretaceous White Chalk, and the area is essentially part of the extensive Lower Chalk plateau that extends northwards towards Swindon. The origin of the name "Silbury" is unclear, though David Field reports[6] that the earliest name is *Seleburgh*, which may derive from Old English *sele* "hall." At 130 feet high, says Wikipedia, Silbury Hill is the "tallest prehistoric human-made mound in Europe, and one of the largest in the world." It is thought to have taken "18 million man hours, or 500 men working 15 years to deposit and shape 8,800,000 cubic feet of earth and fill on top of a natural hill."

According to Richard Atkinson, who excavated the site between 1968 and 1970, the hill comprised "an initial smallish mound of gravel and turf, surmounted later by a second mound of chalk with a surrounding ditch, over which was constructed the massive chalk mound that we see today. The final mound, he thought, was built in tiers like a wedding cake, arguing that the now-invisible lower terraces had become obscured by weathering."[7] Atkinson believed that the hill was Neolithic, and two small trenches cut on the summit (in 2001) by Fachtna McAvoy of English Heritage's Centre for Archaeology "revealed — for the first time — a fragment of antler from a secure context, lying against a chalk wall in a deposit of chalk rubble. This produced a secure radiocarbon date of between 2490–2340 B.C., placing the mound firmly in the Late Neolithic."

Atkinson thought the hill had been built in tiers, but recent survey work by English Heritage suggests otherwise. The "uppermost terrace, when circumnavigated, returns to a point several meters below the starting point — in other words, it spirals down. Weathering has obscured the detail of ledges further down the slope; but if we assume the feature is continuous, it implies a spiral path all the way from the summit to the base." The idea of a spiral path, says Field, is attractive. It would "not only have provided

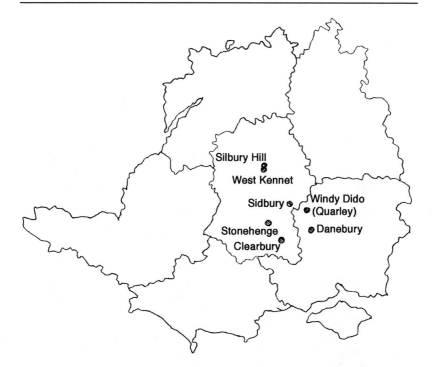

Map 4: Salisbury Plain and surrounding areas c. 1000 B.C. with Neolithic monuments, and sites of early field systems and later "ranch boundaries."

a processional route to the top of the hill, but would also have aided the construction of the mound."

Nobody really knows why Silbury Hill was built — in fact, during Atkinson's and earlier excavations at Silbury, "many more Roman and early medieval finds were produced than Neolithic. In the 19th century, a substantial Roman building was found south of the hill. Cutting into the mound at ground level in 1867, Wilkinson found a platform just below the surface on which was a pile of ashes associated with Romano-British artefacts. Atkinson himself found over 100 Roman coins in the ditch, while numerous Roman shafts and wells were found nearby."

Then, over the past decade, "the Roman evidence increased. A combination of pipeline excavations and aerial photography has revealed the extent of Romano-British settlement on the lower slopes of Waden Hill — a natural hill next to Silbury. It now seems almost inconceivable that, with a Romano-British settlement facing the mound, Silbury was not used in some way." It is possible, says Field,[8] that the mound "was once covered with burials, monuments and memorials, and that what has been found so far is the tip of the iceberg."

Atkinson's medieval evidence

> was no less striking. Small postholes containing iron nails, early medieval potsherds and a silver coin of Ethelred II dating to 1010 suggested that the terraces had been revetted by posts. He also found an iron spearhead, and explained the evidence as defence against the Danish invasions — not unreasonably, given the skirmish at nearby East Kennet in 1006 reported in the Anglo-Saxon Chronicle. He concluded that the original terraces had been recut and fortified. The postholes, however, are located on the inside of each terrace and therefore imply revetment rather than defence.

It seems more likely, says Field, that Silbury Hill "was used as the site for a prestigious building, perhaps a Christian building, in the early medieval period. If the mound had been sacred in the Roman era, it is possible that it retained its religious attraction in later centuries." He suggests[9] that it may have been this prestigious building that gave the mound its name *Seleburgh* ("Hall-Fortress").

The ditch surrounding Silbury Hill, says Field,[10] is often considered a mere quarry from which the mound material was derived. However, its circular nature, and the regularity of its rectangular western extension, indicate that it served more than a functional purpose:

> Archeologists have come to see that ditches, even massive ditches around henges or hillforts, need not always be just utilitarian structures but may have had a metaphysical function too — for example, to keep evil spirits at bay. The rectangular extension at Silbury, if waterfilled, would have served as a cistern or reservoir. Elsewhere in the world, cisterns have often been the focus of ritual and ceremony. The mirror-like quality of standing water may have had symbolic implications too. Given archeologists' fascination with shamanism, it is significant that mirrors are considered symbols of shamanic ceremony and power.

The People of Stonehenge (1): The Builders

While Silbury Hill was being built, some 20 miles to the south, on Salisbury Plain, Stonehenge was also under construction. The Stonehenge site has a very long history. According to Wikipedia's excellent article on Stonehenge, archeologists have found four or five large Mesolithic postholes dating to around 8000 B.C. beneath the nearby tourist car-park. At least three of the posts "were in an east-west alignment which may have had ritual significance; no parallels are known from Britain at the time but similar sites have been found in Scandinavia." The first monument at Stonehenge itself, says Wikipedia, which is dated to around 3100 B.C.,

> consisted of a circular bank and ditch enclosure ... measuring about 360 feet in diameter with a large entrance to the northeast and a smaller one to the south.... The builders placed the bones of deer and oxen in the bottom of the ditch as well as some worked flint tools. The bones were considerably older than the antler picks used to dig the ditch, and the people who buried them had looked after them for some time prior to burial.... Within the outer edge of the enclosed area was a circle of 56 pits, each about 3 ft 3 in. in diameter, known as the Aubrey holes after John Aubrey, the 17th-century antiquarian who was thought to have first identified them.

In the two centuries that followed, at least 25 of the Aubrey holes were used for cremation burials.

The Stonehenge Riverside Project, headed by Mike Parker Pearson of Sheffield University,[11] has carbon-dated a number of burials at Stonehenge, and reports that the cremation burial of an adult found in Aubrey Hole 32 dates from 3030–2880 B.C.; the cremation burial of a young or mature adult from the middle fill of the Stonehenge ditch dates to 2930–2870 B.C.; human skull fragments from the northern ditch fill and the eastern ditch fill date to 2890–2630 B.C. and 2880–2570 B.C. respectively; the ditch was partly dug out between 2570 and 2340 B.C., and a third cremation burial was placed in this new ditch on the ditch's northern side — this burial is dated to 2570–2340 B.C. These finds and dates show that Stonehenge was a cemetery from around its inception until the period of the sarsens (2655–2485 B.C.). An estimated 240 people were buried at Stonehenge over a period of around 500 years, says Parker-Pearson — this amounts to one burial every two years, and suggests they were drawn from a very small and select living population, interred there "because of their special status as members of an elite dynasty of rulers."

Construction on Stonehenge proper is thought to have begun around 2600 B.C. At this time, two concentric arrays of holes (the Q and R Holes) were dug in the center of the site. The holes, says Wikipedia, "held up to 80 standing stones, only 43 of which can be traced today. The bluestones (some of which are made of dolerite, an igneous rock), were thought for much of the 20th century to have been transported by humans from the Preseli Hills, 160 miles away in modern-day Pembrokeshire in Wales. Another theory that has recently gained support, is that they were brought much nearer to the site as glacial erratics by the Irish Sea Glacier."[12]

During the next stage of activity, thought to have taken place between 2600 B.C. and 2400 B.C., 30 enormous sarsen stones were brought to the site. They may have come, says Wikipedia,

> from a quarry, around 25 miles north of Stonehenge on the Marlborough Downs, or they may have been collected from a "litter" of sarsens on the chalk downs, closer to hand. The stones were dressed and fashioned with mortise and tenon joints before 30 were erected as a 110-foot-diameter circle of standing stones, with a ring of 30 lintel stones resting on top. The lintels were fitted to one another using another woodworking method, the tongue and groove joint.... Within this circle stood five trilithons of dressed sarsen stone arranged in a horseshoe shape 45 feet across with its open end facing northeast.

Some time after this, the bluestones "appear to have been re-erected. They were placed within the outer sarsen circle and may have been trimmed in some way. Like the sarsens, a few have timberworking-style cuts in them, suggesting that, during this phase, they may have been linked with lintels and were part of a larger structure." Then, between 2280 B.C. and 1930 B.C., the bluestones "were arranged in a circle between the two rings of sarsens and in an oval at the center of the inner ring.... Soon afterwards, the northeastern section of this bluestone circle was removed, creating a horseshoe-shaped setting (the Bluestone Horseshoe) which mirrored the shape of the central sarsen trilithons." The last known construction at Stonehenge was around 1600 B.C., with the digging of the so-called Y and Z holes, two rings of concentric (though irregular) circuits of near-identical pits (30 pits in each circuit) cut around the outside of the Sarsen Circle.

Who built Stonehenge and where did they live? We know little about the people who first erected the bluestones and sarsens, except that they buried their leaders at Stonehenge, but we know more about those who carried out later work on Stonehenge, thanks to the famous Amesbury Archer and the lesser-known Boscombe Bowmen. The Amesbury Archer was found in 2002 at Amesbury, three miles southeast of Stonehenge, when archeologists from Wessex Archaeology were excavating in advance of a housing scheme. The grave they uncovered, dated to around 2300 B.C., contained the richest array of items ever found from this period. Around 100 objects were found, including the complete skeleton of a man, three copper knives, two small gold hair tresses, two sandstone wristguards to protect his wrists from the bow string, 16 flint arrowheads and five Beaker pots.[13]

According to the Wessex Archaeology website, this makes the grave "the richest Bronze Age find in Britain — there are ten times the usual number of finds from other graves. The gold dated to as early as 2,470 B.C. and is the earliest found in Britain. It seems likely that the objects were buried with the man ... for his use in the next life." Tests on the enamel found on the Archer's teeth revealed that he grew up in central Europe. They could not reveal how long he had lived in Britain, only that he must have lived in the Alps region while a child, either Switzerland, Austria or Germany.

The grave of the Boscombe Bowmen was discovered on Boscombe Down, not far from Stonehenge, during the digging of a trench for a new water pipe in May 2003. The grave, dating to around 2300 B.C., contained the remains of seven individuals — three adult males, a teenage male and three children. Wessex Archaeology notes: "Matching the seven individuals were eight pots. This is the greatest number of people from a single Beaker grave in Britain and it is also the greatest number of Beaker pots from one grave."[14] Seven of the eight pots are decorated all over, six with cord and one with plaited cord. Plaited cord on Beaker pots is "extremely rare" in Britain, and one of the very few British finds was in the grave of the Amesbury Archer. The other finds include five barbed and tanged arrowheads — giving the name the Boscombe Bowmen — some other flint tools, scrapers and flakes, a boar's tusk and a toggle.

Wessex Archaeology notes that in continental Europe "tusks are often found in the same grave as stones used for metalworking, like the one found in the grave of the Amesbury Archer. Sometimes the tusks and stones have been found next to each other together," however: "Only one other bone toggle has been found in Britain, from a later, and rich, Bronze Age burial at Barnack, Cambridgeshire. Most toggles have been found in continental Europe. These finds usually have a central perforation rather than a loop. They have mainly been thought of as decorative pendants but they may have fastened clothing or a hair ornament." The enamel on the Bowmen's teeth shows that the men probably grew up in the Lake District of northwest England, north Wales or southwest Wales, despite their links to the Amesbury Archer and continental Europe.

But where did this Beaker culture come from? The Bell-Beaker culture, as it is formally known, was a cultural movement that spread over wide parts of Europe between 2800 B.C. and 1900 B.C., from the upper Danube in the east, and Germany between the Elbe and the Rhine, through the Low Countries and France (except for the central massif), to Spain, Portugal, Britain and Ireland in the west. Cunliffe[15] sees the "Bell-

Beaker Phenomenon" as "part of the breakdown of traditional social structures and the emergence of a more mobile way of life that began in northern
Europe after 3000 B.C." The name comes from the characteristic drinking
vessel with its inverted bell-shaped profile, which carries incised decoration
in horizontal zones around the body (see Figure 7). These pots were typ-
ically placed in single male burials, often accompanied by weaponry and
covered by a circular mound. It has been demonstrated from pollen grains
found in the bottom of beakers, says Cunliffe,[16] that they were also used
for something like mead, flavored with herbs such as meadowsweet (whose
flowers were used to make Blodeuedd in the Fourth Branch of the *Mabinogion*) or wild fruits. It was these Beaker people, some from as far away as
the Alps, others indigenous adapters of the culture, who blocked West
Kennet Long Barrow with massive stones, and "were associated with the
elaboration and refurbishment of Stonehenge around 2000 B.C."[17]

   While all this work was going on at Stonehenge, where did the huge
labor force live? The answer to this question is to be found in Durrington
Walls, the site of a Neolithic village and henge enclosure two miles northeast of Stonehenge. At some point around 2600 B.C., says Wikipedia, a
large timber circle now known as the Southern circle was constructed. The
circle was "orientated southeast towards the sunrise on the midwinter solstice and consisted of 4 large concentric circles of postholes, which would
have held extremely large standing timbers." Some time later, perhaps 200
years after the circle was first constructed, "another two concentric rings
were added and the henge enclosure was constructed. A ditch some 18 feet
deep was dug, and the earth used to create a large outer bank some 100
feet wide and presumably several feet high." Mike Parker Pearson believes
that Durrington Walls was a complementary structure to Stonehenge —
evidenced by the similar solstice alignments. He suggests[18] that the timber
circle at Durrington Walls represented life and a land of the living, whilst
Stonehenge and the down around it, encircled by burial mounds, represented a land of the dead. The two were connected by the River Avon and
their respective avenues, and a procession route from one to the other represented the transition from life to death.

   Durrington Walls was a land of the living not only because the henge
was made of timber, but also because there was a village there. It was a

   large circular village of many hundreds of houses.... This settlement, with
   a circumference of almost a mile, would have been the largest village
   known in northwest Europe. If the density of houses from the 2004–2007
   excavations (one house per 400sq ft) is representative of their packing

around the settlement then we might expect over 300 houses to survive beneath the henge banks.[19]

Preliminary results from environmental analyses "suggest that this was a seasonal settlement. The absence of carbonized grain or quern stones and the lack of bones from neonatal pigs and cattle, together with the evidence for culling of pigs in the midwinter period, suggest that people journeyed here with their pre-prepared foodstuffs and animals only at certain times of the year."[20]

The People of Stonehenge (2): The Stonehenge God

The Amesbury Archer and the Boscombe Bowmen tell us a good deal about Stonehenge around 2300 B.C., but what of later years? As it happens, we can learn a great deal about the successors of the Amesbury Archer by examining another burial place, the Normanton Down Barrows. The English Heritage website on Stonehenge says that the round barrow cemetery at Normanton dates from around 2600 to 1600 B.C. and it is one of the most impressive groups of burial mounds in the Stonehenge landscape. This barrow cemetery lies to the south of Stonehenge. It contains Bronze Age round barrows of several types, as well as an earlier Neolithic long barrow. There is a "clear line of sight from these barrows to Stonehenge, just over half a mile away."

The earliest ritual use of this site is most likely to have been the construction of the long barrow between 3400 and 3000 B.C. Related to it, and dating from roughly the same time, is an enclosure used for preparing the dead for burial. The body "was left in the open air and progressively cleaned of all flesh by the wind and the birds, leaving the bones ready for the burial — a process of de-fleshing known as excarnation."

According to Stuart Needham, Andrew Lawson and Ann Woodward,[21] the Normanton Down cemetery can be related to the first five phases which Needham has defined for the British Bronze Age. Particular care needs to be given to interpreting the earliest Beaker burials (Period 1, that is, 2500 B.C.– 2300 B.C.) since they are frequently not associated with any surviving mound, and there could be unknown graves almost anywhere. Nevertheless, they suggest early Beaker graves were deliberately sited in the zone of much older long or oval barrows to the west. Later Beaker burials (Periods 2–3, that is, 2300 B.C.–1700 B.C.) reinforce this pattern; some were sooner or later covered by mounds and thus came to be targeted by the early excavators.

The picture, Needham *et al.* say,[22] changes radically in the next phase (Period 3, that is 2050 B.C.–1700 B.C.), actually named after Bush Barrow, which will be discussed shortly.

> Setting aside the late Beaker graves, there are now arguably three foci emerging, most strikingly the famous Normanton "linear" cemetery along the main ridge. Two graves yielded both daggers and belt hooks (Bush itself, and Wilsford G23, where archeologists have found a unique bronze hook corroded against the dagger), and two had just belt-hooks (G15, G18). In addition, there are two graves with classic rich ornament sets (G7, G8) and another with matching bead types (G16).

Assessment of whether the pattern then changes is blurred by the less well dated burials, but the diagnostic Camerton-Snowshill burials (Period 4, that is 1700 B.C.–1500 B.C., and named after a particular type of dagger) are differently sited. More dramatic, they say, is "the marked shift seen in the Middle Bronze Age (1500–1150 B.C.). By the end of the early Bronze Age (Periods 1–4) the great majority of barrows would have existed, but there are some clusters of small mounds with evidence for burials in Deverel-Rimbury urns" (the name of a particular type of pottery) and, by implication, Middle Bronze Age construction. Only "one cluster is attached to a major concentration of earlier barrows, that in the Lake group. There seems to have been an almost complete retreat from Normanton Down; the focus of attention has shifted to the bounded field domains lying just to the west where there is also settlement evidence and the remarkable Wilsford shaft (a very deep feature interpreted as a well or a ritual shaft)," which we mentioned in Chapter 2.

The most famous burial at Normanton Down is undoubtedly the one at Bush Barrow, thought to date from between 1900 B.C. and 1700 B.C. It was excavated in 1808 by Sir Richard Colt Hoare and William Cunnington. As James Dyer says[23]:

> On the floor of the barrow lay the skeleton of a "stout and tall man," a Wessex chieftain. Near his head was a wooden shield with bronze decorations. An axe had been wrapped in cloth and placed by his shoulder. At his side lay two bronze daggers, one with a wooden hilt decorated with thousands of minute gold pins, each 0.04 inches long. There was a small bronze dagger by his right hand, and near his leg "a very curious perforated stone." This seems to have been a stone mace with a head made from a perforated fossil *tubularia* (a plant-like animal closely related to jellyfish) and a handle of wood decorated with bone rings. Although the man's clothes had not survived, some of the objects sewn on to them were found.

On his chest had been a lozenge-shaped plate of sheet gold measuring 7.3 inches (see Figure 8); his belt had a "hook of hammered gold with finely engraved ornament."

Mike Pitts[24] has an interesting theory about the man in the Bush Barrow burial. He points out that in the grave there were three large metal daggers and one axehead. While daggers are not uncommon in these graves, axes are rare. But it is a combination we see in the center of Stonehenge: a single dagger carved on the face of stone 53, surrounded by a group of "at least 14 axes," and further axes on the outer faces of sarsens 3, 4 and 5. It is, says Pitts, "as if the stones have become a symbolic grave, the mythical corpse represented by carvings of precious and distinctive objects normally buried with people granted elaborate and expensive funerary rituals."

Interestingly, there are thirty axes carved on sarsens 3, 4 and 5, the same as the number of megaliths in the ring. Stonehenge, says Pitts, has been "usurped by a man and his retinue, accompanied by objects of mortal existence. The stones are no longer ancestors, but merely an extraordinary version of something everyday, the burial mound. The man is an extraordinary transformation of humanity, something alien to earlier cosmologies: a god." His symbolic tomb is enclosed by two rings of thirty graves (the Y and Z circles), matching the number of stones and axe carvings, just as barrows for the living are surrounded by a ditch. Beyond Stonehenge, the hundreds of round barrows are also arranged in two broad bands, as if in echo of the central "barrow," so that the entire cemetery landscape becomes a symbol of this divine focus.

Controlling the Land: Southern England in the Middle and Late Bronze Age

The rich culture which produced the Bush Barrow burial did not exist in isolation from the rest of Europe. Amber beads found on Normanton Down are thought to have come from the Baltic, and faience beads from later graves may have come from somewhere in Europe or the Mediterranean, possibly exchanged for Cornish tin, one of the basic ingredients of bronze. Some of these trade links may have stretched over long distances. Harding notes[25] that study of particular amber forms has shown that there is a specific connection between southern Greece (Mycenae) and southern England, since the so-called amber spacer-plates of both areas were fashioned in identical ways (spacer-plates were used to separate the strands of a multi-strand necklace); Sciama and Eicher also point out[26] that a gold-framed amber disc found in a tomb at Knossos in Crete "so closely matches Wessex examples that it could be from the hand of the same goldsmith."

These long-distance trade links remind us that when the elite of Stonehenge were being buried on Normanton Down, other civilizations were flourishing in the Mediterranean. Egypt was already an ancient civilization when the Bush Barrow god was laid to rest, using hieroglyphics to record its history and produce a variety of literary texts; the Minoan civilization of Crete was flourishing and keeping records in the undeciphered Linear A script; the Hittite Empire dominated Anatolia for most of the second millennium B.C. and used a script based on the Akkadian cuneiform of Mesopotamia to produce a variety of texts; and from 1600 B.C. the Mycenean Greeks dominated Greece and later Crete, using the Linear B script to keep records in an ancient form of Greek.

What the Stonehenge people knew of these civilizations is unclear, but it is possible that an event in the eastern Mediterranean in the middle of the second millennium B.C. did have a profound impact on them. Some time around this date (possibly around 1628 B.C.), the volcano of Santorini (Thera) erupted. This eruption is believed to have been one of the largest volcanic events on Earth in recorded history, throwing into the stratosphere approximately 24 cubic miles of material, four times the amount of material ejected by Krakatoa. We do not know what effect this cataclysmic eruption had on the people of Stonehenge, but we can make an educated guess.

The dendrochronologist Mike Baillie has studied oaks growing on the surface of Irish raised bogs and has concluded that there was a "large volcanic dust-veil event in 1628 B.C."[27] He notes that ice-core acidity in Greenland peaks at 1644 B.C. ±20, which coincides with the widespread occurrence of narrowest growth rings in Irish bog oaks. In fact, six trees on four different bogs produced their narrowest growth rings in 1624 B.C. — and such extreme single-year

Figure 7: A typical beaker pot, like those found in the graves of the Amesbury Archer and the Boscombe Bowmen.

events occur only nine times in 6000 years. However, it is clear that the "event" at 1624 B.C. is not restricted to a single year, for 1624 B.C. is the low point of a reduction in growth which in general appears to start around 1628 B.C. and lasts for a number of years. This tree ring evidence is supported by data from English bog oaks: Croston Moss in Lancashire has oaks from 3198 B.C.–1682 B.C., and from 1584 B.C.–970 B.C., implying a catastrophic event between 1682 B.C. and 1584 B.C., while the Hasholme chronology spans 1687 B.C. to 1362 B.C. and shows an extremely narrow band of rings in the 1620s B.C.

We don't know what life was like in the 1620s B.C. for the people of Stonehenge, but we can get some idea from A.D. 1816, the Year Without a Summer, thought to have been caused by the huge volcanic eruption of Mount Tambora on the island of Sumbawa, Indonesia, in 1815. Europe, still recuperating from the Napoleonic Wars, says Wikipedia, "suffered from food shortages. Food riots broke out in Britain and France and grain warehouses were looted. The violence was worst in landlocked Switzerland, where famine caused the government to declare a national emergency. Huge storms, abnormal rainfall with floodings of the major rivers of Europe (including the Rhine) are attributed to the event, as was the frost setting in during August 1816." Hungary experienced brown snow, and "Italy experienced something similar, with red snow falling throughout the year."

If the people of Stonehenge experienced anything like this, then it would not be surprising if, keen astronomers as they were, they took this as a sign from the gods and instituted changes in their way of life. And changes did occur after 1600 B.C. There are indications that patterns of worship changed — by around 1450 B.C., votive offerings were being placed in Wils-

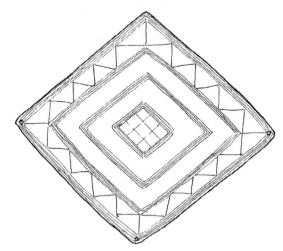

Figure 8: Image of the lozenge-shaped plate of sheet gold found in the Bush Barrow burial near Stonehenge.

ford Shaft, near Stonehenge, similar to those placed in the graves on Normanton Down (see Chapter 2). But the way of life of the people also changed in a much more radical way. Barry Cunliffe, in "Landscape with People," says that in the middle of the second millennium B.C. a major shift away from monument-building occurred. Instead, he says,[28] people focused on control of the land, "with the creation of huge areas of regularly laid out fields often contained by linear earthworks." One such field system that has been studied is at Windy Dido, on the western boundary of Hampshire near Quarley. The fields were first identified in the 1920s when they were photographed from the air; further work has shown that the system "covers 90 hectares and was laid out within large rectangular blocks running downslope from a linear ditch occupying the crest of a ridge to the east."[29] As Cunliffe says,[30] the "magnitude of the scheme and the extreme order with which it was realized implies social organization at a high level motivated by a central coercive power."

The Windy Dido fields do not exist in isolation, for similar field systems belonging to roughly the same period have been identified close to later hillforts at Danebury (west Hampshire) and Woolbury (to the east of Widy Dido), and are "well known on the eastern fringes of Salisbury Plain and on the Marlborough Downs to the north."[31] The impression is given that "over a comparatively short period of time, communities began to take control of the land to a degree never before contemplated."[32] We are witnessing, says Cunliffe, "the deliberate creation of a new landscape but one which appears to have complemented the old by leaving many of the ancestral barrow cemeteries intact in areas of pastureland beyond the boundaries of the arable."[33] It is difficult to know why this reordering of the land occurred, but one reason could be the need for greater efficiency in arable production, which "could have brought about more far-reaching changes in society, forcing the community to focus more closely on the fertility of the land and the deities who controlled it"[34] (which might explain the votive offerings in the Wilsford Shaft). And status, once represented by the richness grave goods, "might now have been displayed in the ability of the lineage to control land by containing it within boundaries"—after all, a "great expanse of ordered and well-tended fields is an impressive sight redolent of power."[35]

Towards the end of the second millennium, says Cunliffe,[36]

> another significant change to the Wessex landscape can be recognized with the creation of extensive systems of linear ditches carving up the landscape into huge blocks. These "ranch boundaries" or "linears" clearly represent a

new concept of land allotment. Whatever practical functions they may have performed — in terms perhaps of livestock management — they were above all a symbol of social reordering on an extensive scale. The sight of these thin white lines seared through the landscape will have impressed on the observer the centralizing power of the central authority.

Many of the linears relate to prominent hilltops, and "five or six centuries later some of these hilltops, like Sidbury, on the eastern edge of Salisbury Plain, Clearbury, near Salisbury, and Quarley were enhanced by enclosing defences, creating what are generally referred to as 'hillforts' ... which suggests that the symbolism of linears was being further reinforced at the time." Interestingly, "some of the new linear ditches cut straight through the earlier field systems, perhaps signifying a cancellation of the values and authority inherent in the preceding system."[37]

All this happened in the 12th century B.C. or thereabouts, but was not confined to the Wiltshire–Hampshire area: on Dartmoor "a complex landscape of linear boundaries, enclosures, settlements and fields created in the middle of the second millennium was widely abandoned, and a similar large-scale abandonment is evident over much of the uplands of northern Britain."[38] What was the reason for this second reordering of the land? The usual explanation is that there was slight increase in rainfall, leading to the development of peat bogs, particularly in upland areas. But Cunliffe points out[39] that there was also a volcanic eruption at Hekla in Iceland in 1159 B.C. Mike Baillie[40] was able to recognize a recurring pattern of a comparatively thick ring for 1160 B.C. followed by ten very narrow rings representing a decade during which there was virtually no tree ring growth. As in 1628 B.C., this volcanic eruption could well have had a profound effect on the people of southern England, forcing them once more to institute changes in their way of life. This second reordering of land use may have reflected "a greater reliance on stock management as opposed to crop growing," as a result of the "failure of the large-scale agrarian system introduced, with so much effort, in the middle of the second millennium."[41] It is possible that after five centuries or more of intensive use the

> thin downland soils showed signs of exhaustion.... Declining yields matched by a rise in population would have caused much social stress perhaps leading to fears that the chthonic deities controlling fertility had ceased to favor humanity. Add to this the *possibility* of a decade of dust clouds in the upper atmosphere affecting the power of the sun and one can begin to picture the sense of foreboding that may have been generated requiring precipitate communal action.[42]

Interlude: At Home and Abroad

Were the people who organized the distribution of land after 1628 B.C., and reorganized it after 1159 B.C., the same people as those whose ancestors were buried in Normanton Down cemetery? We may never know, but what we do know is that Salisbury Plain underwent the same transformations as the surrounding areas, with the rectangular field systems of around 1500 B.C. succeeded by the later "ranch boundaries."[43] We also know that, at some time during the period when the rectangular field systems were being replaced by the "ranch boundaries," possibly around 1100 B.C., the Avenue, the ceremonial route leading to Stonehenge, was lengthened by another mile and a quarter towards the River Avon.[44] And at around the same time, two Bronze Age barrows[45] were constructed on the hill by the River Avon that was later (around 500 B.C.[46]) to become the hillfort of Vespasian's Camp.

All this — the change in the field system, the new work on the Avenue at Stonehenge and the building of barrows on the hill by the River Avon — suggests a people under pressure. This pressure may have been purely internal, given the change in the climate and the disruption that must have ensued, but we cannot entirely rule out external influences. We don't know whether the people of southern England knew much about events in the Mediterranean, though we know they had long-distance trade links which went as far as Mycenae. For a great deal was going on in the Mediterranean at the time: the Mycenean civilization collapsed around 1100 B.C., the Hittite Empire of Anatolia disappeared around 1160 B.C., Troy was destroyed around 1190 B.C., and all written language vanished from Europe for the next four centuries. The reason for the so-called Bronze Age Collapse is unknown, but as in Britain, climate may have been a factor. It seems that there was a period of global cooling from approximately 1250 B.C. to 750 B.C.[47] There is evidence that the Hittite world suffered a severe and prolonged famine in the last decades of the Hittite kingdom, and the Hittites became increasingly dependent on shipments of grain from abroad, probably from the reign of Hattusili III onward, that is, from around 1267 B.C.[48] Herodotus, in *The Histories*, written some 700 years after the event, reports that when the Cretans (Mycenean Greeks) returned from the Trojan war, "famine and pestilence fell upon them, and destroyed both the men and the cattle."[49]

The famine in Anatolia and the famine and pestilence in Crete are signs of a general disruption of life in the Mediterranean, underlined by the emergence of the mysterious "Sea Peoples." This term is derived from the term used by the ancient Egyptians to describe the people who threatened them in two major attacks c. 1210 B.C. and c. 1180 B.C.[50] The Pharaoh Mereneptah tells of his victory c. 1210 in the western desert over Libyans who had brought with them as allies "Sherden-people, Sheklesh-people, Aqaiwasha-people of the foreign lands of the Sea ... Aqaiwasha the foreigners of the Sea." In a list of the northern enemies of Ramses III (c. 1180 B.C.) a Sherden chief is called "Sherden of the Sea"; with him are "the chief of the Pulisati (Philistine) foes." Another inscription of Ramses III mentions as northern enemies "peoples of the sea," literally "the foreign lands, the isles who sailed over against his lands," and they included Philistines and "Tursha from the midst of the sea." Finally, in the Harris papyrus in the British Museum, Ramses II says: "I overthrew all who transgressed the boundaries of Egypt, coming from their lands. I slew the Danuna from their isles, the Tjekkeru and Philistines ... the Sherden and Weshesh of the Sea were made as if non-existent."

Who were all the groups mentioned as being Sea Peoples? The Sherden have been linked to Sardinia, the Sheklesh to Sicily; the Aqaiwasha and Danuna are interpreted as Achaeans and Danaans, that is Greeks; the Philistines are thought to have originated in the Aegean before they settled on the southern coast of Canaan; the Tjekkeru and the Weshesh are obscure; the Tursa are thought to be the Tyrsenoi, or Tyrrhenians, who according to Herodotus,[51] migrated from Lydia to Italy to become the Etruscans (Tusci).[52] Clearly there were large movements of people in the Mediterranean, from Canaan in the east to Italy and Sardinia in the west, all driven by the deteriorating climate and resultant famines to seek new opportunities elsewhere. Whether any of these people reached as far as Britain is a question we will be considering in the next chapter.

The Midden Builders of the Late Bronze Age and Early Iron Age

Meanwhile, in southern England the "ranch boundaries" or linears were being constructed, and to find out what happened after this, we need to go to the Wiltshire village of Potterne, one mile south of Devizes (see Map 5). In an area to the north of the village known as Blackberry, excavations between 1982 and 1985 unearthed a huge prehistoric midden (rubbish heap) that covered an area of 8.6 acres and survives to a depth of 7 feet. A meticulous study of the midden, says Cunliffe,[53] "showed it to have accumulated over a period of some 500 years, from 1100 B.C.–600 B.C., as the result of penning livestock and adding domestic rubbish to the animal waste and bedding material." The excavators identified fourteen successive zones (layers) at Potterne for which a number of radiocarbon dates are available.[54] Zones 14–11 "produced plain pottery of the Late Bronze Age transitional assemblage and are dated to 1100–850/800, while zones 10–2 produced typical All Cannings Cross decorated ware for which the date range 850/800–600 is indicated."

All Cannings Cross pottery (see Figure 9) is named after a farm near the village of All Cannings in the Vale of Pewsey, Wiltshire, 6 miles east of Devizes, and is found throughout central southern England, "centered on the Wessex chalklands."[55] There are two distinctive types of All Cannings Cross pottery: the "large jar with an evenly out-curved rim and a rounded shoulder and body which in most cases is decorated with incised and stamped motifs, often in the form of stab-filled geometric shapes"; and the "bipartite bowl with beaded rim and sharp shoulder angles, between which are bands of decoration, either stamped or incised." The striking, highly decorated pottery of the All Cannings Cross group has "no precedent in Wessex," says Cunliffe[56]:

> While some of the ceramic forms can be explained away as indigenous copies of exotic metal types, the weak profiled jars with stabbed decoration stand out as something very new that cannot be easily paralleled except among Late Urnfield assemblages in eastern France and western Germany.... Thus it is probable that an Urnfield element lies behind the origins of the Early All Cannings Cross group, but it is impossible to define the nature of the link more precisely. There is no firm evidence for a folk movement of any magnitude into the area, but limited infiltrations cannot be ruled out.

This intriguing suggestion that the All Cannings Cross pottery may have come about as the result of "limited infiltrations," possibly from eastern France or western Germany, is a matter we will return to in Chapter 6.

The midden at Potterne is not the only one in the area. John Barrett and David McOmish,[57] have carried out exploratory work at All Cannings Cross and report evidence of a substantial midden less than half a mile to the east of All Cannings Cross. But the best known midden outside the one at Potterne is the midden at East Chisenbury, on Salisbury Plain, 6 miles to the north of Stonehenge.[58] The East Chisenbury midden is circular, and spreads over an area 670 feet in diameter, 8.4–12.4 acres in extent. The mound is 7 feet deep in places, and around 216,000 cubic feet of material still survive. Preliminary results of the excavations carried out there in 1992 show that the mound "had built up rapidly as a complex 'construction' rich in cultural residue dating from between 800 B.C. and 600 B.C." Several thousand shards of pottery have been found, and "display characteristics which are entirely consistent with structured deposition." On the composition of the mound, McOmish notes:

> Initial study of the well-preserved faunal assemblage points to dispropor-
> tionately large numbers of foetal or neonatal sheep; other species such as
> cattle, pig and deer are well represented. Human remains, including two
> fragments of skull, were uncovered. One of these had apparently been
> placed deliberately within the mound, surrounded by shards of pottery
> from the same vessel and a small block of sarsen stone. Linear scarring and
> teeth-marks on its outer surface are inexplicable. Copious quantities of
> coprolites, including human examples, were also noted.

What was the purpose of these mounds? Some have suggested they were created by cycles of feasting, but Cunliffe[59] believes there is another explanation. He hypothesizes that the accumulation of refuse "represents the desire to create communal control over society's midden material thus commanding the potential fertility embedded within it." He notes that in earlier archeological contexts in Wessex there is ample evidence of the use of domestic midden material in complex burial rituals. What is exceptional about the 8th- to 7th-century Wessex middens is "their scale and the degree of social cohesion that their construction implies. They must represent an intense, but comparatively short-lived, communal response to a perceived need in some way associated with an overwhelming desire to control fertility."

The huge mounds were not the only step taken by the people of southern England to control fertility. As Cunliffe says,[60] marl digging became a widespread phenomenon in the first millennium (marl is a lime-rich mud or mudstone), and shallow chalk quarries are frequently found on settlement sites. It seems that many areas of the downland were covered with "clayey acid soils which needed to be broken down and neutralized if they were to become productive." Interestingly, "old chalk diggings were frequently used in Late Bronze and Early Iron Age Wessex for the disposal of the dead."[61]

Of course, during this period the people of southern England left other reminders of their way of life besides refuse mounds, especially in the way of bronze artefacts. From the middle of the 12th century B.C. until the end of the 11th, says Cunliffe,[62] "Britain south of the Humber was served by bronze smiths casting a range of new implements in bronze with a high lead content." The new types constitute what is known as the Wilburton complex (Wilburton is a village in Cambridgeshire): they include leaf-shaped swords, simple socketed spearheads, and socketed axes. The largest find of Wilburton artefacts is the Isleham Hoard from Cambridgeshire, buried around 1000 B.C., and containing some 6500 fragments of bronze, including weapons of the Wilburton complex type, fragments of bronze cauldrons and a series of harness fittings.

At the end of the 10th century B.C., south and east Britain developed a series of new types in parallel with western areas of France, with which close contacts were maintained. The new assemblage, known after the site of Ewart Park (Northumberland), incorporates Continental material of the Carp's-Tongue Sword Complex, including the long sword with narrowed point which gives the complex its name, knives of hog's back and triangular form, various types of socketed axe, socketed knives, pegged and socketed spearheads, and various chisels and gouges.[63]

In addition to these cast bronze implements, "vessels and shields of beaten bronze make their appearance in the British Isles from the 10th century, or perhaps a little earlier, as the result of far-flung contacts with central Europe."[64] Among these were "bronze cauldrons, the earliest of which, from Colchester (Essex) and Shipton (Oxfordshire), are thought to have originated at the end of the second millennium in the wake of contacts with central Europe and were probably manufactured in southern Britain."[65] Beaten bronze shields also appeared in the 10th or 9th century B.C., and were widely distributed over most of the British Isles by the 8th century — recent work, says Cunliffe, indicates a possible Hungarian origin for the type, possibly transmitted via Denmark.[66]

Other "exotic types found their way in at this time, principally from central and northern Europe. Among these must be mentioned the first appearance of bronze fittings appropriate to horse harness, which surely implies the introduction of more sophisticated methods of harnessing and possibly the greatly increased practice of horse-riding. Such developments are largely in parallel with those discernible in Europe in the Hallstatt B phase of the Urnfield culture" (1000 B.C.–750 B.C.).[67]

Hillforts and Iron Age Southern England

By the 7th century, says Cunliffe,[68] a "more stable pattern of agricultural production was under way," and settlements now become "evident and long-lasting after several centuries during which evidence of where people actually lived is somewhat sparse." But in the years following 700 B.C.,[69] a rash of defended sites or hillforts spread across a large area of southern Britain, from Kent and Sussex in the south, westward through Wiltshire, Gloucestershire, Hereford and Worcester, and then up through the Welsh Marches into North Wales. During the period 600 B.C.–400 B.C., says Kristiansen, "densely packed hillforts emerged in Wessex, in the Danebury area, with distances of only 6 miles between each."[70]

The hillforts of southern Britain fall into two types — "small defended village-like hillfort settlements and large hill-top enclosures."[71] The defended village-like hillforts followed the tradition of hillfort building which emerged in the 8th or 7th century B.C., at sites like Breddin (Powys) and Crickley Hill (Gloucestershire). These sites were fairly small and were "set in easily defensible positions — hill-tops, promontories and escarpments"[72]; all have well-constructed ramparts, and many had elaborate gate-towers over the entranceways. Inside these forts occupation was usually fairly dense. At Crickley Hill, two phases can be recognized: the "early phase was characterized by rectangular houses together with 4-post struc-

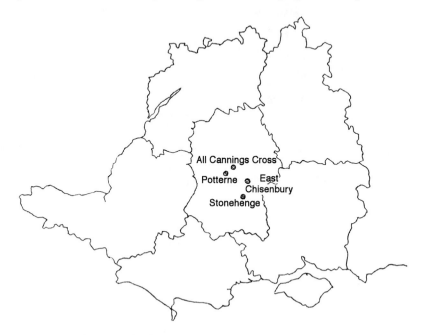

Map 5: Southern England c. 700 B.C. with sites of ritual middens (rubbish heaps) in the modern county of Wiltshire.

tures ... generally interpreted as raised granaries"[73]; later the rectangular houses were replaced by round houses up to 49 feet in diameter. Further south at Danebury (west Hampshire), the early phase, radiocarbon dated to about 500 B.C. ±80, contained "many roundhouses, but instead of 4-posters, which were rather few in number, circular pits or silos were dug into the solid chalk."[74] It was estimated that the total grain capacity of the investigated pits was about 1521 cubic yards, and that the hillfort as a whole had the capacity to store 807 cubic yards of grain, "enough to feed over 1000 people for a year."[75]

Large hill-top enclosures, generally over 40 acres in area, "defended by one or more lines of ramparts..., but more often defined by natural slopes,"[76] include Bathampton, east of Bath, Balksbury, near Andover, Hampshire, and Ogbury, near Salisbury in Wiltshire. The function of these large enclosures is unclear — their "great size and apparent low density of occupation suggest they were stock enclosures and storage places."[77]

The earlier preoccupation with fertility was not forgotten with the building of the hillforts. Cunliffe, during his excavation of Danebury hill-fort, uncovered a large number of storage pits or underground silos, and notes that they are common on all settlement sites. It had earlier been thought that they were constructed to protect the grain from raid, but Cunliffe believes[78] that "the deposition of grain in a storage pit was a deliberate act involving the placing of the seed in the protective custody of the chthonic deities during the dangerous liminal period between the time it was harvested and the moment it was sown." The evidence for this is that once the pit was emptied and the seed was in the soil, the pit became the focus of "acts of propitiation, involving the structured deposition of parts of animals, sets of artefacts and other material"— acts which may have continued "up to the time of the harvest and may have coincided with seasonal festivals." One such propitiatory offering at Danebury[79] involves a

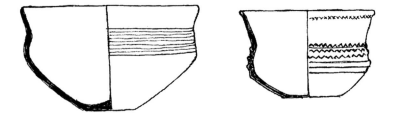

Figure 9: All Cannings Cross pottery like that found throughout Wiltshire, and dating to around 800 B.C.

dog and a horse which has been partially dismembered, its head and one foreleg being placed separately against the pit side.

This ritual dismemberment of the horse in the Danebury pit may be highly significant. Anne Ross notes[80] that in Ireland "a bull-feast, *tarb-feis*, was used to determine by mantic means the rightful successor to the king of Tara: a bull was killed, and a druid ate of its flesh and drank of the broth in which it was cooked. The druids sang a 'spell of truth' over him, and in his dreams he would 'see' the rightful king. Sometimes the prophet had to be wrapped in the hide of the slaughtered animal." The ritual slaughter of three bulls seems to be taking place on one plate of the Gundestrup Cauldron (see Chapter 2), where three warriors hold swords to the throats of huge animals, their immense size in comparison to the men suggesting their own divinity. Three dogs bound beneath the bulls.

There can be little doubt, says Ross, that animal sacrifice took place in Ireland, and she quotes Anne Woodward as saying that many of the sacrificed beasts would have provided meat for feasting, and the numbers of bodies and parts of bodies that have survived on Iron Age sites indicate that the practice of animal sacrifice in Celtic society must have been widespread. All the evidence, says Ross, supports Woodward's contention — Cunliffe's discovery of the heads and legs of horses in various contexts at Danebury "is suggestive of the 'heads and hooves' ritual where the body of the animal was consumed and the hide used to wrap the seer in preparation for his mantic sleep."[81]

But were the people who built Danebury and other early hillforts Celts? We saw in Chapter 4 that Celts probably settled in Britain in the period 450 B.C. to 200 B.C., and the archeological evidence seems to support this. One very distinctive culture which shows Celtic (La Tène influences) is the Arras culture of Yorkshire, characterized by inhumations with the remains of carts — sometimes the carts were placed upright, or the carts were dismantled, the wheels being placed flat; grave goods include iron cart-tires, three-link horse-bits, a fibula (brooch) of the Münsingen type (Münsingen is the site of a La Tène cemetery in Switzerland), and a bracelet similar to those found in Alsace and Burgundy in early La Tène contexts. There is a distinct possibility, says Cunliffe,[82] that the Arras culture "arose as the result of a folk movement into eastern Yorkshire late in the fifth or early in the fourth century." These people may have come from Burgundy via the Paris region (the Celts of the Paris region, the Parisii, have the same name as those of east Yorkshire).

Meanwhile, in the southeast of Britain, from the 5th century on, the ceramic assemblages, says Cunliffe,[83] show strong influences from the adjacent Continent from northern France and the Low Countries. This is most vividly demonstrated by the decorated and painted wares of the Highstead-Dollands Moor group.... The British examples have close similarities with the *vases carenées* and *vases piriformes* of the Continental La Tène cultures. The influence of these ceramic innovations was felt most strongly in the Thames valley and eastern England, contributing to the regional assemblages called here the Long Wittenham-Allen's Pit group, the Chinnor-Wandlebury group, the Highstead-Dollands-Moor group, and the Darmsden-Linton group. Further south in Sussex and west in Hampshire and Wiltshire, elements of the new types, though apparent, are more dimly reflected in contemporary ceramic developments.

The mechanism by which these Continental styles were introduced into Britain "remains unclear. While it is possible a limited folk movement took place bringing new peoples to Kent and the Thames valley region it is no less likely that new ceramic styles emerged as the result of intensifying exchange relations between the two sides of the channel."[84]

It seems unlikely therefore that the early hillforts were built by Celts, though Celtic elites — or fear of Celtic invaders — may have played a part in the so-called developed hillforts. In the 4th century B.C., says Darvill,[85] many of the early hillforts like Crickley Hill "were abandoned and not reoccupied while others were elaborated and extended." These developed hillforts were larger than the early hillforts. Their defenses often "follow the natural contours of a suitable hill, and the area enclosed may be as much as 25 acres." Multiple ramparts are usual, and careful use of existing slopes and natural features to exaggerate the scale of these ramparts suggests that "ostentation was as important as defence." At Danebury, soon after 400 B.C., a second line of ramparts was constructed, and the eastern entrance was particularly heavily defended, with a "strategically placed command post with a clear view over the entire entrance area and ideally suited for slingers."[86] At Danebury, as at many sites of this period, clay sling shot or suitable natural pebbles have been found in considerable quantities, emphasizing the importance of this form of warfare. The "interior of the site was densely occupied with circular houses set around the inner edge of the rampart.... Some areas of the interior were given over to storage, either in pits or in 4-posters. Roadways ran through the site and these were maintained through the period of occupation."[87] The implications, says Darvill, are that "occupation was continuous, intensive and under the control of a strong centralized power." Other developed hillforts include Beacon Hill and St. Catherine's Hill in Hampshire, Maiden Castle in Dorset, Cadbury Castle in Somerset, and Barbury Castle, Fosbury, Yarnbury and Castle Ditches in Wiltshire (see Map 6).

In the Late Iron Age, says Cunliffe,[88] Britain "can be divided into three broad zones: a *core* comprising the south-east which shared many cultural characteristics with the Continent, a *periphery* comprising an arc of coin-issuing tribes stretching from Dorset to Lincolnshire; and *beyond*, that is the rest of Britain west and north of the periphery where coinage had not been introduced into the socio-economic system." The core consists of four tribes, the Trinovantes, Catuvellauni, Atrebates and Cantii, who "shared a number of cultural aspects with the Belgic areas of northern Gaul"—ceramic technology, burial rites, economy and socio-political structure "showed only slight variation from one end of the region to the other."[89] In the past it was believed that the area was settled by the immigrant Belgae referred to by Caesar, but Cunliffe says that a good case can be made that "the undoubted similarities result from regular and intensive social and economic intercourse between the tribes on either side of the Channel."[90] The culture of these four tribes is usually referred to as the Aylesford-Swarling culture, named after two cemeteries in Kent, and dates from around 50 B.C. The tribe of greatest interest to us is the Atrebates, who occupied West Sussex, west Surrey, Hampshire, Berkshire and northeast Wiltshire. Their tribal capital, of course, was Calleva Atrebatum (Silchester in Hampshire), founded around 50 B.C., and Cunetio, on the River Kennet and near the site of the Iron Age hillfort of Forest Hill, was also in their territory.

The four coin-issuing tribes of the periphery are the Durotriges, Dobunni, Iceni and Corieltauvi (see Chapter 2). The Durotriges were a close-knit confederacy, says Cunliffe,[91] centered upon modern Dorset. To the east and north

> their boundaries with the Atrebates seem to have been marked by the Avon, which flows through Salisbury Plain, and its tributary the Wylye, which flows to the south of Salisbury Plain. The New Forest may have served as something of a buffer zone between the two tribes. Further west Durotrigan coins and pottery extend along the valleys of the Yeo and Parrett, in Somerset, and the River Brue in Somerset would approximate to a northern boundary with the Dobunni

The Dobunni[92] were centered on Gloucestershire, "extending into north Somerset, down to the River Brue, north and west Wiltshire, Oxfordshire west of the Cherwell, and most of Worcestershire."

Conclusion

We set out at the beginning of this chapter in search of Mound-People, and we found large numbers of them, from the Neolithic builders of West Kennet Long Barrow, Silbury Hill and Stonehenge to the Late Bronze Age/Early Iron Age midden builders and the Iron Age hillfort builders. We also found early signs of the horse-goddess Epona and Rhiannon of the *Mabinogion*, and of Cunomaglus, the Hound-Lord of Nettleton Shrub. We also saw clear evidence of external influences in British prehistory: the Beaker people from the Continent and the Amesbury Archer from the Swiss or Austrian Alps; the Arras culture of east Yorkshire from Celtic Gaul; the La Tène ceramic forms from Gaul; and the Belgic influences from northern Gaul. It also became clear that a number of powerful families dominated Wiltshire and east Hampshire from around 2300 B.C., initially through Stonehenge, later through the control of land, and later still through the control of fertility and the construction of hillforts.

We have been left with some important questions. The first concerns the extent of Celtic influence in England. Considering how little has remained of Celtic language and even place-names outside Cumbria (where Cumbric was spoken until the 12th century) and Cornwall (where Cornish was spoken until the 18th century), was Celtic spoken only by an elite in southern England, and only for a relatively short space of time before the Romans then the Anglo-Saxons became the dominant force? The second relates to the Mound-People themselves. What became of those who built and watched over Stonehenge for so long, and for those who supervised the building of the middens and hillforts? Did they become the Durotriges, whose territory seems to have included Stonehenge, but who, according to Cunliffe,[93] "remained an isolated body, with an impoverished coinage, showing little sign of wealth accumulation or the emergence of a dominant élite"? Did they become (or were they conquered by) the Atrebates, whose territory seemed to include the northern and eastern fringes of Salisbury Plain? Or did they throw in their lot with the Belgic immigrants who settled south of Danebury around the hillforts of St. Catharine's Hill or Oram's Arbour, in an area which later became Venta Belgarum/Winchester?[94] Or did the people of Stonehenge carry on as normal at Vespasian's Camp? Dennis Price[95] believes that the 4th century B.C. Greek geographer and explorer, Pytheas of Massilia, who made a voyage of exploration to northwest Europe about 325 B.C., visited Stonehenge. The writings of Pytheas have not survived, but Diodorus Siculus quotes a contemporary of Pytheas, Hecataeus of Abdera, in the passage that follows,[96] where he is discussing Britain:

> There is also on the island both a magnificent sacred precinct of Apollo and a notable temple which is adorned with many votive offerings and is spherical in shape. Furthermore, a city is there which is sacred to this god, and the majority of its inhabitants are players on the cithara; and these continually play on this instrument in the temple and sing hymns of praise to the god, glorifying his deeds.... And the kings of this city and the supervisors of the sacred precinct are called Boreadae, since they are descendants of Boreas, and the succession to these positions is always kept in their family.

Price contends that the "sacred precinct of Apollo" refers to Stonehenge, and that the city where the "supervisors of the sacred precinct" live refers to Vespasian's Camp.

The final question raised by this brief prehistory of southern England is this: who were the "limited infiltrations," the small number of people who introduced All Cannings Cross pottery to southern England from eastern France or western Germany, who perhaps became the midden builders of Wiltshire, and who may have been responsible for the construction of the early hillforts? In the next chapter we will attempt to answer this question — and reveal the identity not only of the Mound-People and the Children of Don, but also of those shadowy figures who haunt the pages of *The Spoils of Annwn* and the *Mabinogion*, the Druids.

Chapter 6

Visitors from the East

Brutus in Devon

Did a small number of people from eastern France or western Germany settle in Wiltshire around 800 B.C. or earlier, bringing with them the All Cannings Cross pottery? There are various ways we can approach this question, and the first course I'll be pursuing is to look at the legendary early history of Britain, using as my sources three works in Latin, the *Historia Brittonum* of Nennius, Geoffrey of Monmouth's *Historia Regum Britanniae*, and the *Itinerarium Cambriae* (*Itinerary Through Wales*) of Giraldus Cambrensis; and two works in medieval Welsh, *Lludd and Llefelys* and the *Welsh Triads*.

In Chapter 10 of the *Historia Brittonum*, written around A.D. 830, Nennius gives his version of the founding of Britain. In Homer's *Iliad* one of the leaders of the Dardanians of Troy is Aeneas, a principal lieutenant of Hector, son of the Trojan king Priam. In the *Aeneid*, written by the Roman poet Virgil around 25 B.C., Aeneas survives the destruction of Troy, flees with his son Ascanius and eventually settles in Italy, where he is welcomed by Latinus, king of the Latins, and marries Lavinia, daughter of Latinus, eventually becoming the ancestor of Romulus and Remus, who founded Rome. Nennius writes[1]:

> Ascanius married a wife, who conceived and became pregnant. And Aeneas, having been informed that his daughter-in-law was pregnant, ordered his son to send his magician to examine his wife, whether the child conceived were male or female. The magician came and examined the wife and pronounced it to be a son, who should become the most valiant among the Italians, and the most beloved of all men. In consequence of this prediction, the magician was put to death by Ascanius; but it happened that the mother of the child dying at its birth, he was named Brutus; and after a certain interval agreeably to what the magician had foretold, whilst he was playing with some others he shot his father with an arrow, not intentionally but by accident. He was, for this cause, expelled

114

from Italy, and came to the islands of the Tyrrhene sea, when he was exiled on account of the death of Turnus, slain by Aeneas. He then went among the Gauls, and built the city of Turones, called Turnis. At length he came to this island, named from him Britannia, dwelt there, and filled it with his own descendants, and it has been inhabited from that time to the present period.

Geoffrey of Monmouth, in *Historia Regum Britanniae*, devotes the whole of Book 1 to the story of Brutus. He tells us[2] of the circumstances in which Brutus and his men left Gaul and landed in Britain:

> So without further delay, with the consent of his company, he repaired to the fleet, and loading it with the riches and spoils he had taken, set sail with a fair wind towards the promised island, and arrived on the coast of Totnes.
>
> The island was then called Albion, and inhabited by none but a few giants. Notwithstanding this, the pleasant situation of the places, the plenty of rivers abounding with fish, and the engaging prospect of its woods, made Brutus and his company very desirous to fix their habitation

Map 6: Developed hillforts in southern England c. 100 B.C., showing the modern counties of Wiltshire, Hampshire, Somerset and Dorset.

in it. They therefore passed through all the provinces, forced the giants to fly into the caves of the mountains, and divided the country among them according to the directions of their commander. After this they began to till the ground and build houses, so that in a little time the country looked like a place that had been long inhabited. At last Brutus called the island after his own name Britain, and his companions Britons; for by these means he desired to perpetuate the memory of his name.

The most interesting detail supplied by Geoffrey is that Brutus and his men landed on "the coast of Totnes." Totnes today is a market town at the head of the estuary of the River Dart in Devon, founded by the Saxons around A.D. 900. There are few signs of settlement activity before this time. The earliest signs of occupation near Totnes are a Neolithic cooking site at Hazard Hill some 2 miles to the west, excavated in the 1950s. Two Bronze Age axes have been found between Totnes and Dartington, 2 miles from Totnes. There are Bronze Age earthworks at Dartington North Wood, a Scheduled Ancient Monument, where evidence of Iron Age and Romano-British settlement was also found. The nearest Roman capital was at Isca Dumnoniorum (Exeter), but there is evidence of some form of Roman settlement at Totnes.[3]

However, not far from Totnes is Dartmoor, with human activity going back at least 12,000 years, as shown by "analysis of ancient pollens and charcoal and from the early styles of flint tools still found today."[4] As the website of the Dartmoor National Park Authority also notes, more concrete evidence of human activity can also be found in the chambered tombs, burial chambers built of granite and covered by along earth mounds, which may be up to 6000 years old. There are only a few of these; more numerous are the cairns, or burial places (there are over 1500 of them), which are mostly circular, and date to between 2500 B.C. and 1000 B.C.

Prehistoric Dartmoor obviously enjoyed a rich religious life, for it also contains the largest number of ceremonial sites in northwest Europe, including stone rows, which often terminate in a burial cairn, single standing stones, and stone circles. The people who built these cairns and stone rows lived in stone-built round houses; over 5000 of these have been found, with occupation dating from around 1500 B.C. Like the inhabitants of Hampshire and Wiltshire, those living on Dartmoor devised their own rectangular field system, with low stony earth-covered boundaries called *reaves*.

By 1000 B.C. Dartmoor's climate had turned wetter and cooler (as happened on and around Salisbury Plain) "with its once fertile soil becoming depleted and replaced by a buildup of peat. This led to the slow abandonment of settlement on the higher slopes with evidence of continued occupation limited to a small number of sites."[5]

In Roman times Devon was occupied by the Dumnonii, and after the end of the Roman period, the kingdom of Dumnonia survived in Devon until around A.D. 800. So it is possible that Geoffrey was drawing on old Dumnonian traditions about the former inhabitants of Dartmoor. Interestingly, Geoffrey says that Brutus and his company forced the "giants" living there to "fly into the caves of the mountains"—if by caves he means burial mounds, then these "giants" are the equivalent of the Mound-People living in their *sidi* or *gorsedd*.

Among the most prominent geological features of Dartmoor are the *tors*, rock outcrops formed by weathering, usually found on or near the summit of a hill. The word *tor* is one of the few Celtic words that survives in English, but its origin is unclear, though it is thought to be cognate with Latin *turris* "tower." Curiously, the Latin *turris* is apparently unrelated to any other Indo-European word except for the Greek *tursis*. Equally curious is the fact, first noted by the German linguist Paul Kretschmer (see Wikipedia article "Tower"), that both *turris* and *tursis* appear to be connected with place-names from Lydia, an Anatolian kingdom which developed after the collapse of the Hittite Empire, and with the people called in Greek *Tyrsenoi* or *Tyrrhenioi* (Tyrsenians, Tyrrhenians), as well as with *Tusci* (from *Turs-ci*), the Greek and Latin names for the Etruscans.

But what is the connection between the Lydians and the Etruscans? The Greek historian Herodotus, writing in about 430 B.C., says[6] that as a result of a prolonged famine, the Lydians decided to split in two, with half staying in Lydia and the other half setting off for other lands, finally ending up in Italy, where they became the Tyrrhenians (that is, Etruscans) (see Map 7). The Dutch Professor of Comparative Indo-European Linguistics, Robert Beekes,[7] believes that at the time of the Trojan War, the Lydians lived further north in Anatolia, in Maionia, south of the Sea of Marmara, and were later pushed south by the Phrygians, who came from the southern Balkans. Maionia borders on Troas, the region where Troy was located. Beekes believes that there were two cities in the Troas, one called *Wilusa* by the Hittites, which was inhabited by people speaking an Anatolian (Indo-European) language, and one called *Taruisa* by the Hittites, where the people spoke a non–Indo-European language. After the Trojan war, under pressure from the Phrygians and the famine that resulted from the global cooling we spoke of in Chapter 5, the people of Taruisa migrated to Italy, and their name Tyrsenoi is derived from Taruisa, while their "brothers" in Maionia migrated south into the area of present-day Manisa and the interior of Izmir province to become the Lydians.

Does this mean that *tor* and *turris* are Anatolian words? Not necessarily. The eminent scholar of Iranian languages, H.W. Bailey,[8] believes that *turris* may be derived from one of the Iranian languages, which were spoken north of the Black Sea and possibly as far west as the Danube by peoples known as the Scythians, Sarmatians and Cimmerians. Bailey is discussing Khotanese, an Iranian language spoken in northwest China, and the word *tturaka*. He says[9] that the word means "cover" of a quiver, and he links it to Ossetic *turγa* (where γ represents a voiced velar fricative similar to the final sound in Scottish *loch*) meaning "court, forecourt, vestibule, balcony." He links both words to Sanskrit *torana* "arch, gateway," and Khotanese *ttora* "top," and notes that the base Indo-Iranian *tav-: tu-* has a wide range of meanings: it would seem to have meant "place over, upon, or around." Finally he notes that Ossetic *turγa* as an enclosed place suggests a connection with Greek *tursis*, Lat. *turris* "tower" (Ossetic is an Iranian language spoken in North and South Ossetia, which border on the Republic of Georgia).

Beekes's contention that the Etruscans migrated from Taruisa in the Troas region of northwest Anatolia, and Bailey's hypothesis that the Latin *turris* is derived from an ancient Iranian word used by tribes north of the Black Sea, adds further weight to the theory, put forward in Chapter 5, that the Bronze Age Collapse coincided with mass population movements in the Mediterranean. It also casts new light on the legend of Brutus of Troy, raising the possibility that he gave his name not just to Britain but, more prosaically, to the *tors* of Dartmoor.

Of course, it is unlikely that the name Britain is derived from a man called Brutus. The name was first used by the Greek philosopher Aristotle in the 4th century B.C., when the people were referred to as *Pritteni*. As we implied in Chapter 4, the name Britain is usually derived from the Indo-European root $k^w er$-,[10] which gives Old Irish *cruth* "shape," Welsh *pryd* "shape, time," and perhaps Old Irish *Cru(i)thin*, Middle Welsh *Prydyn*, "Picts," Welsh *Prydain* "Britain," making the British the "tattooed people," and prompting Baudis to suggest that the *Mabinogion*'s Pryderi is in effect "Mr. Britain." But Pokorny himself has cast doubt on this etymology. In a discussion of the etymology of the name of the Swiss town Prättigau, in Rheto-Romance Val Parténs, in older times Pertennis, Pokorny[11] links Pritteni to an Illyrian name, from the Indo-European root *prteno-*, related to

Old Indian *prt-* "Kampf" ("fight, struggle") and "Kampfer" ("fighter, warrior"). This etymology apparently refers to Pokorny's entry[12] for the root *per-* "to hit," which gives Old Indian *prt-/prtana* "fight, struggle," Avestan *peret-* "fight, struggle, battle," and Latin *premo* "push, press." Both *prt* ("fight, battle") and *prtana* ("battle, contest, strife") are listed in Sanskrit dictionaries, and Old Persian *partara* "battle" occurs in a text from the tomb of Darius (486 B.C.).[13] As was the case with *tor*, we are getting more hints of a long-distance connection between Britain and central or eastern Europe.

Elidorus in the Underworld

Giraldus Cambrensis (A.D. 1146–c. A.D. 1223) was the son of a powerful Anglo-Norman baron, Guillaume de Barri, the grandson of a Welsh princess, and a maternal nephew of David FitzGerald, the Bishop of St. David's. In A.D. 1184 he became a royal clerk and chaplain to King Henry II of England. He was chosen to accompany one of the king's sons, John, on an expedition to Ireland, and published a report of what he saw there in *Topographia Hibernica* (*Topography of Ireland*) (1188). He was then selected to accompany the Archbishop of Canterbury, Baldwin of Exeter, on a tour of Wales, the object being a recruitment campaign for the Third Crusade. His account of that journey, the *Itinerarium Cambriae* (*Itinerary through Wales*) (1191) was followed by the *Descriptio Cambriae* (*Description of Wales*) in 1194.

In the *Itinerarium Cambriae* Giraldus was traveling in the Gower Peninsula in Glamorgan, and spent the night at Swansea castle. He then tells a very curious story[14]:

> A short time before our days, a circumstance worthy of note occurred in these parts, which Elidorus, a priest, most strenuously affirmed had befallen himself. "When a youth of twelve years, and learning his letters, ... in order to avoid the discipline and frequent stripes inflicted on him by his preceptor, he ran away, and concealed himself under the hollow bank of a river. After fasting in that situation for two days, two little men of pigmy stature appeared to him, saying, "If you will come with us, we will lead you into a country full of delights and sports." Assenting and rising up, he followed his guides through a path, at first subterraneous and dark, into a most beautiful country, adorned with rivers and meadows, woods and plains, but obscure, and not illuminated with the full light of the sun. All the days were cloudy, and the nights extremely dark, on account of the

absence of the moon and stars. The boy was brought before the king, and introduced to him in the presence of the court; who, having examined him for a long time, delivered him to his son, who was then a boy. These men were of the smallest stature, but very well proportioned in their make; they were all of a fair complexion, with luxuriant hair falling over their shoulders like that of women. They had horses and greyhounds adapted to their size. They neither ate flesh nor fish, but lived on milk diet, made up into messes with saffron. They never took an oath, for they detested nothing so much as lies. As often as they returned from our upper hemisphere, they reprobated our ambition, infidelities, and inconstancies; they had no form of public worship, being strict lovers and reverers, as it seemed, of truth.

Elidorus stayed with these people for some time, frequently returning to "our hemisphere" to see his mother. His mother asked him to bring a "present of gold, with which that region abounded," so he stole, while playing with the king's son, "the golden ball with which he used to divert himself." He then hurried to his mother's house, pursued by two "pigmies," who took the ball from him and departed, showing the boy "every mark of contempt and derision." When the boy tried to return to the underground world, he found no sign of the passage that led there, though he searched for it on the banks of the river for nearly a year. Eventually Elidorus became a priest, but whenever David II, bishop of St. David's, talked to him in his later years of these events, he could never speak of his experience without shedding tears. And, says Giraldus:

> He had made himself acquainted with the language of that nation, the words of which, in his younger days, he used to recite, which, as the bishop often had informed me, were very conformable to the Greek idiom. "When they asked for water, they said Ydor ydorum, which meant bring water, for Ydor in their language, as well as in the Greek, signifies water...; and Dur also; in the British language, signifies water. When they wanted salt they said, Halgein ydorum, bring salt: salt is called *hal* in Greek, and Halen in British, for that language, from the length of time which the Britons (then called Trojans, and afterwards Britons, from Brito, their leader) remained in Greece after the destruction of Troy, became, in many instances, similar to the Greek.

The story of Elidorus is obviously drawn from the same legend or legends that inspired Nennius and Geoffrey of Monmouth, except that Geoffrey's giants fleeing to the mountain caves have been replaced by "pigmies" living underground. What is new in Giraldus is the information that the "pigmies" spoke a language "very conformable to the Greek idiom"—a folk-memory, perhaps, of an Indo-European language spoken in Britain before the Celts came.

The Three Oppressions of Britain

The story of *Lludd and Llefelys* is one of the so-called native tales of the *Mabinogion*, and is thought to have been first written down between A.D. 1225 and A.D. 1250, though it may date to the 11th century. Lludd is Nodens or Nodons, the god of the Roman temple of Lydney Park in Gloucestershire, and the first element of Llefelys is Lugus, as in Lleu of the Fourth Branch of the *Mabinogion*.[15] In this tale, Lludd is the son of Beli, and king of the Island of Britain, and Llefelys his brother is king of France, having married the daughter of the former king. During Lludd's reign, three *gormesoedd*, variously translated as "plagues" or "oppressions," fall on the Island of Britain[16]:

> The first was a certain race that came, and was called the Coranians; and so great was their knowledge, that there was no discourse upon the face of the Island, however low it might be spoken, but what, if the wind met it, it was known to them. And through this they could not be injured.
> The second plague was a shriek which came on every May-eve, over every hearth in the Island of Britain. And this went through people's hearts, and so seared them, that the men lost their hue and their strength, and the women their children, and the young men and the maidens lost their senses, and all the animals and trees and the earth and the waters, were left barren.
> The third plague was, that however much of provisions and food might be prepared in the king's courts, were there even so much as a year's provision of meat and drink, none of it could ever be found, except what was consumed in the first night.

Not knowing what to do about the Coranians, or what might be causing the other two plagues, Lludd consulted his brother Llefelys, the two speaking through a brass horn so the Coranians could not hear them. Llefelys told Lludd that to overcome the Coranians, he would give him some insects, which Lludd should "mash in water" and throw over the Coranians.

> "And the second plague," said he, "that is in thy dominion, behold it is a dragon. And another dragon of a foreign race is fighting with it, and striving to overcome it." And therefore does your dragon make a fearful outcry.... "The cause of the third plague," said he, "is a mighty man of magic, who takes thy meat and thy drink and thy store. And he through illusions and charms causes every one to sleep."

In order to overcome these two plagues, Llefelys made the following suggestions. In the case of the dragons, he should measure the island, and at

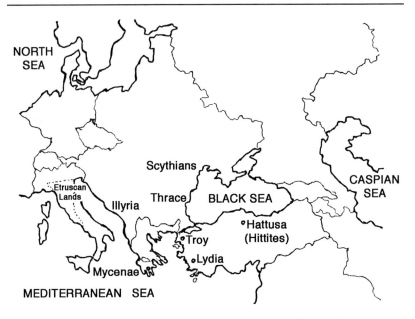

Map 7: The Classical World at and after the time of the Trojan War, showing
Lydian and Etruscan migrations from the area around Troy.

its exact central point, dig a large pit, and put a cauldron of mead in the
pit covered with satin. Eventually the fighting dragons would fall into the
cauldron, drink the mead and go to sleep, whereupon they could be buried
in a strong place. In the case of the food, Lludd should watch over it, with
a cauldron of cold water by his side to stop himself from falling asleep.

Lludd followed this advice: he mashed the insects in water and
destroyed all the Coranians; and he trapped the fighting dragons in the
cauldron of mead, and buried them at Dinas Emrys in northwest Wales.
He then prepared a large banquet, and with a cauldron of water at his
side, he waited. After a time

> he heard many surpassing fascinations and various songs. And drowsiness
> urged him to sleep. Upon this, lest he should be hindered from his pur-
> pose and be overcome by sleep, he went often into the water. And at last,
> behold, a man of vast size, clad in strong, heavy armour, came in, bearing
> a hamper. And, as he was wont, he put all the food and provisions of meat
> and drink into the hamper, and proceeded to go with it forth. And noth-
> ing was ever more wonderful to Lludd, than that the hamper should hold
> so much.
> And thereupon King Lludd went after him and spoke unto him thus.
> "Stop, stop," said he, "though thou hast done many insults and much spoil

erewhile, thou shalt not do so any more, unless thy skill in arms and thy prowess be greater than mine."

Then he instantly put down the hamper on the floor, and awaited him. And a fierce encounter was between them, so that the glittering fire flew out from their arms. And at the last Lludd grappled with him, and fate bestowed the victory on Lludd. And he threw the plague to the earth.

The man of vast size then promised to atone for all the wrongs he had done to Lludd, and to become his faithful vassal.

Before I comment on this tale, I would like first to present one of the *Welsh Triads* Triad 36,[17] which is relevant to *Lludd and Llefelys*:

Triad 36

Three oppressions that came to this Island, and not one of them went back:

One of them (was) the people of the Coraniaid, who came here in the time of Caswallawn (= Lludd?) son of Beli: and not one of them went back. And they came from Arabia.

The second Oppression: the Gwyddyl Ffichti. And not one of them went back.

The third Oppression: the Saxons, with Horsa and Hengist as their leaders.

Triad 36 speaks of the Saxons as one of the "oppressions," and these can readily be linked to the fighting dragons. In the *Historia Brittonum*,[18] Vortigern decides to build a citadel, and collects together building materials, but these keep disappearing overnight. So he calls together his wise men, who tell him: "You must find a child born without a father, put him to death, and sprinkle with his blood the ground on which the citadel is to be built, or you will never accomplish your purpose." So Vortigern sends out messengers to find a child without a father, who find one and bring him before the king. When the king explains to the boy what his wise men told him, the boy reveals to them that under the ground where the citadel is to be built there is a pool, in the pool are two vases, in the vases is a folded tent, and in the tent are two sleeping serpents who begin to struggle with each other:

The white one, raising himself up, threw down the other into the middle of the tent and sometimes drove him to the edge of it; and this was repeated thrice. At length the red one, apparently the weaker of the two, recovering his strength, expelled the white one from the tent; and the latter being pursued through the pool by the red one, disappeared. Then the boy, asking the wise men what was signified by this wonderful omen, and they expressing their ignorance, he said to the king, "I will now unfold to you the meaning of this mystery. The pool is the emblem of this world, and the tent that of your kingdom: the two serpents are two dragons; the red serpent is your dragon, but the white serpent is the dragon of the people who occupy several provinces and districts of Britain, even almost from sea to sea: at length, however, our people shall rise and drive away the Saxon race from beyond the sea, whence they originally came.

One of the three oppressions — the fighting dragons — therefore refers to the Saxons, who certainly came and did not go back. This implies that the man of vast size who stole all the food can be identified with the Gwyddyl Ffichti, or Gaelic Picts, the name used by the medieval Welsh to designate the Scottish Picts. But who were the Picts?

The fact that the food thief appears to be a giant and uses music to cast a spell over people suggests that the Picts belongs to mythological times. This combination of food, music and thievery calls to mind a passage from the *Deipnosophists* (c. A.D. 230) of the Greek writer Athenaeus, where he says, quoting Poseidonius (135 B.C.–51 B.C.)[19]:

> Poseidonius of Apameia, in the twenty-third book of his histories, says, "The Celts, even when they make war, take about with them companions to dine with them, whom they call parasites. And these men celebrate their praises before large companies assembled together, and also to private individuals who are willing to listen to them; they have also a description of people called Bards, who make them music; and these are poets, who recite their praises with songs."

The link to a mythological past is reinforced by the magic hamper carried by the large man, which resembles the magic bag that Rhiannon gave to Pwyll in the First Branch of the *Mabinogion*, and the cornucopia of the goddess of Gloucestershire.

The Picts in some sense do belong to mythological time. They were a confederation of tribes living in the north and east of Scotland from before the Roman conquest of Britain until the 10th century. The Anglo-Saxon historian Bede, writing in the 8th century A.D., tells us[20] that Britain was home to five distinct languages: Church Latin, English, Welsh, Gaelic and Pictish. Bede also relates a legend about the Picts. He says they were descended from a colony of seafarers from Scythia who took possession of northern Britain. The 15th-century Scottish history, the *Scotichronicon*, on the other hand, says that the Picts came from the coasts of the Baltic Sea.[21]

Is there any substance to the legend that the Picts were descended from Scythians? Dunbavin says[22] that W.J. Watson dismissed the legends as "learned embellishment," based on the mention of *picti Agathyrsi* ("painted Agathyrsi") and *picti Geloni* ("painted Geloni") in the *Aeneid* of Virgil. Herodotus, says Dunbavin,[23]

> locates the Agathyrsi on the Black Sea above the Danube, and the Geloni, he says, were Greeks who settled on the upper Dnieper in present-day Ukraine. All these tribes were, at that time, tributary to the Iranian-speaking Scythians. Herodotus also describes the social organization of the Agathyrsi: they held their women in common and were all therefore brothers, as of a single family. This is remarkably similar to the customs attributed to the British tribes by Julius Caesar, Dio Cassius, Solinus and St. Jerome.

According to Dunbavin,[24] the 4th-century Roman writer Solinus "records that the Agathyrsi dyed their hair and faces blue, just as we are told that the Britons did." Indeed, the practice of tattooing and body painting was not restricted to the British Isles. The "tattooing of animal figures on the skin was apparently a widespread custom throughout the Scythian region, as such depictions have been found on the body of a Scythian chieftain excavated at Pazyryrk, in the Altai region of Russia." Interestingly, the Roman historian Pliny implies that the Scythians lived as far north as the Baltic coast,[25] which the *Scotichronicon* gave as the homeland of the Picts.

Of the three oppressions, the most obscure is that of the Coranians, or Coraniaid as they are more generally known. Their name is generally linked to Welsh *cor(r)* "dwarf"[26]; Koch also suggests a connection with Old Irish *corrguinecht* "magic, wizardry," and *corrguinech* "magician, sorcerer." The Coraniaid are said to have the ability to hear any utterance that met the wind—an ability shared by Math in the Fourth Branch of the *Mabinogion*. Asdis R. Magnusdottir[27] links the Coraniaid to the Norse guardian of the gods, Heimdallur, who can hear grass growing, and possesses a horn which can be heard throughout the world.

The method used to destroy the Coraniaid is puzzling. The insects that Llefelys recommends be crushed in water and sprinkled over the Coraniaid apparently are not found in Britain, and could be a reference to Spanish fly, which is found only in southern Europe, including France. Spanish fly is a species of blister beetle which secretes a poison called cantharidin—cantharidin can cause blisters, and if accidentally ingested by horses can be toxic. The fact that the crushed insects can kill the Coraniaid but can't harm Lludd's people suggests that there may be a close association between the Coraniaid and horses which, in magical terms, makes them especially vulnerable to cantharidin.

Perhaps most puzzling of all is that the Coraniaid are said to come from Arabia. In the Third Branch of the *Mabinogion* (see Chapter 4), Manawydan, when he became a saddle-maker, made pommels colored with "blue azure," as he had seen Llassar do. In medieval times, blue pigment was made from lapis lazuli, which originally came from Afghanistan — the word *lazuli* comes from the Arabic *lazaward*, which ultimately comes from the Persian *lazhvard*, the name of a place where lapis lazuli was mined. This word is also the origin of the color *azure*, and may also be the origin of the name *Llassar*. It seems likely therefore that the Coraniaid were thought to come from the same place as lapis lazuli, here glossed as Arabia, but more plausibly signifying the vast expanse of eastern Europe where Scythians and other Iranian-speaking tribes lived. It was Llassar, after all, who escaped from the Iron House in Ireland and brought Bran the cauldron of regeneration — and as was pointed out in Chapter 5, the technology for making cauldrons of beaten bronze probably originated in central Europe.

Thracians and Cimmerians

The legendary history of Britain speaks of Trojans, Greeks, Scythians and people from the Baltic, and there are tantalizing hints that there is indeed some connection between Britain and lands far to the east. To make sense of this, we need to look at a culture usually referred to as Thraco–Cimmerian, and associated with two ethnic groups, the Thracians and the Cimmerians. For Homer (*Odyssey* 1.14), the Cimmerians were a people "living in a mythical land of fog and darkness on the fringes of the habitable world"[28]; while the Thracians, a more flesh-and-blood people, were allies of the Trojans in the *Iliad*.

The Thracians were an Indo-European people speaking a language that is now extinct, and centered on present-day Bulgaria, the European part of Turkey, and parts of Romania, Serbia, Greece and the Republic of Macedonia. The Thracians were neighbors of the Greeks and figure prominently in the historical record, unlike the Cimmerians. Herodotus[29] says that the Cimmerians originally inhabited the region north of the Caucasus and the Black Sea, in what is now Ukraine and Russia, but were driven out by the Scythians. The Assyrian annals of 714 B.C. report that a people called the Gimirri helped the forces of Sargon II, king of Assyria, defeat the kingdom of Urartu, in the Lake Van area of Anatolia; at the time, the

Gimirri seem to have lived in northwest Iran, but later settled in what is now the Republic of Georgia.

The concept of a Thraco–Cimmerian culture was originally proposed by Paul Reinecke in 1925, and reinforced by researchers in the 1930s.[30] These researchers "saw the presence of equestrian bronzes and weapons in central and southeastern European graves and hoards that showed East European steppe-bound analogies as a reflection of the invasion of mounted warriors. These putative invaders were identified with the historic Cimmerians who were thought to have caused major disruptions in the cultural development of the Carpathian basin and beyond into Central Europe," superimposing themselves on the prevailing Urnfield culture. They were linked to the Thracians because parts of the Black Sea coast were under Thracian influence at the time, the Thracians were rich in mineral resources, especially iron ores, and they were renowned for their horses and mounted warriors.[31]

Where the Cimmerians originated and where they lived still remains a matter of debate. Kristian Kristiansen notes[32] that from about 900 B.C., rich, well-organized "kingdoms" or "chiefdoms" developed in the Caucasus, interacting with the civilizations to the south. Here, he says, "we also find typical horse-bits and cheek-pieces of early Thraco–Cimmerian type." During the 9th and 8th centuries, says Kristiansen, "a grouping or complex of related cultural traits ... were expanding into Central Europe" which can be identified as Thraco–Cimmerian. Among the artefacts belonging to this complex, says Bouzek, are horse-bits and Cimmerian bimetallic daggers, with bronze handles and iron blades, which are found as far west as Silesia (now part of Poland), Moravia (now part of Czechoslovakia), Leibnitz (Austria), Neundorf (in Lausitz, in the eastern German state of Brandenburg)[33] (see Map 8).

Horses and wagons were an important feature of the Thraco–Cimmerian culture, which brought with it some important technological innovations. Kristiansen points out[34] that Thraco–Cimmerian horse-bits "were of the two-joint type, meant for riding, as opposed to the rigid Urnfield bits, which were more suitable for traction, as they are hard on the mouth of the horse. Second, compared to Urnfield bits with a diameter normally of 3 inches, the new types are 4 to 4 and a half inches, implying larger breeds of horses. Third, the wagons and wheels demonstrate a newer and more complex technology." From this, says Kristiansen, we may conclude that "riding had now become fully developed in warfare, demanding the specialized breeding and training of horses."

The process of expansion says Kristiansen,[35] was "highly complex, trade alternating with elite conquest." In Hungary, "pastoral overlords brought with them a new burial ritual and a completely new material culture," while in Slovenia "there was more a mixture of foreign and local traditions." A "new princely social organization emerged in the 8th century, characterized by large fortified settlements and tumulus burials," as at Sticna (Slovenia), Ödenburg/Sopron (in Hungary, on the Austrian border) and Novo Mesto (Slovenia). Large "tumulus barrows, another aspect of the new eastern ideology, were raised outside new royal courts at Sticna and Novo Mesto ... to signal the presence of new elites," as at Seddin (in Branbenburg) and Voldtofte (in Denmark) in the north during the same period.[36]

It seems therefore that the Thraco–Cimmerians were horse-riding nomadic warriors who spread westward from the steppes of present-day Ukraine and Russia, bringing with them new types of weapons and horse-riding technologies. The influence of Thraco–Cimmerian culture seems to have been strongest in Hungary, but also extended as far west as Austria and even Switzerland — a Thraco–Cimmerian bronze horse-bit has been found at the settlement of Zürich-Alpenquai on the shores of Lake Zürich.[37] Obviously the Thraco–Cimmerian culture did not spread as far as Britain, but it may well have influenced Britain indirectly. The All Cannings Cross pottery discussed in Chapter 5 may well have been introduced by a small number of settlers from eastern France. Nancy K. Sandars says[38] that this pottery comes from the Jura region of France, which borders on Switzerland, not far from the westernmost spread of Thraco–Cimmerian bronzes.

It was noted in Chapter 5 that the introduction of the All Cannings Cross pottery was accompanied by the construction of large-scale middens in places like Potterne and East Chisenbury. But these were not the only changes that occurred. The period between 900 B.C. and 600 B.C. saw the emergence of the first hillforts — large hilltop enclosures and small strongly defended forts.[39] The hilltop enclosures include Danebury, site of a later hillfort, and Balksbury, both in west Hampshire. Balksbury has been extensively excavated, and work has shown that

> the enclosure bank and ditch was built in the 9th–8th centuries B.C., and the enclosure continued in use for about two centuries, during which time the bank and ditch was refurbished on at least two occasions. Internally the only significant features of this phase to be identified were a number of small four-post "granaries" and a few lightly-built circular "huts." The most interesting aspect of the recent work has been the examination of the

build-up of colluvium, containing midden material, against the inside of the enclosing bank. Analysis suggested that the high organic component of the deposit probably derived from animal waste and other organic material brought in for fodder and litter.[40]

The evidence suggests that

the primary function of these hilltop enclosures was pastoral, to provide corral space for livestock at certain times during the year. In this context the four-post structures could be interpreted as fodder ricks, while the light circular buildings could have provided shelter for those tending the beasts. The size of the enclosures might suggest that they served large communities, and this raises the possibility that they were places where the community could gather at certain times during the year for ceremonies and feasting, when the more practical tasks of culling, castration and the redistribution of stock were being undertaken. Some supporting evidence for this comes from Balksbury, where it was found that the colluvium contained midden material possibly derived from feasting. As to the size of the territory to which the enclosure belonged, it may be relevant to note that some of the pottery found in these deposits came from as far away as 6–10 miles.[41]

The small strongly defended forts include Budbury (west Wiltshire); Lidbury Camp, near Enford, Wiltshire, not far from the midden at East Chisenbury; and Oliver's Camp, near Devizes, Wiltshire, in the general area of All Cannings Cross and the midden at Potterne (see Map 9). The sites are of less than 7 acres in extent, they "favour ridge-end locations (although some are found in less defensible and more open central downland settings) and often have more than one line of defence. All seem to have been intensively occupied with the exception of Oliver's Camp, which produced comparatively little material and no major internal structures."[42] Cunliffe suggests that they "might have been elite settlements of some kind, the prominent location and impressive defences being the symbols of elite status distinguishing them from contemporary farmsteads."[43] According to Cunliffe, the overall impression gained from this and other evidence is that "this was a period of transition in the course of which the economic, social and belief systems changed rapidly."[44]

Before I leave the Cimmerians, I need to say something about legends that link the Cimmerians to the Germanic tribe known as the Cimbri, and to the Cymry, or Welsh. The Cimbri lived in Jutland, Demark, in the area known as Himmerland, where the Gundsetrup Cauldron was found, and the classical writers Strabo, Diodorus Siculus and Plutarch all link them to the Cimmerians. The etymology of Cimmerian and Cimbri is unknown. One possibility is that Cimbri is from the Indo-European root *kei* "to lie down,"[45] which gives Greek *keitai* "lies," *kome* "village," Hittite *kihthta* (*kitta*) and *ki-it-ta-ri* (*kittari*) "lies," Latin *civis* "townsman," Gothic *haims* "village," Old Norse *heimr* "homeland, world," Old High German *heim* "homeland, house, dwelling." Other scholars[46] have seen the root as *tkei* "settle, found," and also derived from it Sanskrit *kseti* "dwell." Thus Cimmerian and Cimbri would mean "settlers, villagers."

The other possible etymology of Cimmerian is linked to the etymology of the Welsh *Cymry*. This is said to be derived from the Celtic words *com* plus *brog*; *brog* is cognate with Latin *margo* "frontier, margin," Gothic *marka* "frontier," Old High German *marcha* "limit, boundary," Old English *mearc* "boundary," Armenian *marz* "border, land," Ukrainian *meza* "border, margin," Persian *marz* "border, land"[47]; *com* is cognate with Greek *koinos* "shared, common." The earliest mention of the Persian word *marz* is during the Persian Sassanid Empire (A.D. 205–A.D. 651), when there was a position called *marzban*, that is, governor of a frontier province. However, given the fact that Sassanid Persian is not likely to have been influenced by Celtic or Latin, it is probable that the Middle Persian and Armenian words *marz* either developed independently, or borrowed from each other. Therefore, it would seem that the name Cimmerian developed from Indo-European words similar to *kom* and *marz*, and meant "those sharing a common land." So even if the Cimmerians, Cimbri and Cymry are not related, at least two of the names have a similar Indo-European derivation.

The Thracian Horseman

What Cunliffe says about Wessex between 900 B.C. and 700 B.C. suggests that the people who brought the All Cannings Cross pottery probably lived in small strongly defended forts at Lidbury Camp and Oliver's Camp, and kept their stock and conducted communal feasts in hilltop enclosures at Danebury and Balksbury. If Cunliffe's interpretation is to be believed, they worshipped chthonic deities — fertility gods — by constructing huge middens at East Chisenbury and Potterne, where all that the earth produced was returned to the earth. If I understand Cunliffe correctly, it was these same people who, from around 600 B.C., built the hillfort at Danebury, on the site of the earlier hilltop enclosure, digging out pits in which grain was stored, placing the grain under the protection of these same chthonic deities, and later making sacrifices to the gods in these pits, including the ritually dismembered horse referred to in Chapter 5.

Continuity seems to have been maintained at Danebury until the end of the 4th century, when there is "evidence of a widespread fire followed by diminished use."[48] Cunliffe believes that this is evidence of social disruption: it coincides with a major change in pottery style recognizable over a considerable area, perhaps indicating a social dislocation of more than regional significance. After this "distinctive horizon many of the early hillforts show no sign of any further use, while others continued to be utilized, their enclosing earthworks being refurbished." The simplest explanation of the phenomenon, says Cunliffe,[49] is that there was "a widespread social crisis brought about perhaps by the emergence of competing polities. Once it was resolved some of the old polities, who had maintained their integrity and dominance, continued while others were disbanded or absorbed. This could explain the abandonment of some of the hillforts and the development of others." Although Cunliffe does not say this, one factor here could be the emergence of Celtic elites in the Thames Valley and eastern England, where pottery styles were strongly influenced by Continental La Tène cultures from northern France and the Low Countries, and conflict could easily have arisen in the Berkshire Downs and the Cotswolds, at the frontier between two groups of people represented by the more conservative saucepan pot continuum of the south of England[50] and the innovative La Tène pottery north of the Thames.

All this points to the fact that the culture which predominated in southern England until around 400 B.C. or later was not Celtic and had probably evolved from the culture which made the All Cannings Cross pottery and accumulated the massive middens. We have two pointers to the nature of this culture: it appears to have worshipped chthonic deities, and it appears to have included horses in its religious ritual. Let's start with the horses, which clearly played an important part in the life of the Thracians and Cimmerians who may have indirectly influenced the makers of the All Cannings Cross pottery.

We know nothing of the religion of the Cimmerians, but a good deal about Thracian religious beliefs. Horse-gods have a long history among Indo-European peoples: Linear B tablets from Pylos in southern Greece (see Map 10), dated to around 1200 B.C., mention a *po-ti-ni-ya i-que-ya*, or Potnia Ikkʷeia, "Mistress of Horses"[51]; and the ancient Indian religious text the *Rigveda* refers many times to the divine twin horsemen known as the Ashvins. But in Thracian religion or mythology the first mention of

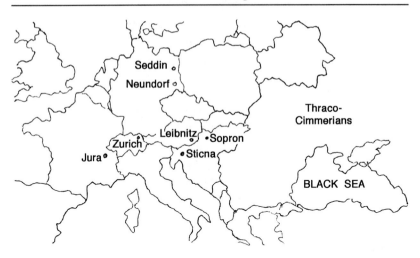

Map 8: Furthest extent of Thraco–Cimmerian migrations westward early in the 1st millennium B.C.

a figure connected with horses is found in the *Iliad* of Homer, thought to have been composed around 800 B.C. In Book 10, Dolon, an ally of the Trojans, says to Odysseus[52]:

> If you're keen to infiltrate
> the Trojan army, over there are Thracians.
> fresh troops, new arrivals, furthest distant
> from the rest, among them their king Rhesus,
> son of Eioneus. His horses are the best.
> the finest and largest ones I've ever seen,
> whiter than snow, as fast as the winds.
> His chariot is finely built — with gold
> and silver. He came here with his armour —
> an amazing sight — huge and made of gold.
> It's not appropriate for mortal men
> to wear such armour, only deathless gods.

Homer implies that Rhesus was a god or at least god-like figure, and this is borne out by the later cult, attested from the 4th century B.C., of the rider-god called the Thracian Horseman, also known as *Heros* ("Hero"). Robert Turcan[53] notes that this being is depicted on stelae found in all regions of Thrace, including Odessos and Romula (see Map 11). In these depictions, mostly from the time of the Roman Empire, the Thracian horseman "advances, sometimes at a walk" (see Figure 10), sometimes at a gallop, "towards an altar erected in front of a tree around which a snake is entwined"[54] (the walking pace recalls the horse of Rhiannon when Pwyll sees her for the first time). We also see him "leaping forward with a spear in his hand to hunt boar, or astride a lion. Sometimes he holds game — a doe or a hare, for instance — which he has flushed out and killed. A dog usually accompanies him"[55] (as in the ritual depositions at Danebury).

Raffaele Pettazzoni points out[56] that that on at least five stelae (from Philippopolis and Oiskos) the Thracian Horseman, or Thracian Rider, as Pettazzoni calls him, has three heads, and in one stela he has two heads. One inscription with the Rider includes a Thracian word interpreted as *panthopto*, that is, "all-seeing," whose Greek equivalent *panoptes* is used to describe Helios, the Sun. According to Pettazzoni, there are numerous indications that the Thracians worshipped the sun: in a fragment of Sophocles' tragedy *Tereus*, dating from the 5th century B.C., the sun is invoked with the words: "O Sun, whose splendour is most revered by the horse-loving Thracians"[57]; and according to a myth preserved in the astronomical work the *Catasterismi* attributed to Eratosthenes, a Greek astronomer of

Map 9: Small forts and large hilltop enclosures in the vicinity of Salisbury Plain around 800 B.C.

the 3rd century B.C., and probably derived from a lost play of the 5th century B.C. by Aeschylus, the *Bassarids*, Orpheus, originally a Thracian, used to rise while it was still dark to climb before dawn to the summit of Mt. Pangaion and salute the sun as it rose.

However, Herodotus[58] says that the Thracians "worship no gods but Ares, Dionysus, and Artemis. Their princes, however, unlike the rest of their countrymen, worship Hermes above all gods and swear only by him, claiming him for their ancestor." No mention is made of the Thracian Horseman, and Pettazzoni tries to explain why. He believes that ordinary Thracians worshipped the god that Herodotus calls Dionysus, while aristocrats worshipped the god interpreted as Hermes.[59] A parallel can be found, he says, among the Scythians, who, according to Herodotus, had a certain number of national divinities, including an "Apollo," while the Royal Scythians, the clan to which the kings and lords belonged, venerated another god.[60] The opposition between the religion of Dionysus and the religion of the Sun is underlined in the *Bassarids* of Aeschylus, where Dionysus gets his revenge on the sun-worshipping Orpheus by having him killed by his followers, the Bassarids.

It appears from this that the sun-god was interpreted as Hermes, but why? Pettazzoni believes that "an infernal aspect is common to both Hermes as *psychopompos* ('soul-guide') and to the Sun, as setting daily in the west and vanishing beneath the horizon to lighten the underground world of the dead during the night and reappear at sunrise in the east."[61] This helps to explain the Greek interpretation of the Persian god Mithra. In inscriptions from the tomb of Antiochos of Commagene (a kingdom in what is now south-central Turkey), the sun-god Mithra "is identified not only with Helios and Apollo, but also with Hermes." Interestingly, "Mithra was invoked by the rulers of Persia to witness their oaths and asseverations,"[62] just as the Thracians swore all their oaths by "Hermes." Pettazzoni concludes that the "Hermes" of Herodotus is the Thracian Horseman, sometimes described on inscriptions as *genikos* or *geniakos*, Progenitor of the Thracians, and as all-seeing sun-god, well placed to ensure that all oaths were kept by those who made them.[63]

Is there any connection between Rhesus of the *Iliad*, the cult of the Thracian Horseman, and the dismembered horse found in the storage pit at Danebury? I think there is, and I am not alone in thinking so. David Rankin,[64] following on from Henrich Wagner's 1971 work, *Studies in the Origins of the Celts and of Early Celtic Civilization*, links Rhesus and the Thracian Horseman if not to Danebury and the dismembered horse, then to the Irish god the Dagda, also known as *Eochaid Ollathair* ("Horse Great-Father"), and links the Thracian Hermes to Lugh in the Irish tradition. Of course from the British and Welsh perspective, the closest match to the Thracian Rider-god is Rhiannon, the horse goddess that both Pwyll and Manawydan marry. The concept of marriage to a horse-goddess is given extra piquancy by that indefatigable traveler, Giraldus Cambrensis, in his *Topography of Ireland*. He is traveling in the northwest of Ulster, in the area of Kenelcunill (Cenel Conaill), when he comes across a people "accustomed to appoint its king with a rite altogether outlandish and abominable"[65]:

> When the whole people of that land has been gathered together in one place, a white mare is brought forward into the middle of the assembly. He who is to be inaugurated, not as a chief, but as a beast, not as a king, but as an outlaw, has bestial intercourse with her before all, professing himself to be a beast also. The mare is then killed immediately, cut up into pieces, and boiled in water. A bath is prepared for the man afterwards in the same water. He sits in the bath surrounded by all his people, and all, he and they, eat of the meat of the mare which is brought to them. He quaffs and drinks of the broth in which he is bathed, not in any cup, or using his hand, but just dipping his mouth into it round about him. When this unrighteous rite has been carried out, his kingship and dominion have been conferred.

As Daniel Bray points out,[66] this ritual of horse-sacrifice has distinct parallels in the Vedic inauguration rite, the *asvamedha*, which

> involved the sacrificial slaughter of a stallion, whereupon the queen symbolically slept with it under covers, and afterwards the flesh was cooked and eaten by the assembled people. As this activity was carried out, hymns were sung to praise the horse, to direct its dismemberment, and to petition favourable returns, phrased as follows: "Let this racehorse bring us good cattle and good horses, male children and all-nourishing wealth. Let Aditi make us free from sin. Let the horse with our offerings achieve sovereign power for us."

The Druids of Dodona

We saw in Chapter 5 that the deposition of the dismembered horse in the storage pit at Danebury was linked by Anne Ross to the "heads and hooves" ritual of the bull-feast, first described in the Irish epic tale *The Destruction of Da Derga's Hostel* (c. A.D. 1100). Presumably the "heads and hooves" ritual and the kingship ritual described by Giraldus were super-

Map 10: The Mycenean world around 1200 B.C., showing settlements in Crete, Greece and Asia Minor (Anatolia).

vised by priests of some sort, and we must assume that the priests who supervised these rituals in the 12th century A.D. were in a sense the same priests who presided over the ritual deposition of the dismembered horse at Danebury in the 6th century B.C. I will now argue that these priests were Druids, and that this priesthood was born in the 8th century B.C. around the middens and small strongly defended forts of Wiltshire.

The first piece of evidence for this claim lies in the etymology of the name. In fact the etymology of *druid* is disputed, but the most common explanation is that it means something like "oak-seer." As West points out,[67] this interpretation of the name links the Druids to the ancient oracle of Dodona in Epirus, northwestern Greece, which, says West, is an Illyrian rather than a Greek institution. Susan Guettel Cole says[68] that the oracle of Dodona, located in a distant valley deep in Epirus,

> had the reputation of great antiquity. Priests called *Selloi* went barefoot with feet unwashed. Zeus himself, possibly represented by the great oak tree that grew in his sanctuary, was attended by three priestesses and accompanied by doves. Ancient traditions differ in the precise details. Just how responses were delivered is not divulged; some believe the god's will was interpreted from the rustling of the oak leaves, others from the cries of the doves. Enquiries were inscribed on small lead tablets, written by the petitioners themselves.

Dodona is mentioned in the *Iliad*[69] when Achilles prays to "Lord Zeus, Dodonean, Pelasgian Zeus; you that live far away and rule over wintry Dodona." Sotiris Dakaris, who excavated Dodona, "dates the beginning of the cult from the late early–Helladic to early middle–Helladic, hence to about 2000 B.C. He also points to the close connection of the dove with

Figure 10: Image of the rider-god, also known as the Thracian Horseman, found on the Lincolnshire/Nottinghamshire border, near the village of Brough (Roman Crocolana). British Museum. Note the exaggerated walking pace of the horse.

Cretan-Mycenean religion, in which the dove is venerated as a divine symbol and sacred animal,"[70] and believes that Zeus first became established at Dodona in the 13th century B.C.

This was not the only sacred oak in Greece. On Mount Lycaeus in Arcadia, where Zeus is said to have been reared, there is a spring called Hagno, named after one of the nymphs who reared Zeus. Pausanias tells the following story about this spring[71]:

> Should a drought persist for a long time, and the seeds in the earth and the trees wither, then the priest of Lycaean Zeus, after praying towards the water and making the usual sacrifices, lowers an oak branch to the surface of the spring, not letting it sink deep. When the water has been stirred up there rises a vapor, like mist; after a time the mist becomes cloud, gathers to itself other clouds, and makes rain fall on the land of the Arcadians.

Classical writers linked the Druids to bards and vates, and the etymology of these two words is instructive. The word *bard* is said to derive from *g^wera-* "to raise the voice, to praise," which also gives Avestan *(aibi) jaretay* "praiser" and Sanskrit *jaritar* "singer, praiser."[72] On the other hand, Raimo Anttila says[73] that Enrico Campanile derives *bard* from Indo-European *g^wera-dhe-o-s* "the one who puts up (makes) praise(s)," which Campanile links to Sanskrit *giro dha* and Avestan *garo da*, Vedic *giram dha* and Avestan *garem da*. These derivations are supported by other sources. In the *Sanskrit Lexicon*, the meaning of *gir* is given as "addressing, invoking, praising"; "invocation, addressing with praise, praise, verse." According to the *Old Avestan Glossary, gar-* means "song of praise; to sing (songs of praise)"; in Kanga's *Avesta Dictionary, garô* or *gar* means "invocation," and in the *Altiranisches Wörterbuch, garah* means "hymn, song of praise."

The word *vates* is said[74] to be related to a set of Germanic words that link the ideas of poetry and possession: Gothic *woths* "possessed," Old High German *wuot* "frenzied," Old English *wod* "song," Old Norse *othr* "possessed, inspired; mind, poetry," and to the Norse god Odin, and his Anglo-Saxon counterpart Woden. N.D. Kazanas speculates[75] that Woden/Odin may be a development of an Indo-European deity appearing as Vedic *Vata* (= wind: a variant of the more common *Vayu*) who "exhibits traits pertinent to the Germanic god. Thus Vata's swiftness is a standard of comparison for swift motions"; his "wrath can be roused easily"; he "blows down from heaven with rainstorms" and "roars in the sky thundering," and has "the treasure of immortality in his dwelling whereby he gives life to his devotees": these traits are found also in Wodan. It may be recalled that the Taliesin-poet drew on something he called *awen* ("inspiration"),

Map 11: Significant sites in Arcadia and Macedonia (c. 700 B.C.), plus Greek cities in Italy associated with Pythagoras, and the distribution of the cult of the Thracian Horseman.

which is cognate with Welsh *awel* "breeze" — obviously the equation *breeze = inspiration* is very similar to the equation *wind = prophetic* fury.

The second piece of evidence that the priests of Wiltshire around 800 B.C. were Druids, or at least came from those distant lands where the oak was venerated, is to be found in the other burials at Danebury. It was noted earlier that beside the dismembered horse in the pit at Danebury was the skeleton of a dog, and we have said little so far about the dog. J.P. Mallory and Douglas Q. Adams confirm[76] that the association of dogs with death is a common Indo-European theme. Yama, the lord of death in the ancient Vedas of India, has two four-eyed dogs, who are guardians and "keepers of the path to the afterworld." In Iranian tradition, "a four-eyed dog was brought before a dead body in order for its gaze to expel the demons. The Daena or 'inner self' of the dead person, in the shape of a beautiful woman, escorts the souls of the righteous to Paradise accompanied by two dogs whose function is to guide the soul to the proper path by barking." The three-headed Cerberus is the best-known other-worldly dog, first attested in the *Theogony* of the Greek poet Hesiod, written around 700 B.C. Green points out[77] the ritual importance of dogs at Danebury. In one of the pits constructed before 500 B.C. the bodies of two dogs were found, "together with a selection of twenty other bones representing a range of wild and domestic species. After the animals had been positioned, chalk blocks were laid over the bodies and then a huge timber structure was erected over the middle of the whole deposit." Green adds that horses and dog "occur together repeatedly enough for their association to be considered statistically significant at Danebury."

Another animal overrepresented at Danebury is the raven.[78] In Romano-Celtic iconography, says Green,[79] ravens were associated with a number of beneficent deities. The god who presided over the Burgundian healing spring shrine at Mavilly, in northeastern France, "was depicted in company with a large raven"; the goddess Nantosuelta appears on images at Sarrebourg, near Metz (northeastern France), and Speier (Germany), accompanied by a raven. In Luxembourg "a distinctive type of goddess was worshipped, a deity whose image consisted of a lady seated within a house-shaped shrine and accompanied by a raven." Interestingly, one representation of the horse-goddess Epona, at Altrier in Luxembourg, depicts her with a dog and a raven.[80]

However, the raven or crow also has ancient connections with Greece and other Mediterranean lands. In Fragment 89 of the *Catalogue of Women*, attributed to Hesiod, the poet tells us that a crow came to Apollo to warn him that his lover Coronis had wed Ischys. Herodotus also tells that Aristeas, the semi-legendary Greek poet of the 7th century B.C., who came from Proconnesus (the Turkish island of Marmara), had traveled to the Issedones (an ancient tribe of Central Asia), transported by Apollo.[81] Herodotus tells us that Aristeas reappeared 200 years later in Metapontum in southern Italy, telling the people of Metapontus that he had accompanied Apollo in the shape of a raven.

Metapontum is associated not only with Aristeas, but also with the Greek philosopher Pythagoras (c. 570 B.C.–c. 495 B.C.), who believed in reincarnation and who has been linked to the Druids (see Chapter 1). Pythagoras was born on the Greek island of Samos, but in later life moved to Croton, in southern Italy, and subsequently to Metapontum. Pythagoras was "regarded by his followers as the reincarnation of Hyperborean Apollo."[82] Legend has it that Pythagoras met the legendary sage, healer and priest of Apollo, Abaris the Hyperborean — who, according to Herodotus, traveled round the world on an arrow — and took away his arrow and made him his follower.

Apollo is an ancient god, mentioned in the *Iliad* Book 1, where, angry that the Greeks have taken the daughter of his priest Chryses, he shoots his plague-arrows at the Greeks for nine whole days, causing widespread destruction to animals and men. Morris Silver[83] mentions Cook's hypothesis that the cult of Apollo "actually made its way along the old amber route from the land of the Hyperboreans," thought to live north of the Thracians and Scythians. Support for Cook's theory is found in a tradition cited by Pausanias[84] that Hyperboreans founded the cult of Apollo at Delphi. There is also the report of Apollonius Rhodius[85] that Apollo shed tears of amber when he was sent from heaven to Hyperborea. On the other hand, Pausanias[86] cites another tradition that Delphi's second temple, which replaced a mere hut, was *sent* to Hyperborea by Apollo. Herodotus reports[87] that in his time "the cereal offerings arriving for Apollo's summer festival at Delos were accompanied by Hyperborean maidens and sacred couriers called Perpherees." Farnell, says Silver, reasons, however, that the Hyperboreans were "not a people at all, but real ministers of the god who performed certain sacred functions north of Hellas."[88]

The Doors to the Otherworld

To say that the Druids were "oak-seers" certainly links them to ancient religious practices of the Mycenean Greeks or earlier, but it scarcely captures the essence of the priests who must have directed the activities of the underworld cult of southern England and the ritual deposition of the horse and dog at Danebury. So I would like to suggest another possible etymology for the word *druid*, one that takes us back to that mysterious poem, *The Spoils of Annwn*. In line 24, the poet refers to "the Fortress of Four-Peaks, isle of the strong door," and we said (Chapter 3) that the four-peaked or four-cornered fortress referred to the sky, and the "strong door" referred to the door between our world and the otherworld. The Welsh word used is *dor*, and this word is universal in Indo-European languages, with *dvar* in Old Indian, *dvarem* in Avestan, *thura* in Old Greek, *duris* in Baltic languages, *foris* in Latin, and *Tor/Tür* in German. I would argue therefore that the first element of *druid* is from the Indo-European word for "door," and that a *druid* is in fact a "door-knower," or "doorkeeper," where "door" can be understood as the door to the Otherworld.

I say this because there is some evidence that early in the 1st millennium B.C. the classical world was already seeing doors/gates as entrances to the Otherworld and linking them to divine figures. Hesiod in his *Theogony* (c. 700 B.C.) refers to the "gates of strong Hades and awful Persephone,"[89] which are guarded by Cerberus. The very ancient Roman god Janus was associated with doors, but is not clearly related to any other Indo-European deities. Frazer sees Janus as sky-god,[90] and derives his name from the same root *di* which gives us Zeus; interestingly, he also links Janus to the oakwoods of the Janiculum, the hill on the right bank of the Tiber where Janus is said to have reigned as king. The name Janus may alternatively be connected to the Etruscan Ani, a sky-god[91] (and the Etruscans, as we have seen, could have come from northwest Anatolia, close to the area where the "visitors from the East" may have originated).

Although Janus cannot be easily compared to any other European god, Norman Oliver Brown points out[92] that he can be linked to Hermes, the god of the boundary-stone: Janus, like Hermes, is a trickster and carries a magic wand; he was said to be the protector of enterprises of all sorts, and the inventor of various arts, including religious ritual. Hermes, of course, is another aspect of the rider-god, the Thracian Horseman, who, like Janus, looks in at least two directions at once, and is sky-god, sun-god, and god of the underworld — a god who indeed is in charge of many doors.

Arthur of Arcadia

If the Druids who came to Wiltshire in the 9th century B.C. were from the Thracian lands to the north or northwest of Greece, then they must have officiated over a religion which venerated the oak as sacred, or was well-versed in doors to the Otherworld, worshipped a horse-god like Rhesus or the Thracian Horseman, and considered themselves to be descended from a chthonic deity like the Thracian "Hermes" (Julius Caesar's Dis Pater). They may also have believed in some form of reincarnation or transmigration of souls, inspired by early miracle-workers like Aristeas and Abaris, whose trance-journeys are one probable source of Pythagoras's doctrine of metempsychosis (these trance-journeys were presumably enhanced by cannabis, which was used by the Scythians and Thracians.[93] They must also have been students of astronomy, like the priests of Stonehenge with whom they could well have joined forces, and it is astronomy which provides the most compelling evidence for the early presence of Druids in Wiltshire.

Arthur was no astronomer, but his name is inextricably bound up with the stars. There are various ways to interpret his name. One possible derivation has been popularized by C. Scott Littleton and Linda A. Malcor,[94] who contend that the name comes from Artorius ("plowman"), the second name of Lucius Artorius Castor, who brought over a group of Sarmatians to northern Britain as Roman cavalry. The Sarmatians, like the Cimmerians, were Scythians, and Littleton and Malcor see the Arthur stories as variations of the tales of Batraz, hero of the Nart sagas of the Iranian-speaking Ossetians of the North Caucasus.

Another possible derivation, says Thomas Green,[95] is from British *Arto-uiros* "bear-man"—a derivation supported by the fact that *art(h)* in Welsh is used figuratively to denote a warrior. Rachel Bromwich has shown[96] that *Arcturus*, deriving from the Greek word for "Keeper of the Bears" and denoting a bright star associated with the Great Bear (Ursa Major) constellation, was a genuine non–Galfridian variant form of Arthur's name,

> and one for which there is good reason to believe there was traditional authority. *Arcturus*, like *Arctos* (= Ursa Major or "the bear") was often used to denote the polar region, the far north, and there are references in Latin literature to the savage and tempestuous weather associated with the rising and setting of the star *Arcturus*. By extension, the name of the star gave rise to the adjective used by Lucan for the Gauls as *arctoas gentes* "people of the (far) north," *Bellum Civile* V, 661. To name a hero *Arcturus* could therefore be taken to imply that he belonged to the north (i.e. to north-west Europe), and that he was "bear-like" in his characteristics.

Graham Anderson takes the identification between Arthur and Arcturus a step further. Anderson points out[97] that the star Arcturus was already referred to in the agricultural poetry of the early archaic period (c. 700 B.C.), when it was used interchangeably with the name of its constellation, Boötes[98] (see Figure 11). Hesiod says in his *Works and Days*[99]:

> When in the rosy morn Arcturus shines,
> Then pluck the clusters from the parent vines; ...
> and again, but for a different season of the year: ...
> When from the Tropic, or the winter's sun,
> Thrice twenty days and nights their course have run;
> And when Arcturus leaves the main, to rise
> A star bright shining in the evening skies;
> Then prune the vine.

Anderson confirms[100] that the spelling Arcturus is found in medieval texts, and notes that the form Arthurus was used for the star itself: John of Howden's 13th-century *Cythera* refers to the *giram Arthuri*, "Arthur's round," when discussing astronomical movement of the star.

As Bromwich observes, Arcturus was associated with savage and tempestuous weather. Richard Hinckley Allen points out[101] that Pliny called it a *horridum sidus* ("horrible star"), and that

> Demosthenes, in his action against Lacritus 341 B.C., tells us of a bottomry bond, made in Athens on a vessel going to the river Borysthenes — the modern Dnieper — and to the Tauric Chersonese — the Crimea — and back, that stipulated for a rate of $22^{1}/_{2}$ percent interest if she arrived within the Bosporus "before Arcturus," *i.e.* before its heliacal rising about mid–September; after which it was to be 30 per cent. Its acronychal rising fixed the date of the husbandmen's *Lustratio frugum*; and Vergil twice made allusion in his 1st *Georgic* to its character as unfavorably affecting the farmers' work. Other contemporaneous authors confirmed this stormy reputation, while all classical calendars gave the dates of its risings and settings.

The heliacal rising of a star is when the star makes its first seasonal appearance on the eastern horizon just before dawn, and the achronycal or acronychal rising is when the star first becomes visible above the eastern horizon at nightfall. In antiquity the heliacal rising occurred mid–September, and the acronychal rising occurred mid–February, which Allen says coincided with the *lustratio frugum* or "purification of the fruits."

The mythology of Arcturus is as ancient as the references to it. In a fragment attributed to Hesiod and quoted in the *Catasterismi*, the following story is told of the nymph Callisto[102]:

> The Great Bear.] — Hesiod says she (Callisto) was the daughter of Lycaon and lived in Arcadia. She chose to occupy herself with wild-beasts in the mountains together with Artemis, and, when she was seduced by Zeus, continued some time undetected by the goddess, but afterwards, when she was already with child, was seen by her bathing and so discovered. Upon this, the goddess was enraged and changed her into a beast. Thus she became a bear and gave birth to a son called Arcas. But while she was in the mountains, she was hunted by some goat-herds and given up with her babe to Lycaon. Some while after, she thought fit to go into the forbidden precinct of Zeus, not knowing the law, and being pursued by her own son and the Arcadians, was about to be killed because of the said law; but Zeus delivered her because of her connection with him and put her among the stars, giving her the name Bear because of the misfortune which had befallen her.

There is also another story attributed to Hesiod which Anderson quotes[103]:

> It is said that Arkas is the son of Callisto and Zeus ... and Lycaon pre-
> tended not to be aware that Zeus had raped his daughter: he entertained
> Zeus, according to Hesiod, cut up the child and laid him on the table. At
> which Zeus overturned the table — from which the city gets its name
> Trapezous — struck his house with a thunderbolt, and changed Lycaon into
> a wolf. He then put Arkas together again and made him whole; and the
> child was nourished by a herdsman.

The Latin writer Hyginus, in his *Fabula*, from the 1st century A.D., says[104]:

> But the sons of Lycaon wanted to test Jupiter to see whether he was a god;
> they mixed human flesh with other flesh and put it in front of him at a
> feast. After he became aware of this, he overturned the table in a rage, and
> killed Lycaon's sons with a thunderbolt. In that place Arkas later fortified a
> town which he called Trapezous.

Arcas, who was also changed into a star to protect his mother, was the founder of the Greek state of Arcadia. Anderson draws a parallel[105] between Arcas/Arcturus, who founded a community called Table, and King Arthur, who built the Round Table. Arthur built his Round Table to avoid bloodshed that quarrels at a table had caused among his men, just as Arcas/Arcturus founded the city of Table to take the place of the table where Zeus had shown his anger at human sacrifice.

There is another very distinctive detail about Arcas/Arcturus, says Anderson.[106] He is described by a commentator of the Hellenistic poet Aratus's astronomical poem the *Phaenomena* (3rd century B.C.) in the following terms:

> And behind Helice the Bear someone like a driver is being carried along,
> the so-called Arctophylax (Arcturus). As to his resemblance to a driver, this
> is because he is carrying a *kalaurops* (Aldine edition *kalabrops*) in his right
> hand, as if holding on to the cart, the bear, with his left. For he himself
> seems to be the guardian of the cart, called the bear, as Bootes (the herds-
> man), who is driving the oxen (from it), carries a *kalaurops*, which is a club.

The *kalaurops* or *kalabrops* held by Arcturus sounds very similar to Arthur's sword Excalibur,[107] first given by Geoffrey of Monmouth as Caliburnus.

But if Excalibur has an Arcadian origin, the Sword in the Stone has a Scythian origin, according to C. Scott Littleton and Linda A. Malcor.[108] They point to a passage from Herodotus[109] where he describes Scythian sacrifices to their war-god:

> In every district, at the seat of government, there stands a temple of
> [Mars], whereof the following is a description. It is a pile of brushwood,

made of a vast quantity of fagots, in length and breadth three furlongs; in height somewhat less, having a square platform upon the top, three sides of which are precipitous, while the fourth slopes so that men may walk up it. Each year a hundred and fifty wagon-loads of brushwood are added to the pile, which sinks continually by reason of the rains. An antique iron sword is planted on the top of every such mound, and serves as the image of Mars: yearly sacrifices of cattle and of horses are made to it, and more victims are offered thus than to all the rest of their gods. When prisoners are taken in war, out of every hundred men they sacrifice one, not however with the same rites as the cattle, but with different. Libations of wine are first poured upon their heads, after which they are slaughtered over a vessel; the vessel is then carried up to the top of the pile, and the blood poured upon the scymitar. While this takes place at the top of the mound, below, by the side of the temple, the right hands and arms of the slaughtered prisoners are cut off, and tossed on high into the air. Then the other victims are slain, and those who have offered the sacrifice depart, leaving the hands and arms where they may chance to have fallen, and the bodies also, separate.

Much later, Ammianus Marcellinus, writing around A.D. 390, says this of the Scythian Alani, who lived northeast of the Black Sea[110]: "Nor is there any temple or shrine seen in their country, nor even any cabin thatched with straw, their only idea of religion being to plunge a naked sword into the ground with barbaric ceremonies, and then they worship that with great respect, as Mars, the presiding deity of the regions over which they wander."

However, the aspect of the Arthur story that interests us most is the cauldron of *The Spoils of Annwn*, which later became the Holy Grail of medieval Arthurian romances. As Anderson points out,[111] Herodotus tells a story of the Scythians which is reminiscent of Grail stories[112]:

According to the account which the Scythians themselves give, they are the youngest of all nations. Their tradition is as follows. A certain Targitaus was the first man who ever lived in their country, which before his time was a desert without inhabitants. He was a child — I do not believe the tale, but it is told nevertheless — of Jove and a daughter of the Borysthenes. Targitaus, thus descended, begat three sons, Leipoxais, Arpoxais, and Colaxais, who was the youngest born of the three. While they still ruled the land, there fell from the sky four implements, all of gold — a plough, a yoke, a battle-axe, and a goblet. The eldest of the brothers perceived them first, and approached to pick them up; when lo! as he came near, the gold took fire, and blazed. He therefore went his way, and the second coming forward made the attempt, but the same thing happened again. The gold rejected both the eldest and the second brother. Last of all the youngest brother approached, and immediately the flames were extin-

Figure 11: Stylized representation of Boötes the ox-driver or plowman, some-times also referred to in classical antiquity by the name of its brightest star Arcturus, here shown on the left knee of the ox-driver/plowman.

guished; so he picked up the gold, and carried it to his home. Then the two elder agreed together, and made the whole kingdom over to the youngest born. The sacred gold their kings guard very carefully, and hon-our it with magnificent sacrifices. And if any guardian of the gold falls asleep in the open air during the festival, the Scythians say he will not last out the year.

Here the equivalent of the Grail is the golden goblet, which like the other three golden objects, can only be claimed by someone worthy, in this case the youngest son. The parallels with the cauldron and Grail are more clear in the much later Nart sagas, which were only written down in the 19th century. Three of the Narts lay claim to the *Nartamongae*, the cauldron of the Narts — they are called Uryssmaeg, Soslan and Sosryquo. There are, says Anderson,[113] a number of variants: in one tale, each of the Narts has a little cask in front of him: if his boast is true it overflows three times. In story 16 it is a magic cup which rises of its own accord and goes to the lip of the bravest man. Three other cauldron tests are offered in nos. 41ff.: the *Nartamongae* will only go to the warrior without fault, and only Batraz qualifies, while Uryssmaeg, Soslan and Sosryquo fail; only Batraz can cause ice in the cauldron to boil merely by reciting his exploits; or can win the ladle of the cauldron by emptying the vessel of noxious animals.

The cauldron of renewal is also found in Greek mythology. There is an early tradition, in a fragment of Hesiod, that Medea, daughter of the king of Colchis and therefore from the regions north of the Black Sea, "was able to renew Aeson, the father of Jason, in a golden *lebes*"[114] (cauldron). The cauldron theme is also taken up indirectly in the foundation myth of the Macedonians, recounted by Herodotus[115]:

> Now of this Alexander the seventh ancestor was that Perdiccas who first became despot of the Macedonians, and that in the manner which here follows:— From Argos there fled to the Illyrians three brothers of the descendents of Temenos, Gauanes, Aëropos, and Perdiccas; and passing over from the Illyrians into the upper parts of Macedonia they came to the city of Lebaia. There they became farm-servants for pay in the household of the king, one pasturing horses, the second oxen, and the youngest of them, namely Perdiccas, the smaller kinds of cattle; for in ancient times even those who were rulers over men were poor in money, and not the common people only; and the wife of the king cooked for them their food herself. And whenever she baked, the loaf of the boy their servant, namely Perdiccas, became double as large as by nature it should be. When this happened constantly in the same manner, she told it to her husband, and he when he heard it conceived forthwith that this was a portent and tended to something great. He summoned the farm-servants therefore, and gave notice to them to depart out of his land; and they said that it was right that before they went forth they should receive the wages which were due. Now it chanced that the sun was shining into the house down through the opening which received the smoke, and the king when he heard about the wages said, being infatuated by a divine power: "I pay you then this for wages, and it is such as ye deserve," pointing to the sunlight. So then Gauanes and Aëropos the elder brothers stood struck with amazement when they heard this, but the boy, who happened to have in his hand a knife, said these words: "We accept, O king, that which thou dost give;" and he traced a line with his knife round the sunlight on the floor of the house, and having traced the line round he thrice drew of the sunlight into his bosom, and after that he departed both himself and his fellows.

Anderson says[116] that Gauanes is the equivalent of Gawain in Arthurian stories, and Lebaia is related to *lebes*, a cauldron or broad dish, supplying the place-name "vesselville" or "platter-ville" (that is, Grail town). Gawain is traditionally the son of Lot, and a *temenos* is a lot, in the sense of an allocation of land. Perdiccas seems to play the same role here as the youngest son in the Scythian tale — the Scythian youngest son was granted the gold implements, while Perdiccas took possession of the symbolic gold of the sun.

All this happened around 700 B.C., and Pettazzoni says[117] that in this story we see "traces of an ancient devotion to the sun on the part of the Macedonian royal house. This sun-worship continued in later times, for the Roman historian Livy tells us that in 181 B.C. Philip V of Macedonia, accompanied by his son Perseus, climbed a peak of Mt. Haemus, in present-day Bulgaria, and descended again in haste, after having dedicated two altars, one to Jupiter and the other to the Sun." The fact that Perdiccas's bread swells to double its normal size may be linked to Perdiccas's solar powers — in any case, it recalls the cornucopia and the magic hamper or bag in the First Branch of the *Mabinogion* and the story of *Lludd and Llefelys*.

Arthur and Ancient Astronomy

It would clearly be helpful if we could look at the story of Arcturus in the context of ancient beliefs about the stars, and an insight into such beliefs is provided by the Canadian physicist and student of ancient astronomy and religion F. Graham Millar, in "The Celestial David and Goliath." His thesis is that the Biblical story of David and Goliath has an astronomical origin, with David representing the constellation of Boötes (also known by the ancients as Arcturus), his sling representing the nearby Corona Borealis, Goliath representing the constellation of Orion on the other side of the sky, and Saul, who gives David his armor, representing the constellation Hercules. Linked to the story of David and Goliath is the Irish myth of Lugh and Balor.[118] In Irish legend Balor was a famous warrior who had one eye in the middle of his forehead; another, his baleful eye, was in the back of his skull. With it he could strike people dead by looking at them, but he kept it covered except when he wanted to petrify his enemies. Millar says that according to Mac Cana,[119] when Lugh saw Balor open his eye against him, Lugh cast one of his father Aed's thunderbolts at him with a slingshot, driving the thunderbolt through the back of Balor's head and killing him. The version that Millar gives is one of several — the Aed he mentions is another name for the Dagda, but in another version it is a spear made by the weapon-forger of the gods, Goibniu, that kills Balor, and in yet another version it is, appropriately, a sling-stone.

The investigation of the David and Goliath story as a myth of the stars, says Millar,[120] "must begin with noting the effect of precession of the equinoxes. It is the slow conical swing of the axis of the Earth, acting as a huge spinning top. The result is that, in a period of 25,800 years, the pole of the heavens moves as a circle on the celestial sphere on a radius of 23.4°."

Precession "caused the ancients to fear that the sky was falling.... Vega was near the celestial pole of 11,000 B.C., and may have been regarded in ancient times as the supreme god, who supported the apex of the universe." The Akkadians called it the Life of Heaven, and the Assyrians the Judge of Heaven.[121] By 8000 B.C. they must have noticed that it had "fallen" from its place, and it has continued to fall. The fall may be mentioned in the Bible (Isaiah 14:12):

> How you have fallen from heaven,
> O morning star, son of the dawn!
> You have been cast down to the earth,
> you who once laid low the nations!

Today Vega, says Millar, is 51° from the pole.

Among those who feared the sky was falling were the Celts: when Celtic ambassadors discussed a treaty with Alexander the Great in 335 B.C., says Rankin,[122] they admitted fear of nothing except, perhaps, that the sky should fall (Strabo 7.38, Arrian *Anabasis* 1.4.6). Their form of words, which may have been close enough to an oath, actually referred to a substantial fear that the world might sometime end (Livy 40.58.4–6).

The concept of the sky falling, says Millar, helps us to interpret the rock carving of the first millennium B.C. from Camonica in northern Italy.[123] This shows a tall figure, apparently with horns, with arms upraised; on his right arm is a torc; to his left and at the level of his arms is a ring or circle, and below this, and just beneath his arms is a snake. Millar believes that this figure, the Horned One, depicts the combined constellation of Hercules and Ophiucus ("Snake-Holder"). The combined asterisms possibly constituted the obsolete constellation of Menat.[124] Mac Cana, says Millar, "pronounced the tall figure to be the antlered god Cernunnos." He observed the serpent in his left hand, which Millar sees as the constellation Serpens Caput (to the west of Ophiucus). Mac Cana also "commented upon the torc (heavy circlet) on his right arm; Celtic figures have frequently been depicted as wearing the torc as an amulet." The ring or circle to the left of the figure is, according to Millar, "in the right position for Corona Borealis."

Millar goes on to say[125] that the "hands of Cernunnos are raised in the weight lifter's pose," often called the "orans position," and argues that the god is holding up the sky. Mircea Eliade has described[126] how the Siberian shamans "believed that the high branches of the sacred birch reached to the sphere of the fixed stars, and would erect birch pillars to support the sky." Like the pillars, the antlers of Cernunnos may perhaps be interpreted as supporting the sky.

The pole of the heavens was midway between the upraised arms of Hercules at 8000 B.C. Hence, the idea that Cernunnos supported the sky is likely to have originated broadly near that date. When precession continued, the "persona of the Horned One moved into the constellation of Boötes," where he was known as Lugh.

Millar contends[127] that the Gundestrup Cauldron also provides clues to ancient astronomical beliefs. Four panels on the Cauldron depict divinities as busts with arms upraised in the orans position. Some or all of them were probably "replications resident in the constellation of Hercules, inheriting from Menat the function of supporting the sky." One of the panels with a figure having upraised arms on the Gundestrup Cauldron is accompanied by a wheel, which Millar interprets as the Corona Borealis.

The most famous panel on the Gundestrup Cauldron is Plate A, the one with the horned figure (see Chapter 2), and Millar interprets this in astronomical terms. The central image, the Horned one, is the constellation of Boötes, and other images are the neighboring constellations:

> Subject to artistic license, they are in the right places. Ursa Major is turned around to face the Horned One to express his vassalship. Clockwise from the lower right, the following constellations can be recognized: Leo Major and Minor, Hydra, Boötes, Hercules/Ophiuchus (bearing horns), the Ass (an obsolete constellation), Ursa Minor, Delphinus, and Capricornus. On comparing the central Horned One with Boötes on the star chart, one sees a compelling likeness: the Buddhic position of the legs, and the torc on his right arm corresponding in position with Corona Borealis; this was also Lugh's sling.

As Millar points out,[128] there is no Balor on the Gundestrup Cauldron. For him we may look elsewhere for one or more of the motifs — "a single eye, blindness, a weapon piercing the eye in the back of his head, the piercing of the head, or beheading." Orion "is reputed to be blind"[129]; no other constellation bears this attribute. The head of Orion is represented by only one star, Meissa.[130] It is a double in which the brighter star is pale white and of magnitude 3.5. To the naked eye "this is a dim star, not visible through hazy cloud, so on occasion Orion is blind or lacks a head." Astrologically, then, Balor can be identified with Orion.

This just leaves the question of the weapon fired at Goliath or Balor, and Millar believes[131] that the weapons in the myth

> may have been inspired by a meteor shower. A meteor, or shooting star, is vividly mythologized as a thunderbolt, a thrown spear, a glinting sword, or a sword half-drawn from the scabbard and reinserted....
>
> From year to year showers may vary in the maximum number visible per hour. A shower comes from a definite direction in space, and by perspective the meteors seem to radiate from a point on the celestial sphere called the radiant. A shower takes its name from the constellation in which the radiant lies.
>
> Of all the constellations, only three bear the name of a mythical hero and at the same time contain a meteor radiant. Perseus is one, but he can be identified with Mithra and so is disregarded here. Hercules and Orion remain, the possessors of the thrown weapons. Never in any age has Orion been visible at the time of the Herculids, since at that time the Sun is invariably close to Orion, outblazing him.

Boötes, says Millar, is not the radiant for a major meteor shower, and neither is Corona Borealis. However, the constellation Hercules is the origin of a shower of meteors, and it could have seemed to the ancients that Hercules (Aed or Goibniu in Irish mythology) was forging weapons and giving them to Boötes, who then flung the bolts with his sling, Corona Borealis. Around 3000 B.C., Orion was visible from August to October, and Boötes, low in the north on August 4th, "was in position to bombard him until his heliacal setting" — his last seasonal appearance on the western horizon just after sunset.

Toward the end of his paper,[132] Millar refers to the Welsh story that comes closest to the story of David and Goliath or Lugh and Balor, an episode in *Culhwch and Olwen*. The giant Ysbaddaden has three poisoned darts: the first night he throws one at Bedwyr, who catches it and throws it back at the giant, wounding him in the knee; the second night he throws one at Menw, who catches it and throws it back at the giant, wounding him in the center of the breast. They return on the third night, and the giant says:

> "Shoot not at me again unless you desire death. Where are my attendants? Lift up the forks of my eyebrows which have fallen over my eyeballs, that I

may see the fashion of my son-in-law." Then they arose, and, as they did so, Yspaddaden Penkawr took the third poisoned dart and cast it at them. And Kilhwch caught it and threw it vigorously, and wounded him through the eyeball, so that the dart came out at the back of his head.

In fact, there is also the episode in the Fourth Branch of the *Mabinogion* where Lleu, the Welsh equivalent of Lugh, takes aim, presumably with his needle, and hits a wren between the sinew and the bone of its leg — a very pale imitation of the Lugh-Balor encounter.

Both of these tales have links to ancient astronomy, if only indirectly. Lleu can get his name only with the help of his mother Arianrhod (= Corona Borealis), and shoots at the wren to achieve this. Culhwch, is associated with pigs and through this to the Otherworld, like Arthur in *The Spoils of Annwn*, and perhaps is taking Arthur's place in the Ysbaddaden episode — after all, at one point, his followers urge Arthur to go home and not bother himself with "such small adventures as these," implying that Arthur may in earlier versions have been involved in "adventures" like the Ysbaddaden episode, whose significance was not appreciated by later storytellers. So it is possible that Arthur/Arcturus was originally the equivalent of Lugh, originally charged with preventing the skies from falling, and fighting off celestial enemies with the help of the divine sling of the Corona Borealis, but reduced in the *Mabinogion* to fighting giants like Ysbaddaden with poisoned darts, or hitting wrens with needles to get a name from Arianrhod (the Corona Borealis).

Conclusion

We have attempted to show, through British legendary history, through archeology, through an exploration of Thracian and Greek religion and mythology, and through ancient astronomical beliefs, that the Mound-People of Wiltshire in the 9th century B.C. could have come from somewhere in eastern Europe, possibly by the amber route, from Thrace through "Hyperborea" to the Baltic and western Germany, possibly via the Thaco–Cimmerian expansion from Thrace through Hungary, Austria, Switzerland and eastern France. What language did these people speak? It could have been one of the extinct languages of eastern or Central Europe like Thracian or Illyrian, or one of the extinct languages of western Europe like Ligurian, spoken in northwestern Italy and southeastern France, or even an Indo-Iranian language. There is one tiny and ambiguous clue provided by the name of the river which passes near Stonehenge, the Avon (which is, admittedly, found in other parts of England). The name is usually said to be Celtic. Matasovic[133] links it to Old Irish *ab*, *aub*, Middle Welsh *afon*, Gaulish *ambe*, and ultimately to Hittite *hapa* "river," Old Indian *apa* "water," Old Greek *apeiros* "coast," Latin *amnis* "stream." In Chapter 3 we saw that Varuna lost his identity in Zoroastrianism, becoming *Apam Napat*, "Grandson of the Waters." So the river of Stonehenge could have acquired its name long before the Celts, as a tribute to a long-forgotten god.

We have also proposed in this chapter that the Druids are not Celtic, but preceded the Celts into Wiltshire at the same time as the people who brought the All Cannings Cross pottery. We have linked their veneration of oak trees to the ancient Illyrians of Dodona, their possible interest in doors to the earliest Greeks and Romans and possibly to the Etruscans, and their burial practices to Indian, Iranian and Greek views of the afterlife. We have seen that their doctrine of reincarnation could have come from the same sources that Pythagoras drew on. And most importantly, we have shown that the story of Arthur/Arcturus could have originated in eastern or central Europe, as part of an astronomical tradition going back thousands of years. But the story of Arthur is not about prehistory, but about a period of history after the Roman army left Britain, and we will be looking at this Arthur in the final chapter.

Chapter 7

Brutus of Troy Town

The Truth Lovers

But before we can look at the historical Arthur, we need to review all the evidence we have assembled for the origins of the Mound-People and the Druids, and to advance any new evidence which may seem relevant to the question. The first piece of evidence comes from an unexpected source — the tale of *Culhwch and Olwen*, first discussed in Chapter 1. In this tale, Arthur's men have to find Mabon son of Modron, and to do this they must ask a number of long-lived animals: first they ask the ousel (blackbird) of Cilgwri, who does not know where Mabon is, but advises them to consult an older animal, the stag of Redynvre; the stag can't help, but takes them to an even older animal, the owl of Cwm Cawlwyd; the owl can't help either, but leads them to the "oldest animal in this world," the eagle of Gwern Abwy; the eagle doesn't know, but takes them to an animal even older than he is, the salmon of Llyn Llyw, who finally tells them that Mabon is a prisoner in Gloucester.

The "oldest-animal" format of this story is not unique to *Culhwch and Olwen*. In a fragment attributed to Hesiod[1] it is reckoned that the crow lives nine human generations, the stag four times as long as a crow, the raven three times as long as a stag, the date-palm nine times as long as a raven, and the Nymphs ten times as long as the date-palm. West notes[2] that the verses were often quoted in late antiquity and more than once rendered into Latin, so could have been known to anyone with a classical education. However, he says,[3] "neither Classical learning nor any other form of horizontal transmission can account for the extraordinary parallel" between *Culhwch and Olwen* and an episode in the *Mahabharata*, the Indian epic composed between 800 B.C. and 400 B.C. In the *Mahabharata*, it is related that the royal seer Indradyumna fell from heaven because no one any longer remembered him. He asked the sage Markandeya if he recognized him. Markandeya did not, but told him that there was an owl in the Himalaya who was older than himself and might know him. They went there. The owl said that he did not recognize Indradyumna, but that there was a crane living by a lake who was older than he. The crane was also unable to identify the seer, but said there was a tortoise in the lake who was even older than he was and might know more. The tortoise was summoned and after much reflection recognized the seer, who had formerly built his fire altars on the tortoise's back.

The link between Britain and ancient India is reinforced by *The Spoils of Annwn*. In Chapter 3 we noted that (Caer) Sidi, the Mound-Fortress, was cognate with Vedic Sanskrit *sadas*— the ritual space belonging to the gods where the *soma* sacrifice took place, and, more importantly, that (Caer) Pedryuan, the Four-Peaked or Four-Cornered Fortress, could be best explained by reference to "four-cornered Varena" of Zoroastrianism, and "four-faced" (*caturanika*) Varuna (more properly, Indra-Varuna) of the *Rigveda* with his "four-cornered" (*caturasrir*) thunderbolt. This link to Varuna is reinforced in another poem attributed to Taliesin, *Song Before the Sons of Llyr*, which refers to the "Distributor"— in Indo-Iranian texts, Varuna was sometimes called Baga, which can be translated as "The Distributor." As we noted in Chapter 6, Varuna was called Apam Napat, "Grandson of the Waters," in India and ancient Persia, which gives an alternative etymology for the river of Wiltshire, the Avon.

Kazanas says[4] that Varuna is the

> king of the gods, like Odin in Asgard and Zeus on Olympus. He personifies more than the sky (space or substance) which encompasses everything. An ethical god, he lays down laws for every level of creation and rules through *maya*, measuring knowledge or unfathomable power. He watches everything from his golden palace in highest heaven and has spies everywhere. He binds the sinner with fetters but also liberates and grants victory in war. He is also associated with waters and oceans and retains only this feature in post–Vedic texts. Varuna is almost invariably lauded with *Mitra* and often with *Aryaman* as well, in a trinity. Both Varuna and Mitra are called *samraja* (emperors), and guardians of cosmic order (*rta*) in highest heaven. In some hymns and later texts Varuna is associated with night and Mitra with day. Mitra is a daytime aspect of the sun connected with friendship and contracts.... In the Iranian *Avesta*, the supreme god is Ahura Mazda, who resembles Varuna is his ethical aspect and kingship; his power of light is Mithra.

These connections hint at an Indo-Iranian origin, which might not be inconsistent with legends that see Britain as founded by a Brutus of

Troy—Indo-Iranian peoples may have lived north of the Black Sea and around the River Danube, which from a British perspective is not far from northwest Anatolia. At any rate, further weight is given to an Indo-Iranian origin by Pokorny's contention that Pritteni is derived from Indo-Iranian *prtana/partara* "battle," implying that Pryderi of the *Mabinogion* was originally a fighter, and Britain was originally Land of the Fighters. If such warriors did indeed settle in Britain, they did have other more prosaic concerns, if I am correct in assuming that the tors of Dartmoor take their name from an Indo-Iranian word identified by H.W. Bailey as cognate with Sanskrit *torana* "arch, gateway" and Khotanese *ttora* "top," and derived from a root meaning "place over, upon, or around." Such long-range migrations might seem out of the question, but Beekes argues that the Etruscans of Italy migrated from northwest Anatolia, in the region around Troy, in the 12th century B.C., at the same time that their Lydian "brothers" headed south for Manisa and Izmir province. If the whole eastern Mediterranean was suffering from famine, war and civil unrest, then it seems highly likely that mass migrations took place, which could have led some people as far as Britain.

Further evidence is provided by the story of Elidorus, reported by Giraldus Cambrensis after his travels through Wales. The mound-people that Elidorus encountered had no form of public worship but were "lovers and reverers of the truth." This of course may be simply a way of describing an ideal society, like that envisaged in Plato's *Republic* (4th century B.C.), or Augustine's *City of God* (5th century A.D.). Plato believed that society should be ruled by philosophers, who are "lovers of the truth"; but Plato's works were virtually unknown to western Europeans scholars in the 12th century. Augustine, in his *City of God*, touches on Plato, observing that if a philosopher is a lover of truth, then he must be a lover of God. So it is more likely that the legend of Elidorus refers to something else. Giraldus tells us that the mound-people "never took an oath," which seems to rule out a link with the Thracian "Hermes."

One possibility is that the mound-people's love of truth is connected with Varuna and *rta*. James Hastings, in discussing *rta* as moral order, says[5] that "the conception of moral order is doubtless Indo-Iranian," that "the conception cannot be more recent than the 15th century B.C.," and that "it was developed before the Vedic Aryana entered India." He says that the gods themselves are not merely born of the *rta*, but they follow the *rta*; they are practicers of the *rta* and knowers of it. The special guardian of the *rta* is Varuna, the great guardian of morality, who moves about discerning the truth and the unrighteousness of mankind. As mentioned earlier the Zoroastrian equivalent of Varuna is Ahura Mazda—*mazda* means "intelligence, wisdom," and is cognate with Sanskrit *medha*, whose adjectival form *medhira* "wise" is used to describe Varuna. It may be significant that the name of Pwyll, who becomes Lord of the Otherworld and marries the horse-goddess Rhiannon, means "mind, spirit, reason," suggesting a possible link to Mazda—and to Math, the master magician of the Fourth Branch and the brother of Don.

In Zoroastrianism the equivalent of *rta* is *asha* or *arta*, and the opposite is *druj*. John Waterhouse says[6] that *druj*, or Lie, was the enemy who attacked man from within, and was the foe of Truth. As the opponent of Asha (Truth) the Druj represented the falsehood of the old gods,[7] and later, in the Acheamenian age (550 B.C.–330 B.C.), the Druj became identified with Ahriman, the devil. In an account of the Persians, Herodotus remarked: "They teach the boys, from five years old to twenty, three things only—to ride, to shoot, and to be truthful.... Most disgraceful of all is lying accounted."

Lies and Labyrinths

The word *druj* may possibly be found in England and Wales in an unexpected place. W.H. Matthews, in *Mazes and Labyrinths*, discusses the relationship between Troy and labyrinths. In *Historia Regum Britanniae*, Geoffrey of Monmouth said that the founder of Britain, Brutus, was descended from Aeneas, who left Troy and sailed to Italy. Once in Britain, Brutus founded a city called New Troy, a name presumably based on the tribe called the Trinovantes—though Geoffrey was Welsh and presumably knew that Trinovantes had nothing to do with Troy. However, Matthews provides a new insight into the legendary link between Troy and Britain.

Matthews explores labyrinths of all kinds, but in Chapters 10 and 11 he focuses on turf mazes, which are found all over England with various names such as Mizmaze, Julian's Bower, Troy Town or Shepherd's Race.[8] Julian's Bower is at Alkborough in Lincolnshire; the Mizmaze is at Breamore, near Fordingbridge in Hampshire[9]; there is a squarish Mizmaze at St. Catherine's Hill near Winchester in Hampshire[10]; there was a maze near Dorchester—the memory is still preserved in the name of a farm, Troy Town, near Puddletown[11]; there was a Walls of Troy in the marshes of Rockcliffe in Cumbria[12]; there is a Troy Town at Somerton, near Banbury in Oxfordshire[13]; in Surrey a Troy Town was formerly well known in the neighborhood of Guildford, at Hillbury, between Guildford and Farnham.[14] In Chapter 12 Matthews also mentions[15] a "curious custom formerly prevalent among Welsh shepherds," which "consisted of cutting in the turf a figure in the form of a labyrinth, which they called Caerdroia, *i.e.* the walls, or citadel, of Troy." Finally he points out[16] that there are labyrinths in northern Europe, not of turf but stone-lined, which also have Troy in their name, for example Trojeborg or Tröborg.

Matthews believes that the name Troy Town is quite ancient, and quotes a French account[17] of a voyage to Jerusalem in 1418. The Seigneur de Caumont stopped off at Crete and wrote of "that intricate house made by Dedalus ... which was named Labyrinth and today is vulgarly called by many the city of Troy." But the link between Troy and labyrinths is much older than that, as shown by an Etruscan vase found at Tragliatella. This was "very roughly decorated with incised figures, representing amongst other things a circular labyrinth of the traditional type and some horsemen who are thought to be engaged either in the attack on Troy or in the game known as the *Lusus Trojae* or Game of Troy. That there can be no doubt about the artist's identification of the labyrinth in some way with the celebrated city in question is clear from the word *Truia* scratched within it."[18]

The meaning of the Game of Troy is found in Virgil's *Aeneid.* In Book 5, Aeneas's son Iulus is taking part with his companions in a sport called *Ludus Trojae* or *Lusus Trojae* ("Game of Troy"), or simply *Troja.*[19] The game "consisted of a sort of processional parade or dance, in which some of the participants appear to have been mounted on horseback." Virgil draws a comparison between the complicated movements of the game and the convolutions of the Cretan Labyrinth:

> As when in lofty Crete (so fame reports)
> The Labyrinth of old, in winding walls
> A mazy way inclos'd, a thousand paths
> Ambiguous and perplexed, by which the steps
> Should by an error intricate, untrac'd
> Be still deluded.

But Virgil is not the first to mention a ceremonial dance.[20] Homer, in the *Iliad* (Book 18), is describing Achilles's shield[21]:

> Next on that shield, the celebrated lame god made
> an elaborately crafted dancing floor, like the one
> Daedalus created long ago in spacious Cnossus,
> for Ariadne with the lovely hair. On that floor,

> young men and women whose bride price would require
> many cattle were dancing, holding onto one another
> by the wrists.

Sometimes, says Homer, "they would dance deftly in a ring with merry twinkling feet, as it were a potter sitting at his work and making trial of his wheel to see whether it will run, and sometimes they would go all in line with one another." The tradition of a ceremonial dance associated with the Cretan labyrinth continued long after Homer. It was said that Theseus "killed the deadly Minotaur and fled with his Athenian comrades to Delos, where they celebrated their triumph through song and dance."[22] This victory dance was called the "Crane dance" (*Geranos*), after the complicated flight patterns of the crane. Plutarch (1st century A.D.) describes this dance in his *Parallel Lives*[23]: "Theseus, when he sailed away from Crete, touched at Delos; here ... he and the youths with him danced a measure which they say is still practiced by the people of Delos to this day, being an imitation of the turnings and windings of the Labyrinth expressed by complicated evolutions performed in regular order. This kind of dance is called by the Delians 'the crane dance.'"

Matthews speculates[24] on the possible origins of the word *Troy* in Troy Town. It may, he says, "have originated not with the name of a town, but with some ancient root signifying to wind, or turn." He also links Troy to the Druja or Draogha of Persian legends and the *druh* "demon" of the Rigveda. The first suggestion derives Troy from the Welsh *tro*, which is from the Indo-European root *tragh*,[25] which gives Latin *traho* "pull," Old Irish *traig* "foot," Welsh *troed* "foot," Old Irish tragud "tide," Welsh *treio* "flow back to the sea," Welsh *tro* "turn, variation, time," Welsh *troi* "to turn, roll," and English *drag*. A variation on this theme is provided by Henning Eichberg[26]—in discussing northern European stone-lined labyrinths, he links Troy to German *drehen* "to turn," cognate with English *throw*.

But the suggestion that interests us most is the link with Druja and Druh. Pokorny[27] derives these words from the Indo-European root *dhreugh-*, which gives Avestan *druẑaiti* "lies, cheats," Old Indian *drṓgha-*, *drṓha-* "insult, damage, betrayal," Avestan *draoga-* "fallacious," m. "lie, falsity, deception," Old Persian *drauga-* "fallacious," Old Indian *drúh-* "fiend, demon," Old High German *triogan* "deceive," Old Norse *draugr* m. "ghost," Old Norse *draumr*, Old High German *troum*, Anglo-Saxon *drōm*, English *dream* "dream."

This brings us right back to Elidorus's mound-people and their love of truth, and to the Zoroastrian *asha/arta* and its opposite *druj*. If a group of Iranian-speaking people did settle in southern England, what might they have associated with deception, demons and, possibly, labyrinths? Dennis Price[28] claims that Stonehenge was once a labyrinth, and its association with music and dancing may be reflected in the name that Geoffrey of Monmouth uses for it — the Giant's Dance. It is certain that any prehistoric visitor to England would have heard of Stonehenge, and might well have given it a name which reflected their belief that it was a place of deception, or a place made by demons.

The People of the Cauldron

The antiquity of such settlers seems to be implied in the story from the Second Branch of the *Mabinogion* concerning the origin of the cauldron of regeneration. Bran, it will be recalled, got the cauldron from an Irishman called Llasar Llaes Gyfewid and his wife Cymidei Kymeinvoll, who had escaped from the Iron House in Ireland. The story goes that while the Irish king was hunting, he was on top of a tumulus (*gorsedd*) above a lake in Ireland called the Lake of the Cauldron. A large, monstrous man emerged from the lake with a cauldron on his back, accompanied by an even bigger woman. Matholwch took them in, but they insulted and injured people, and made themselves generally hated. However, the two, plus their children, would not go of their own free will, nor could they be forced to go. So the Irish king and his people decided to forge a solid iron chamber, surround it with charcoal, and fire it until it was red hot. The man and woman escaped and fled to Wales with their cauldron.

As Cunliffe points out,[29] the first bronze cauldrons in Britain are thought to have emerged at the end of the second millennium in the wake of contacts with central Europe. Early in the first millennium Ireland seems to have taken over as the main production center, which might explain why the cauldron of regeneration comes from Ireland. It tells us little about Llasar's origins, but a detail in the Third Branch is more revealing. When Pryderi, Manawydan, and their spouses go to England to look for work, we are told that "Manawydan began to fashion pommels, and they were coloured in the way he had seen Llassar Llaes Gyfnewid do with blue azure." This suggests that Llasar or Llassar is derived from Persian *lazhvard*, which gives us the word *azure* and the stone (*lapis*) *lazuli*, raising at least the possibility that the name Llasar/Llassar has an Iranian connection. This may be strengthened by the relationship between Bran's cauldron and that of Medea, with her origin in the Black Sea kingdom of Colchis.

Much of the argument for eastern or central European origins has been based on the connection between the horse-sacrifice at Danebury and the horse-goddess Rhiannon on the one hand, and the Homeric Rhesus and the Thracian rider-god on the other. At this point we should also mention the Vedic ritual known as the *asvamedha* or "horse-sacrifice." This is described in detail in the *Yajurveda* (1400 B.C.–1000 B.C.). The ceremony could only be conducted by a king — the horse (a stallion) was anointed with ghee and decorated with golden ornaments; the horse was then slaughtered, and three queens walked around the horse reciting mantras; the chief queen then had to mimic copulation with the dead horse, while the other queens ritually uttered obscenities. The chief queen spent the night with the horse, and the next day the horse was ritually dissected and roasted.

Reincarnation and the Cosmic Order

If the Mound-People seem to have Indo-Iranian ancestors, what of the Druids? Their name is said to be Celtic and to mean "oak-seers," but other origins are possible. In Sanskrit *druva* means "eternal," so they could be "knowers of the eternal"; and *druh*, as we have just seen, means "demon" or "deception," so they could the "demon-knowers" or the "deception-knowers," able to see through all falsehood. However, the most compelling etymology is one that interprets *druid* as "doorkeeper," in the sense of one who knows the door to the Otherworld, either the underworld that was such a feature of religion in southern England, or the celestial Otherworld of the star-god Arcturus. In fact, as *The Spoils of Annwn* shows, the Otherworld seems to be both underground (Caer Sidi) and in the heavens (Caer Pedryuan), and the Druids held the key to the door of both these realms. The association between the Druids and doors also casts new light on the poem we discussed in Chapter 1, "What man is the gatekeeper?," which could be interpreted as Arthur seeking entry to the Otherworld (at the very least, it seems that Arthur may be invisible at the beginning of the poem[30]).

The Druids are famously said to have believed in reincarnation, and in Chapter 6 we quoted Jan Bremmer as saying that the Pythagorean doctrine of reincarnation had Greek rather than Indian origins. However, a somewhat different point of view is put forward by Thomas McEvilley. He believes that there are so many similarities between the Greek and Indian concepts of reincarnation that they must have been drawing on a common source. For example, on the question of vegetarianism, he notes[31] that Empedocles (c. 490–430 B.C.), a Greek philosopher born in Sicily, who was influenced by the Pythagoreans, preached to meat-eaters: "Do you not see that you are devouring each other in the thoughtlessness of your minds?"; while in India, the mythical progenitor of mankind, Manu, is supposed to have said: "He whose flesh I eat in this life, will devour mine in the next."

McEvilley also believes that Greeks and Indians had a similar attitude to what he calls[32] "the knowledge that frees." This knowledge "is not the ordinary discursive kind," but rather a kind by which "the unhearable becomes heard, the unperceivable becomes perceived, the unknowable becomes known."[33] The Orphics, says McEvilley,[34] "held that release is obtained through recollection of one's own god-nature.... We may understand the cosmos not by merely beholding it, but by tuning ourselves to its tuning." As Plato (c. 428–c. 348 B.C.) says in *Timaeus*: "The motions akin to the divine part in us are the thoughts and revolutions of the universe; these, therefore, every man should follow, and correcting those circuits in the head that were deranged at birth, by learning to know the harmonies and revolutions of the world, he should bring the intelligent part, according to its pristine nature, into the likeness of that which intelligence discerns." This doctrine goes back in some degree to Bronze Age Mesopotamia, says McEvilley, where the trail of the idea of macrocosm/microcosm leads. By about 2000 B.C. in Mesopotamia,[35] the universe was seen as a "single huge anthopomorphic being," as shown in a poem relating the myth of the goddess Inanna. When "her father Enki gives her kingship, Inanna uses the imagery of the cosmic being to describe her newly expanded state: 'The heavens he set as a crown on my head, the earth he set as sandals on my feet.' By the Late Bronze Age this mode of imagery in which the elements are assigned to parts of an anthropomorphic body had virtually replaced the old narrative mode in which individual deities or heroes clashed about specific willed projects." The gods and goddesses "began merging into a single cosmic being who bore within himself or herself the old deities as aspects or parts." A Babylonian hymn from around 1000 B.C. absorbs the pantheon into Marduk as his attributes or aspects[36]:

> Ninurta is Marduk of the hoe,
> Nergal is Marduk of the attack,
> Zababa Marduk of the hand-to-hand fight,
> Enlil is Marduk of lordship and counsel,
> Nabium is Marduk of accounting,
> Sin is Marduk, the illuminator of the night,
> Shamash is Marduk of justice,
> Adad is Marduk of rains....

Other hymns identify the universe with the human body[37]:

> O lord, your face is the sun god, your hair, Aya,
> your eyes, O lord, are Enlil and Ninlil....
> The appearance of your mouth, O lord, is Ishtar of the stars
> Anu and Antum are your lips, your command ...
> your teeth are the seven gods who lay low the evil ones.

Returning to Greek and Indian concepts of reincarnation, McEvilley points out[38] that in India there is the concept of *jivanmukta*, a "human who will not be reborn after the death of his present body-habitation." Empedocles seems to have regarded himself as such a man, saying: "I surpass mortal men, who are subject to many deaths.... I walk among men as a god, no longer mortal — I have been set free." It was also said of Pythagoras that he belonged to "a class between gods and humans," meaning perhaps that he would not be "born again as a mortal but as an immortal," a released soul. In Indian tradition the *jivanmukta*, before passing out of the body forever, would use their last incarnation to teach others how to achieve the same status.

Special powers are attributed to the released soul. In Greece "the lore about early philosophers called *theologoi*, and about the Orphic movement in general, is full of stories of teaching masters who worked in part through super-powers" (e.g. Abaris, Aristeas, the miracle-workers discussed by Bremmer). Released souls "were credited with special abilities, often including recognition of past incarnations. Porphry says of Pythagoras: 'When he strained with all his mind [says Empedocles], he could easily see everything there is in ten, yes even twenty human lifetimes.'"

McEvilley reports[39] that the philosopher Xenophanes, in a fragment written about 525 B.C., says of Pythagoras: "Once they say that he was passing by when a puppy was being whipped and he took pity and said: 'Stop — don't beat that animal; it is the soul of a friend. I recognized its voice when it cried out.'" McEvilly notes that this voice-recognition "has resonances in shamanic tradition round the world, as well as in the yogic

tradition of India; in both cases the spiritually or magically advanced personality is believed to understand the 'speech' of animals and birds."
Pythagoras is often linked to Orpheus, and it is widely believed, says
McEvilley,[40] that Orpheus "represents in part Greek contact with a tradition
of Thraco–Scythian shamanism — his famous descent to the underworld
to bring back Eurydice answers to the shaman's role as psychopomp."

We know next to nothing, of course, about how the Druids viewed
reincarnation. In the poems attributed to Taliesin, *Angar Kyfyndawt* (*Cruel
Bondage* or *Hostile Alliance*),[41] and *Kat Godeu* (*The Battle of the Trees*), the
poet appears to be alluding to a series of reincarnations[42]:

> I was a blue salmon,
> I was a dog, I was a stag,
> I was a buck on the mountain,
> I was a trunk, I was a spade (?)
> I was a drinking horn in the hand,
> I was a peg in forceps
> for a year and a half
> I was a speckled white rooster
> among chickens in Edinburgh.
>
> I have been a course, I have been an eagle.
> I have been a coracle in the seas:
> I have been compliant in the banquet.
> I have been a drop in a shower;
> I have been a sword in the grasp of the hand
> I have been a shield in battle.

However, the fact that he has been reincarnated not only as living beings
but also as inanimate objects suggests something closer to the Babylonian
hymns, and implies that the poet is identifying himself with the cosmos,
or with aspects of the one cosmic being. A comparison could also be made
with the *Bhagavadgita* (c. 500 B.C.), in which the god Krishna says to
Arjuna, one of the heroes of the *Mahabharata*[43]:

> I am the flavor in the waters, Kaunteya;
> I am the radiance of the moon and sun,
> the sacred word in all the *Vedas*,
> the sound in the air, the virility in men,
> and the pure fragrance on the earth;
> and I am the brilliance in flame,
> the life in all beings,
> and I am the austerity in ascetics.
> Know me as the primeval seed of all beings, Partha.
> I am the intuition of the intelligent;
> the brilliance of the brilliant am I.

The Druids of course conducted their ceremonies in *nemeton*, which as Jane Webster says[44] is commonly glossed as "sacred grove," though it may also have designated a small shrine or chapel. The word is attested mainly in place-names, for example Augustonemeton and Nemetodorum in Gaul, Nemetobriga in Spain, and Medionemeton in Britain. The origin of the word *nemeton* is unclear. In Old Irish, says Koch,[45] *nemed* is an important sociolegal term meaning "privileged person, dignitary, professional, sacred place, land owned by a privileged person, sanctuary, privilege"; in Early Welsh the cognate word *nyfed* occurs in the heroic elegies of the *Gododdin* in the phrase *molut nivet*, to be understood as "the [poetic] praise of dignity, rightful privilege, privileged places, persons." Therefore one possible etymology is the Indo-European root *nem-* "to bend, bow,"[46] which gives Old Indian *namaiti* "to bend, bow," *namas* "bow, obeisance," Avestan *nemah*, *nemaiti*, "bend, bow," Latin *nemus* "grove." Here again we have a possible link between a Druid term and both Sanskrit and Avestan.

Conclusion

But how does this story of Indo-Iranian ancestry fit in with the priests of Dodona, with the star Arcturus, later Arthur, with Arcas, the legendary founder of Arcadia, with Lugh and Balor, and Culhwch and Ysbaddaden? The answer must lie in the civilization of Mycenae, which dates from around 1600 B.C., reached its peak around 1400 B.C., and collapsed around 1100 B.C. We know that the Myceneans worshipped a horse-goddess, *po-ti-ni-ya i-que-ya*, or Potnia Ikk*eia "Mistress of Horses," who in classical Greece became Poseidon Hippios and/or Hera Hippia/Athena Hippia. We also know that the sacred site of Dodona was in use during the Mycenean period. It is also clear that by the time of Hesiod, Arcturus had long been known as a star by which agricultural activities could be regulated, and the myth of Arcas and Callisto was well established. As for the Iranian-speaking peoples of the Black Sea and Danube area, we have already noted that Homer refers to the Cimmerians, and there is a passage in the *Iliad*, Book 13, where Homer shows further knowledge of the Black Sea area[47]: "Now when Jove had thus brought Hector and the Trojans to the ships, he left them to their never-ending toil, and turned his keen eyes away, looking elsewhither towards the horse-breeders of Thrace, the Mysians, fighters at close quarters, the noble Hippemolgi who live on milk, and the

Abians, justest of mankind." The *Hippemolgi* or "Horse-Milkers" who live on milk are generally thought to be the Scythians, as are the Abians. The Mysians are said to have fought in the Trojan War as allies of Troy, and to have settled in Mysia, in northwest Anatolia. They spoke a language which could have been related to Hittite, or could have been a form of Paionian, a language spoken in Thrace. Strabo says[48] that the Mysians, "in accordance with their religion ... abstain from eating any living thing, and therefore from their flocks as well; and that they use as food honey and milk and cheese."

The origin of the Mysians is unclear. Edwards[49] notes that the Hittite Empire collapsed around 1200 B.C., and "When the curtain rises again, central Anatolia is ruled (or at least occupied) by an invading people, a horse-rearing military aristocracy called the Phrygians." According to the traditions preserved among the Macedonians, says Herodotus,[50] the Phrygians crossed the straits into Anatolia from Macedonia and Thrace, where they had until then been known as the Bryges or Briges. The Greeks in general, says Edwards, "believed that this event took place before the Trojan war, enshrining it in legend; though Xanthus, a Lydian historian, held it took place after that event, in a joint invasion with the Mysians." Excavations in Troy VIIb have "revealed the introduction, after the destruction of the city by fire, of a new population using a coarse ware apparently of central European origin, and this may reasonably be held to mark the passage of the Phrygians and Mysians."[51]

All the evidence points to the fact that at some time between 1100 B.C. and 800 B.C., a group of people either speaking an Iranian language or influenced by Iranian speakers, and living close enough to the Mycenean Greeks to have assimilated aspects of their culture, migrated to Britain, landing somewhere in the neighborhood of Totnes and Dartmoor. It is not possible to say whether these "immigrants" were responsible for the "ranch boundaries" or "linears" that were constructed as early as 1100 B.C. and well into the beginning of the 1st millennium, but they would certainly have been appropriate to people whose lives were focused on horses and who kept herds of sheep, goats and horses.[52] It is likely that these people, or people related to them, brought the All Cannings Cross Pottery to Wiltshire, and constructed the huge middens at Potterne and East Chisenbury.

Chapter 8

Arthur, King of Wessex?

Ambrosius and Vortigern

The most puzzling thing about Arthur is that he not quite a figure of myth, but not quite a figure of history. There is no mention of a divine Arcturus or Arthur in Britain during Roman times, which suggests that he is a post–Roman historical figure. On the other hand, there is no mention of an historical Arthur until A.D. 830, when Nennius has him fighting battles against the Saxons. In Chapter 1 we linked Arthur via his father Uther Pendragon to the comet of A.D. 539 and the subsequent plague, and I will now pursue this theme a little further.

Much of our knowledge of British history immediately after the Roman army left Britain is due to a British monk, Gildas, who wrote a long sermon entitled *De Excidio et Conquestu Britanniae* ("On the Ruin and Conquest of Britain"). The dates of Gildas and his work are much debated — Thomas D. O'Sullivan concludes[1] that the sermon was probably written between A.D. 515 and A.D. 530, while Higham[2] dates it to no later than A.D. 485.

The work itself does seem to provide clues in a number of well-known passages. In this first passage, the Britons appeal to Rome for help against the Picts and Scots[3]: "The wretched remnant, sending to Aetius, a powerful Roman citizen, address him as follows:—'To Aetius, now consul for the third time: the groans of the Britons.' And again a little further thus:— 'The barbarians drive us to the sea; the sea throws us back on the barbarians: thus two modes of death await us, we are either slain or drowned.' The Romans, however, could not assist them." Since the Romans could not help them, an alternative had to be found: "Then all the councillors, together with that proud tyrant Gurthrigern [Vortigern], the British king, were so blinded, that, as a protection to their country, they sealed its doom by inviting in among them (like wolves into the sheep-fold), the fierce and impious Saxons, a race hateful both to God and men, to repel the invasions of the northern nations."

Eventually these "impious Saxons" overran the country, until the British

> took arms under the conduct of Ambrosius Aurelianus, a modest man, who of all the Roman nation was then alone in the confusion of this troubled period by chance left alive. His parents, who for their merit were adorned with the purple, had been slain in these same broils, and now his progeny in these our days, although shamefully degenerated from the worthiness of their ancestors, provoke to battle their cruel conquerors, and by the goodness of our Lord obtain the victory.
>
> After this, sometimes our countrymen, sometimes the enemy, won the field, to the end that our Lord might this land try after his accustomed manner these his Israelites, whether they loved him or not, until the year of the siege of Mons Badonicus, when took place also the last almost, though not the least slaughter of our cruel foes, which was (as I am sure) forty-four years and one month after the landing of the Saxons, and also the time of my own nativity. And yet neither to this day are the cities of our country inhabited as before, but being forsaken and overthrown, still lie desolate.

Later in his sermon, Gildas castigates five British whom he considers cruel, rapacious and living a life of sin: Constantine of Dumnonia, Aurelius Caninus, Vortiporius of the Demetae (Dyfed), Cuneglasus, and Maglocunus, or Maelgwn.

The first clue is provided by the appeal to Aetius, a Roman general who fought a number of campaigns in Gaul against Burgundians, Visigoths and Alans, and who was consul three times, the third time in A.D. 446. The second clue is provided by the name Vortigern. It is not clear whether Gildas actually used the name, but Bede, writing in A.D. 730, did refer to Vortigern, and he was presumably using Gildas as his source for the period. The name Vortigern is usually seen as a title rather than a name, meaning in Celtic something like "Over-Lord"—in fact, Gildas calls him in Latin *superbus tyrannus* ("proud tyrant"), which may be a play on the name Vortigern. According to the genealogies of Powys, he was king of Powys from around 420 or 425, and was probably based in the Romano-British Viroconium (Wroxeter in Shropshire) (see Map 12): excavations have shown, says Castleden,[4] that after the collapse of Roman control Viroconium "was substantially rebuilt, timber buildings replacing stone: ... big elaborate buildings of classical design, with symmetrical facades, colonnades and often a second storey." The central focus of Viroconium was a "massive winged building raised on the site of the Roman basilica; it was a pseudo-classical building with a clutch of ancillary buildings and outhouses, and it seems likely that this was Vortigern's palace."[5]

The third clue is provided by the name Ambrosius Aurelianus, whose parents were "adorned with purple." Higham says[6] it is possible that Ambrosius was "a distant relative of one of the imperial families sprung from the west," such as the house of Theodosius (A.D. 379–395) which "had branches flourishing in Spain, at least until the campaigns of Constantine III" (A.D. 407–411). Castleden sees Ambrosius as a Celtic aristocrat, and argues[7] that the "Ambros" place-names

> may represent the stations of units raised and led by Ambrosius and styled "Ambrosiaci." The location of these garrisons is significant. One group seems to surround and protect the territory of the Dobunni (known as Calchvynydd "Chalk-Hill" in the dark ages). A second group of Ambrosiaci was positioned in the Lee and Stort valleys, well located to defend London, then a British enclave, against attack by the East Anglians along the Roman roads from Cambridge and Colchester.

Myres, says Castleden,[8] proposes that Ambrosius owned land at Amesbury, which was originally *Ambresbyrig*.

Frank D. Reno[9] links Ambrosius to Riothamus, mentioned by the Roman historian Jordanes in his history of the Goths, written around A.D. 551, as "king of the Brittones." According to Jordanes, Riothamus fought on the side of the Romans against the Visigoths led by Euric, and was defeated in around A.D. 470. Reno argues that Riothamus then went to Britain around 475, where he became known as Arthus (from the Welsh *arddus*, meaning "high"[10]), and that Arthus is an epithet of Ambrosius Aurelianus.

Ambrosius Aurelianus is a little like Arthur, in that it is difficult to find him in the historical record. His name means literally "Golden Immortal," and it is tempting to link him to Arthur, though for different reasons from those proposed by Reno. Arcturus is a prominent star in the constellation Boötes, and it would be appropriate to give Arthur/Arcturus the title of Golden Immortal. The suggested link between Ambrosius and Amesbury may also be significant, providing a possible link between Ambrosius and one of the families that ruled over Salisbury Plain and surrounding areas for so long before the coming of the Romans.

This interpretation of Ambrosius is reinforced by *Historia Brittonum*, which seems to be drawing on at least two set of legends about Ambrosius. In Chapter 31, Nennius tells us[11] that while Vortigern was king, the British "had cause of dread, not only from the inroads of the Scots and Picts, but also from the Romans, and their apprehensions of Ambrosius." In Chapter 42 we are told that the "boy without a father," who told Vortigern about the dragons fighting under the site of his citadel (see Chapter 6), was called Ambrose. In Chapter 48, Nennius reports that Pascent, son of Vortigern, became ruler of Builth and Gwrtheyrnion, which "were granted him by Ambrosius, who was the great king among the kings of Britain." Finally in Chapter 66, there is an enigmatic piece of chronology: "And from the reign of Vortigern to the quarrel between Guitolinus and Ambrosius, are twelve years, which is Guolopum, that is Catgwaloph." Guitolinus (Latin Vitalinus) is also mentioned in Chapter 48 as the son of Gloui (Gloucester) and one of Vortigern's ancestors; Guolopum and Catgwaloph are thought to refer to Wallop and the battle of Wallop, now a village in western Hampshire, 9 miles southwest of Amesbury, and not far from Danebury hillfort (see Map 13). All these details from Nennius suggest that Ambrosius was based in Wiltshire or Hampshire, may have fought a battle with Vortigern, and like Arthur, had become part historical figure, part wonder-worker.

The last clue provided by Gildas is the battle, or siege, of Mons Badonicus (Mount Badon). It has proved extremely difficult to establish where this battle or siege took place: candidates include Badbury Hill, near Faringdon in Oxfordshire; Liddington Castle above the village of Badbury, near Swindon in Wiltshire; Badbury Hillfort, also known as Badbury Rings, near Wimborne Minster in Dorset (though this was not really on the frontline between the Saxons of eastern England and the British of western England); and Solsbury Hill, near Bath (though it is unlikely that Gildas would refer to Aquae Sulis by its later Germanic name). The date is also unknown, with estimates ranging from around A.D. 480 to around A.D. 520—given O'Sullivan's dating of the *De Excidio* to the 520s, then a date of around 480 seems more likely.

Not surprisingly, perhaps, the *Anglo-Saxon Chronicle*, written around A.D. 891, is silent on this battle or siege. The only evidence it provides is negative evidence: the Chronicle gives a list of *Bretwaldas*— Saxon rulers who had achieved overlordship over some or all the other Anglo-Saxon kingdoms — and there is a gap between Aelle of Sussex, whose dates are given as 488–514, and Ceawlin of Wessex, who is said to have been Bretwalda from 562 to 593. These dates are highly suspect, but they do show a gap of almost fifty years during which Saxon expansion was apparently halted.

Let's assume for the sake of argument that the *De Excidio* was written

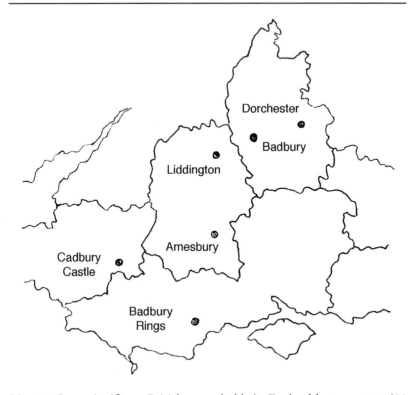

Map 12: Some significant British strongholds in England between A.D. 400 and A.D. 500, and possible sites of battles between British and Saxons, showing modern Wiltshire, Somerset, Dorset, and Oxfordshire.

around A.D. 520 and that the battle/siege of Mons Badonicus took place around A.D. 480. What was life like then in southwestern Britain? It is almost certain that most of the Romano-British towns were abandoned by about A.D. 450 or perhaps a little later, and that some people at least had moved into hillforts. This is underlined by the history of Cadbury Castle in south Somerset, 5 miles northeast of Yeovil. It is not far from the Romano-British town of Lindinis (Ilchester), one of the capitals of the Durotriges. Cadbury Castle, says Costen, was refortified in the second half of the 5th century, and continued to be used into the 6th century.[12] The "scale of the refortification is such that it cannot be compared with any other site in the region." It was refortified so that the 3,940-ft perimeter enclosed 18 acres of land; the new rampart used over 20,000 meters of timber. The "presence of a large hall on the hilltop is good evidence of occupation by individuals of high status," as is the presence of imported

Mediterranean pottery: "It seems unlikely that Cadbury Castle would have been reoccupied and the walls rebuilt so lavishly unless it was used at some point by military forces. The site looks eastward, and guards access to Somerset from the southeast and east, acting both as a bulwark against advance from the east and as a dominant site for the central Somerset basin. As such it is the successor to Ilchester as the focal point for commerce and politics in the district."

Cadbury Castle was not the only site in Somerset to be refortified after the Roman withdrawal. According to Barbara Yorke, Cadbury Congresbury, also known as Cadbury Hill, in north Somerset, near Yatton, had "part of its Iron Age perimeter refurbished in the sub–Roman period."[13] Cadbury Congresbury "has produced more imported pottery than any other English site, apart from Tintagel in Cornwall, as well as evidence of fine metalworking and substantial feasting. Cannington hillfort, near Bridgwater in Somerset, also seems to have been reoccupied in the post–Roman period and a substantial cemetery in use at the same time has been excavated in its vicinity."[14]

It is possible that the authority responsible for the refurbishment of Cadbury Castle and other hillforts in the area may have been responsible for the erection of the earthwork, West Wansdyke, which, says Yorke, "consists of a discontinuous north-facing bank and ditch running parallel and to the south of the River Avon, from Maes Knoll, south of Bristol, to just south of Bath."[15] It was probably built in the late 5th and 6th centuries, as a reaction to the extension of Saxon settlement into the Kennet Valley in the late 5th century.

So Somerset was clearly in British hands at the time of Gildas, but what of areas adjoining Somerset? Excavations have suggested, says Yorke, that "Bokerley Dyke on the easterly edge of Cranborne Chase in Dorset was built in the post–Roman period when it would have controlled access to the Dorchester area along the Roman road of Akling Dyke. A substantial part of the land between Bokerley Dyke and West Wansdyke was occupied by the formidable natural obstacle of Selwood Forest,"[16] and Yorke speculates[17] that Selwood, West Wansdyke and Bokerley Dyke may represent a "negotiated frontier between Britons and Saxons."

West Wansdyke is not the only earthwork from this period. East Wansdyke ran for some 15 miles "from Morgan's Hill near Devizes, across the Marlborough Downs to just west of Savernake, in east Wiltshire, and so separated the Kennet Valley from the rest of Wiltshire. East and West Wansdyke used to be considered as one monument, but there is no trace

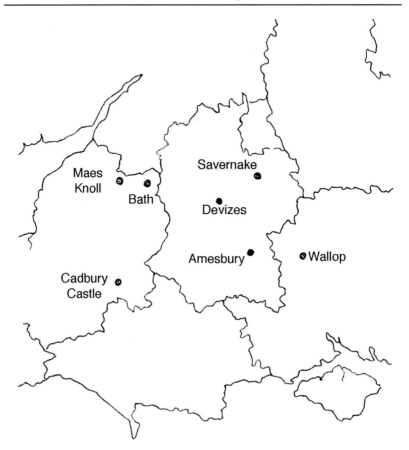

Map 13: British fortifications in Somerset and Wiltshire between A.D. 400 and A.D. 550, and some sites associated with Ambrosius Aurelianus.

of a bank or ditch running between them, although they are linked by the Roman road from Silchester to Bath."[18]

Unlike Somerset, there is little evidence of widespread reoccupation of hillforts in the area to the south of East Wansdyke. Excavation of a hillfort at Whitsbury Castle, near Fordingbridge in East Hampshire, 10 km south of Salisbury, "produced positive evidence for the refurbishment of its defences."[19] There is also "evidence for hillforts becoming estate centers in the early Middle Ages." Margaret Gelling, says Yorke,[20] has discussed the examples of *Æscesbyrig* (Uffington Castle), now in Oxfordshire but formerly in Berkshire, and Blewbury (Berkshire).

Gelling notes[21] that there are two types of place-names: habitative, which "contain a word for settlement," and topographical, which "make a statement about the setting of the village but do not mention buildings." Topographical names, says Gelling,

> may be specially characteristic of areas where the English are known to have established themselves at a particularly early date, and in such areas the more important settlements, the ones which became the centers of large estates, are more likely to have topographical names than habitative ones. Lambourn ("lamb river"), Blewbury ("variegated hill-fort"), and Faringdon ("fern down") are examples of such estate-centres in Berkshire. This is a county where documentary records from before the Norman Conquest are particularly rich, and with the help of these it can be shown that habitative names some times replace topographical ones in the 10th century or later.

And Gelling gives the example a large estate called *Æscesbyrig* ("Ash-tree fortification"), which was split into two estates called Uffington ("Uffa's farm/settlement") and Woolstone ("Wulfric's farm/settlement").

Yorke believes that Amesbury, Malmesbury and Old Sarum (*Searoburh*) are probably similar examples from Wiltshire. Old Sarum in Roman times was the fort of Sorviodunum, and there is archeological evidence of a Romano-British village in and around Stratford Sub Castle, next to Old Sarum,[22] so it is possible that the hillfort was occupied in the 5th century.

Amesbury may have been named after Ambrosus Aurelianus, who could have occupied Vespasian's Camp in the 5th century. Certainly there was a Romano-British village at Butterfield Down on the outskirts of Amesbury, where a hoard of late Roman gold coins was found, and a cemetery nearby, including at least one high-status grave.[23] Moreover, as McOmish *et al.* have shown,[24] during Roman times there were at least eleven flourishing villages on what is now Salisbury Plain Training Area, one of which, on Charlton Down, covered over 25 ha. The range of artefacts from the sites, they say, points to established sedentary agricultural communities.

What does all this tell us about Ambrosius and Vortigern? The evidence — and that is exceedingly slim — is that Vortigern was an early 5th-century ruler, possibly ruling from Viroconium, who enlisted the Saxons as allies against the Irish and Picts. Ambrosius was a later ruler — from the period A.D. 450 to A.D. 500 — who in some sense succeeded Vortigern and, from a base in Wiltshire, rallied the British against the Saxons. As Reno points out,[25] it is possible that Ambrosius is the figure who later became known as Arthur, but it is equally possible that the story of Arcturus involves another much more surprising figure.

Caratacus and Cunorix

As we saw in Chapter 1, Europe witnessed a spectacular comet in A.D. 539, and this was followed a few years later by an outbreak of the plague. At this time, large areas of western England, including Somerset, Dorset, Devon and Cornwall, and north of the Thames, Gloucestershire, Herefordshire, Shropshire and northwest England were still controlled by the British, and eastern England, including Essex, East Anglia, Sussex and the Isle of Wight were under the control of Angles, Saxons or Jutes.

Throughout this book we have focused on Salisbury Plain and its surroundings, in particular the Marlborough Downs and west Hampshire, and it is plain that from A.D. 500, if not earlier, this area was on the front line between the British and the Saxons, as the construction of East Wansdyke demonstrates. But what actually happened there, in the struggle for the ancient heart of southern England? The best place to start is the *Anglo-Saxon Chronicle*, which reports the following events[26]:

> A.D. 495. This year came two leaders (*aldormen*) into Britain, Cerdic and Cynric his son, with five ships, at a place that is called Cerdic's-ore. And they fought with the Welsh the same day.
> A.D. 508. This year Cerdic and Cynric slew a British king, whose name was Natanleod, and five thousand men with him. After this was the land named Netley, from him, as far as Charford.
> A.D. 514. This year came the West-Saxons into Britain, with three ships, at the place that is called Cerdic's-ore. And Stuff and Wihtgar fought with the Britons, and put them to flight.
> A.D. 519. This year Cerdic and Cynric undertook the government of the West-Saxons; the same year they fought with the Britons at a place now called Charford. From that day have reigned the children of the West-Saxon kings.
> A.D. 527. This year Cerdic and Cynric fought with the Britons in the place that is called Cerdic's-ley.
> A.D. 530. This year Cerdic and Cynric took the Isle of Wight, and slew many men in Carisbrook.
> A.D. 534. This year died Cerdic, the first king of the West-Saxons. Cynric his son succeeded to the government, and reigned afterwards twenty-six winters. And they gave to their two nephews, Stuff and Wihtgar, the whole of the Isle of Wight.
> A.D. 552. This year Cynric fought with the Britons on the spot that is called Sarum, and put them to flight.
> A.D. 556. This year Cynric and Ceawlin fought with the Britons at Beranbury.

Netley is on the south coast of Hampshire, near Southampton, while Charford is in Hampshire, near Fordingbridge and south of Salisbury. Cerdic and Cynric are said to be Saxons but, as Yorke points out,[27] both the Isle of Wight and the Hampshire coast were settled by Jutes. Bede says that the Hampshire coast was still known in his time as the *Iutarum natio* "nation of the Jutes," and place-names survive identifying various southern Hampshire locations as Jutish, including the New Forest (*Ytene*), Bishopstoke (*Ytingstoc*) on the River Itchen, a few miles south from Winchester, and a valley near East Meon (*Ytedene*).

In that case we can discount the early details, except the assertion that in A.D. 519 Cerdic and Cynric "undertook the government of the West Saxons," and that their descendants had ruled the West Saxons ever since. But who were Cerdic and Cynric, and if they did not rule in south Hampshire where did they rule? The *Anglo-Saxon Chronicle* gives a clue in its entry for A.D. 635, when it tells us that one of the descendants of Cerdic and Cynric, Cynegils, "was baptized by Bishop Birinus at Dorchester [see Map 14]; and Oswald, king of the Northumbrians, was his sponsor." Bede gives us another clue when he says (Book 3, Chapter 7) that the West Saxons "in early days were called the Gewisse."[28] And there is another clue: Cerdic and Cynric are, or could be interpreted as, British names.

The simplest of these clues is the name, *Gewisse*. This Germanic word is usually translated as the "the sure ones," "the reliable ones," implying they were people the Anglo-Saxons could trust. However, Hoops and Beck[29] link the word to Gothic *gawidan*, "join," and Old High German (*gi-)wetan* "to bind," suggesting that Gewisse meant "confederation" or "confederates," and implying something similar to the *foederati* of the late Roman Empire — entire tribes paid, in cash or in kind, to fight for Rome.

The matter of Dorchester, that is Dorchester-on-Thames, Oxfordshire, is also fairly straightforward. Dorchester was originally a Roman town called Durocina. In the late Roman period, says Daniel G. Russo,[30]

> Dorchester was not a *civitas*-capital but rather a "small town" or *vicus* (c. 14 acres) which had likely grown from minor civilian settlements (*canabae*) attached to an earlier legionary fortress. Nonetheless it was strategically important enough to receive stonework defenses during the third century, and it seems to have had some local administrative and commercial prominence as well. Excavations have shown that life continued in Dorchester into the early 5th century. Evidence of this sub–Roman occupation includes two-storey timber buildings on stone foundations and quantities of Theodosian-period coinage. One of the town's late Roman cemeteries

to the north was found to have been in use in the early 5th century but not beyond.

Recent research suggests "the Romano-British town was virtually deserted by A.D. 450."

As post–Roman Dorchester declined, Saxon influence grew. In fact, as Yorke points out,[31] Dorchester provides some of the earliest evidence of Anglo-Saxon settlement:

> Three early Germanic burials have been found near Dorchester-on-Thames, a man and a woman at Dyke Hills and a woman at Minchin recreation ground. The man was buried with the most complete late Roman official belt-set so far discovered in England [and] the belt-set is probably of early 5th century date, thus making the Dorchester man a candidate for a Germanic soldier in the employ of a British rather than Roman authority....

In the vicinity of Dorchester a number of cremation and inhumation cemeteries seem to have been established on both banks of the upper Thames and its tributaries in the first half of the fifth century. By the end of the fifth century settlement may have spread to the Vale of the White Horse and the Kennet Valley, and it could have been this expansion which provoked the building of one or both of the Wansdykes.

According to Russo,[32] concentrated settlement in and around Dorchester

> did not commence, however, until the late sixth century. The context for this intensification seems to have been the campaigns of the West Saxon *Bretwalda* Ceawlin ... against the sub–Roman enclaves in the Chiltern and Severn valleys.... Indeed, there are strong indications that Dorchester had become the headquarters of some prominent Anglo-Saxon ruler or leading family at this time. Excavations within the town disclosed Byzantine and early Anglo-Saxon gold coinage, along with gold ornaments and personal jewelry dated c. A.D. 600–625. Another "princely" or royal site of the early Thames Valley Saxons has been identified at Cuddesdon, some 6 miles north of Dorchester. The unusually rich finds there were contemporary with those within Dorchester and probably represent a rural *villa regalis* (royal estate centre) of the same family. It has also been observed correctly that some place in this region, probably Dorchester, was serving as a central, perhaps royally controlled redistribution or production centre for early Anglo-Saxon prestige items and raw materials. The sum of the archaeological evidence thus strongly points to Dorchester as an important multifunctional central place of the Thames Valley Saxons and a likely headquarters of their kings by the opening of the seventh century.

Map 14: Sites associated with the West Saxon Gewisse between A.D. 550 and A.D. 660, in Wiltshire, Hampshire, Somerset, Dorset, Devon, Gloucestershire and Oxfordshire.

The most perplexing aspect of Cerdic and Cynric is their apparently British names. Cerdic appears to be the Anglo-Saxon rendering of the Welsh Ceredig, itself a later version of Caratacus, the leader of the Catuvellauni who resisted the Roman invasion of Britain. There were several people of this name in Britain at the time: Matthews[33] mentions the British king Coroticus addressed by Saint Patrick in an open letter (St. Patrick excommunicated some of Coroticus's soldiers for taking some of St. Patrick's converts into slavery), and Ceredig, the last king of Elmet, a British kingdom in west Yorkshire; Reno[34] mentions Ceretic, the fifth son of Cunedda, the founder of the Welsh kingdom of Gwynedd; and Ceretic, described in *Historia Brittonum* Chapter 37 as the interpreter for Hengist and Vortigern in their negotiations over Hengist's beautiful daughter. Reno thinks[35] that Cerdic and the interpreter Ceretic are the same individual, though their dates appear to be different.

Cynric could be a Saxon name, meaning "Kin-Ruler," but it is more likely to be British and mean "Hound-King," like the god of Nettleton Shrub Roman temple, Cunomaglus or "Hound-Lord." Matthews links it to an Irish name Cunorix found at Wroxeter, but given the long association between southern England (especially Wiltshire) and otherworldly dogs, I see Cunorix as more probably a native Briton. The possibility that Cerdic and Cynric were British may be subtly hinted at in the *Chronicle* when it describes them as *aldormen* (high-ranking royal officials)—perhaps an admission that they were high-born British working to further the Saxon cause.

A Tale of Two Hillforts

The *Anglo-Saxon Chronicle* has Cerdic and Cynric doing nothing much in southern Hampshire until A.D. 534, and Cynric doing the same until A.D. 552. The *Chronicle* says that Cerdic assumed the kingship in A.D. 519, tough Dumville[36] has calculated that Cerdic became king somewhat later, around A.D. 538. This period of apparent inactivity may be the *Chronicle*'s way of dealing with the long pause in Anglo-Saxon expansion westward after the battle of Mons Badonicus. Interestingly, Cerdic may have become ruler around the time of the comet, and the end of the pause may have come after the outbreak of plague that followed the comet.

It is difficult to reach any conclusions about Cerdic because the only activities attributed to him are ones which seem historically implausible. However, he must have enjoyed great prestige among the Gewisse/West Saxons who succeeded him, since they were all keen to claim him as their ancestor. The most likely explanation is that he was a British aristocrat from somewhere in the region of Dorchester-on-Thames who spoke both Celtic and Saxon. He may have been a descendant of the Ceretic who was Vortigern's translator, or he may have had some connection with the court of Powys, which by this time is thought to have abandoned Viroconium/Wroxeter and moved to Pengwern (possibly Shrewsbury).

More can be said about Cynric, however, because he is credited with some very specific deeds. In A.D. 552 he is said to have captured Old Sarum (see Map 14), though as Yorke points out,[37] the area had already been settled by Saxons: the Anglo-Saxon cemetery at Harnham Hill, Salisbury, has burials going back to around A.D. 500; the graves at Petersfinger, just to the south of Salisbury, date from the 5th century; the cemetery at Winterbourne Gunner, northeast of Salisbury, has graves from the 5th and 6th centuries; and the Anglo-Saxon graves at Collingbourne Ducis, on Salisbury Plain, date from a round A.D. 500.

Then in A.D. 556 he is said to have captured Beranbury (Barbury Castle) along with Ceawlin, of which more later. Barbury Castle is an Iron Age hillfort near Wroughton in northeast Wiltshire, just south of Swindon. It is on the Ridgeway, an ancient trackway from Buckinhamshire to the Kennet Valley, which passed near Dorchester-on-Thames — control of Barbury Castle would have secured the route from Oxfordshire to Wiltshire for the Gewisse.

This implies that Cynric and the Wiltshire Gewisse had a base somewhere in north Wiltshire, and one possibility for this base is Ramsbury, in northeast Wiltshire, near the border with Berkshire, 7 miles south of Barbury Castle. Ramsbury was made a bishopric in 909, and this suggests, says Haslam,[38] that Ramsbury was at the time a *villa regalis*. Ramsbury is only 4 miles from the Roman fortified *vicus* of Cunetio, which was the successor to the Forest Hill Farm hillfort. Cunetio appears to have been refortified in A.D. 367. The "concentration of Roman villas around Cunetio marks its immediate environs as being a highly organized agricultural region, comparable to the environs of Bath and to Cirencester."[39]

Haslam argues,[40] following the lead of Cunliffe, that during the late Roman period, some villa estates increased in size at the expense of others, and resources became concentrated at a few estate centers. What followed after the withdrawal of Roman forces is suggested by a model for the transition of Roman to Anglo-Saxon Winchester put forward by Biddle,[41] who has suggested that

> a ruling element which emerged from the mercenary presence in Winchester in the late 4th century assumed "power and territorial control from the last remnants of the Romano-British administration, supplanting the social order which it had been their first duty to defend." The find of a military belt buckle of Hawkes's type IIA at Cunetio might suggest that this town could also have survived through the support of "mercenaries" (whatever their precise origins) as some sort of political focus after the general collapse of the Roman industrial economy.

Haslam believes that the large estate centers survived into the 6th century, and would have been the natural focus for anybody wishing to establish a military presence in the area. He argues[42] that

> the proximity of Ramsbury to Cunetio, the presence there of probable Roman villa and presumably a late Roman estate centre, and its position in

the probable avenue of Saxon penetration up the Kennet valley, all suggest that it could well have become the focus of the area in succession to Cunetio, and could have taken on some of the administrative functions of the former late Roman and sub–Roman town, subsequently becoming a *villa regalis* on the consolidation of the West Saxon kingdom.

The probability is strengthened, says Haslam,[43] by the name *Ramsbury*, where the *burh-* element means "fortified dwelling" rather than hillfort (the nearest hillfort is Membury, 5 km to the northwest), and the whole name means "Fortified Dwelling of the Raven" (which has intriguing associations with the Wiltshire past and British mythology).

North and South

Let us now return to the *Anglo-Saxon Chronicle* and continue the story of the Gewisse:

> A.D. 560. This year Ceawlin undertook the government of the West-Saxons.
> A.D. 568. This year Ceawlin, and Cutha the brother of Ceawlin, fought with Ethelbert, and pursued him into Kent. And they slew two aldermen at Wibbandun, Oslake and Cnebba.
> A.D. 571. This year Cuthulf fought with the Britons at Bedford, and took four towns, Lenbury, Aylesbury, Benson, and Ensham. And this same year he died.
> A.D. 577. This year Cuthwin and Ceawlin fought with the Britons, and slew three kings, Commail, and Condida, and Farinmail, on the spot that is called Derham, and took from them three cities, Gloucester, Cirencester, and Bath.
> A.D. 584. This year Ceawlin and Cutha fought with the Britons on the spot that is called Fethan leag. There Cutha was slain. And Ceawlin took many towns, as well as immense booty and wealth. He then retreated to his own people.
> A.D. 591. This year there was a great slaughter of Britons at Woden's Barrow; Ceawlin was driven from his kingdom, and Ceol reigned six years.

Ceawlin is said to have become king of the Gewisse and Bretwalda in 560, though the actual date is more likely to be around 580. Ceawlin is likely to have been another Briton, but like Cerdic and Cynric, his origins are obscure. One possibility is that the name is related to the British name Coel, as in the Welsh Coel Hen, the Old King Cole of nursery-rhyme fame. Koch[44] notes that Coel is said to be the ancestor of many early medieval north British rulers, known collectively as the *Coeling*. They are associated with Rheged (Cumbria) and Elmet (Yorkshire) though one of the Coeling, Llywarch Hen, is said to have fled south to Powys, in Shropshire. Welsh *coel* as a common noun means "belief or omen"; Old Irish *cel* means "auspicious."

The chances are, then, that Ceawlin, like Cerdic, originated in or had links to the Midlands or the north of England. It is perhaps significant that, unlike Cynric, his battles all occurred north of London, and were all fought alongside a supposed relative or relatives known variously as Cutha, Cuthwine or Cuthwulf. Their names suggest that they were Saxons, derived from *cuð* "well-known," *wine* "friend," *wulf* "wolf," and therefore allies of the Dorchester-on-Thames rulers.

Of the battles he fought, the first, against Aethelberht, king of Kent, was presumably a border dispute; the location of Wibbandun is unclear (the supposition that it was Wimbledon is now rejected). The battle at Bedford is puzzling, since this area is thought to have already been in the hands of the Angles of East Anglia. The most interesting of the battles is the one at Dyrham in which Cuthwin and Ceawlin captured Cirencester, Gloucester and Bath and killed three kings, Conmail, Condida, and Farinmail. Patrick Sims-Williams[45] believes these names represent Welsh Cynfael, Cynddylan, and Ffernfael or Ffyrnfael — two of these names are unknown, but Cynddylan is the same as the name of a 7th century king killed in Shropshire fighting with Penda of Mercia against Oswald of Northumbria. However, Gloucestershire did not remain long in the hands of the Gewisse, for by 603 it was part of the kingdom of the Hwicce.

The last battle that Ceawlin fought was at Fethan leag, thought to be Stoke Lyne in Oxfordshire. In Swanton's translation of the entry for 584, the last sentence is given as "and in anger he turned back to his own [territory]."[46] This suggests strongly that he lost the battle, and may account for the entry of 591, in which Ceawlin was "driven from his kingdom." This battle is said to have taken place at Woden's Barrow, now called Adam's Grave, near Alton Priors, east of Devizes in Wiltshire. The fact that it took place in Wiltshire suggests conflict between the Wiltshire Gewisse and the Oxfordshire Gewisse.

Ceawlin's successor as ruler of the Gewisse was Ceol, the son of Cutha, who is said to have become king in 591 or A.D. 592. The name is likely to be British, but its origins are obscure. In Old Irish there are related words *giall* "captive," "promise," *giall* "to serve, obey," *gell/gill* "to pledge, promise."[47] Perhaps his name indicates that he was a sub-king who had pledged allegiance to the Dorchester-on-Thames kings. He reigned for only five or six years, and was succeeded in A.D. 597 by his brother Ceolwulf. The second element *wulf* sounds Germanic, but may be British — there is an Old Irish word *olc*, genitive *uilc* "mad, wicked, evil,"[48] which is cognate with *wulf*. His name, like that of Ceol, may indicate that he also was a sub-king who had pledged allegiance to the Dorchester-on-Thames kings. This casts some doubt on whether Cutha, Cuthwine and Cuthwulf were indeed Saxons — it is possible that the name Cutha is somehow connected with that of the goddess Cuda (see Chapter 2), known from a relief found at Cirencester, whose name is said to denote prosperity.[49]

Very little is known of the reign of Ceol and Ceolwulf, who were followed in A.D. 611 by Cynegils, whose relationship to Ceolwulf is uncertain. The name Cynegils is also British, being the equivalent of Cuneglas or Cuneglasus, also the name of one of the "tyrants" denounced by Gildas in his *De Excidio Britanniae*. The first element of Cuneglas is presumably the word for "dog," and the second element *glas* is a color word that means something like "blue-grey." Cuneglas ("Blue/Grey-Hound") is obviously similar to Cunorix ("Hound-King"), so it seems likely that Cynegils belonged to the same Wiltshire branch of the Gewisse as Cynric. During his reign, he is said to have fought alongside Cwichelm (presumably a Saxon ally) at Beandun in A.D. 614, and killed 2046 of the Welsh (Beandun is though to be Bindon in Devon). He and Cwichelm are also said to have fought Penda of Mercia at Cirencester, and it is likely that Penda was victorious. Two points emerge from this list of battles: the Gewisse were under pressure from Mercia, and they were already beginning to turn their attention to lands in the south and west of England. The pressure from Mercia may explain Cynegils and Cwichelm's conversion to Christianity in the 630s, and the establishment of a bishopric at Dorchester-on-Thames (King Oswald of Bernicia was their godfather, and presumably became a useful ally).

Apparently Cynegils's decision to convert to Christianity did not meet with the approval of his successor Cenwalh. He is said to be the son of Cynegils, and his name is also British, possibly Cunovalus ("Hound-Strong"). Bede says that Cenwalh refused to be baptized, and abandoned his wife, the sister of Penda, king of Mercia, whereupon Penda forced him into exile. During his time in exile with the Christian king Anna of East Anglia, however, Cenwalh did convert to Christianity and became king of the Gewisse around A.D. 650. After this, the push toward the south and west began in earnest. In A.D. 652 Cenwalh defeated the British at Bradford-upon-Avon, and in A.D. 658 at Penselwood in east Somerset, giving him control of the eastern part of Dumnonia. It is also likely that around this time Cenwalh gained control of parts of Dorset, since he is named as the first Saxon patron of Sherborne Abbey in Dorset. In around A.D. 660, Cenwalh established a bishopric at Winchester, probably because the Gewisse no longer had effective control of Dorchester-on-Thames.[50]

Winchester became the second bishopric of the Gewisse for a number of reasons. Dorchester-on-Thames was no longer viable because of pressure from the Mercians; Winchester was some distance from the Mercians, but close to the Jutish and British kingdoms that the Gewisse presumably coveted; it was relatively close to Salisbury Plain, the traditional center of southern England; and it had a settled population of Saxons.

Winchester, of course, was originally the Roman *civitas* of Venta Belgarum, the capital of the Belgae, whose territory in Roman times may have included Salisbury Plain. Russo says[51] that "by the end of the fourth century, new public and private construction had virtually ceased" in Venta, the cemeteries had gone out of use by A.D. 420, and by A.D. 450 "Venta's sub–Roman town life had virtually ended." The first sign of an Anglo-Saxon presence dates from the late fifth century, with burials in the large pagan cemetery at King's Worthy, some 2 miles north of Venta. Inside the town, the "earliest actual evidence of Anglo-Saxon settlement are some pottery sherds," from around A.D. 480.

The first references to Winchester in Anglo-Saxon documents "occur in connection with the foundation of its episcopal see toward the middle of the seventh century." The *Anglo-Saxon Chronicle* records that "in A.D. 648 Cenwalh ordered the church of Winchester to be built and identifies it as St. Peter's, evidently the Old Minster." So by this time Winchester "was under royal West Saxon control and termed a *ceaster* (*castrum*) 'fortified place.'"[52] Archeological evidence

> does indicate limited concentrations of seventh century intramural occupation in the central and northeast town quadrants.... Indeed, the presence of an early Anglo-Saxon royal residence adjacent to or within the old Roman forum-basilica complex is considered very likely.... In addition, excavations have shown that late Roman Winchester's main south gate was blocked during the late fifth and sixth centuries, first by a ditch and then by a mortared wall. Traffic from the south thereafter had to enter the town via more easterly gate (known significantly enough as Kingsgate) leading precisely to the forum and proposed early Anglo-Saxon palace site.... The Lower Brook Street excavations of 1971 ... disclosed an early Anglo-Saxon residential complex with a seventh century burial that

included an elaborate necklace of gold and garnet pendants and a collar of silver rings.[53]

It is clear from this that Winchester, or at least the areas surrounding Winchester, had been in Saxon hands for some time before Cenwalh established the bishopric there. The fact that the bishopric was established there rather than in north Wiltshire may tell us something about the Wiltshire Gewisse. Cynric first entered the historical record when he captured Old Sarum, and was next mentioned when he fought at Barbury Castle with Ceawlin. This suggests that Cynric may have come from Venta Belgarum or the surrounding area, or even from Amesbury or from one of the villages on Salisbury Plain.

Why did the Wiltshire Gewisse not adopt Calleva Atrebatum (Silchester) as their capital? Yorke notes[54] that some form of life did continue in Silchester between 400 and 600, as shown by fragments of three Celtic brooches "which would be otherwise more at home in western Wessex." It may be that Silchester was too close to Mercia and Essex to be a secure capital, but I suspect there may be a historical reason. The Atrebates and the powerful families of Salisbury Plain and surrounding areas must have come into conflict — indeed, the Atrebates probably controlled territory that had previously been in the hands of the Wiltshire elite. Cunliffe points out[55] that the abandoned hillfort of Bury Hill, in northwest Hampshire, was reinforced around 100 B.C., presumably by the Atrebates, just at the time that Danebury went out of use, and speculates that the polity that constructed Bury Hill "was in some way challenging the authority of the nearby, long-established, Danebury," presumably under the control of the ancient rulers of Salisbury Plain.

So what became of the displaced rulers of Wiltshire and Hampshire? Those from the north of the region may have moved to Gloucestershire in the territory of the Dobunni, but returned to north Wiltshire after the Roman invasion — both Gloucestershire and north Wiltshire seem to have been dominated by a wealthy and sophisticated elite during Roman times. Those from the south may have moved to hillforts like Cadbury Castle in Somerset, and moved back later in Roman times, when the territory of the Atrebates was divided among the Atrebates, the Regnenses and the Belgae, with their capital at Venta Belgarum/Winchester. Given the history between the old ruling families of Salisbury Plain and its surroundings and the Atrebates, the abandonment of Calleva Atrebatum may have been a conscious decision on the part of the Gewisse to get revenge on their erstwhile enemies.

The Druid Arthur

What does all this tell us about southern England between A.D. 400 and A.D. 600? It seems that between A.D. 400 and A.D. 500 there was conflict between two groups: the Wiltshire group led by Ambrosius, which was opposed to seeking help from Germanic mercenaries, and the Viroconium/Powys group led by Vortigern, which was happy to use Saxons in their fight against the Irish and Picts. Ambrosius was most likely a Christian, and supported by the ancient families that had for so long dominated Wiltshire and east Hampshire, but in spite of that, he seems to have become celebrated in later legend as Arcturus/Arthur.

However, it is probable, as we saw in Chapter 1, that Arcturus/Arthur only came to prominence after the comet of A.D. 539 and the ensuing plague. Arcturus was a figure of the Wiltshire Druids, perhaps another name for Rhesus, the Thracian Horseman, or for the Thracian "Hermes," the ancestor god of the Thracians, or for Lugus, who held up the heavens. Arcturus, or Boötes, or Lugus, was the giant-killer who used the shower of meteors to slay Goliath or Balor or Ysbaddaden. The Druids, or those who survived the centuries of Roman persecution, were keen astronomers, and when they witnessed the comet, then experienced the ravages of the plague, they must have seen these events as a sign, just as the aftermath of the volcanic eruptions in 1628 B.C. and 1159 B.C. must have been interpreted as omens. Their response to these events was to rally the British with the tales of Arcturus/Arthur, a celestial figure well able to deal with celestial events. But Arcturus/Arthur could not stop the Saxons, and at least one descendant of the Wiltshire/east Hampshire families who had built and controlled Stonehenge, parceled up the land for agriculture, organized the middens and supervised the construction of the hillforts, decided that to maintain any semblance of the power they had exercised for centuries or even millennia, they must join forces with the Saxons and create a kingdom that preserved the interests of the British living in the ancient heart of southern England.

They seem to have done this rather successfully, since the capital of Wessex was Winchester, not far from their former seats of power on Salisbury Plain and Danebury. While Arthur/Arcturus was fighting mythical battles, the Wiltshire Gewisse were fighting real ones — against Saxons who threatened them, but also against British who did not share their view of the future of southern England. Eventually, of course, after the Danes had destroyed Northumbria and east Anglia and cut Mercia in half in the 890s,

Wessex under King Alfred became in effect the only English kingdom, and the center of a unified England from the 10th century until the Norman invasion in 1066.

There is an intriguing piece of evidence, however, that the kings of Wessex never forgot their roots. In A.D. 979 the Dowager Queen Ælfthryth founded a Benedictine monastery at Amesbury, the Abbey of St. Mary and St. Melor. The abbey was named after St. Melor, because the saint's relics were kept there. Melor was Breton saint, whose story is very revealing. His uncle Riwal killed Melor's father St. Miliau, and wished to kill Melor, who was only seven at the time. A council of bishops dissuaded him, so he decided instead to maim the boy, cutting off his right hand (later replaced by a silver prosthesis) and left foot (replaced with one of bronze). The silver hand links Melor directly to Lludd (Nodens, the god of Lydney Park), the king who experienced the three "oppressions," and whose full name was Lludd Llaw Ereint ("Lludd of the Silver Hand") — which suggests that the Wessex royal family had long memories.

The length of their memories may explain another curiosity in the Wessex story. In Henry of Huntingdon's account of the Battle of Burford in A.D. 752, the forces of Cuthred of Wessex were preceded into battle against Aethelbald of Mercia by the *aldorman* Edelhun carrying the royal emblem of a golden dragon, and in the scene of the Battle of Hastings on the Bayeux Tapestry, Harold is seen fighting under a pennant-style standard which is clearly a dragon.[56] Was this the Wessex answer to the red dragon of the Welsh, or does it preserve distant memories of the comet which perhaps gave birth to their kingdom?

Ambrosius, Arthur and Glastonbury

The descendants of Cerdic and Cynric ruled Wessex and then England until 1066. In that year Edward the Confessor died childless, and William of Normandy claimed the throne, on the basis that he was the great-nephew of Emma of Normandy, Edward's mother. To enforce this claim, he invaded England in 1066 and killed the English king Harold at the Battle of Hastings. The *Anglo-Saxon Chronicle* records in the entry for 1066 that "this year appeared a comet on the fourteenth before the kalends of May" — suggesting that the kingdom of Wessex came to an end very much as it had come into being.[57]

From 1066 England became a Norman kingdom, and the Anglo-

Saxon nobles were displaced: some became prisoners in Normandy, or in monastic communities; some fled to Scotland, including the last of the Anglo-Saxon royal line, Edgar the Aetheling, who was named king after the death of Harold but was never crowned, together with his sisters Margaret and Christina; and others, like Harold's mother Gytha and Gospatrick Earl of Northumbria, fled to Flanders.[58] William seized the lands of the displaced Anglo-Saxon nobility and handed it over to Norman aristocrats; by the time of the Domesday Book in 1086, says Daniell,[59] "the dispossession of the Anglo-Saxon nobles was practically complete."

Daniell says[60] that the period from 1080 to 1120 was the "lowest point" of the fortunes of the Anglo-Saxon aristocracy. By the reign of Henry I their fortunes began to recover, especially when the Norman king Henry I married Matilda, the daughter of Margaret and niece of the last Anglo-Saxon king Edgar the Aetheling. Matilda "displayed an interest in her West Saxon roots, received a genealogical table from the monks of Malmesbury and was eventually buried in Westminster Abbey near Edward the Confessor."

Following the Conquest, Anglo-Saxon culture was under threat, but "was kept alive by the monasteries, which preserved the traditions of their own communities against the changing religious and political world."[61] Daniell points out[62] that one of the defining works of the 12th century was Geoffrey of Monmouth's *Historia Regum Britanniae*. An important element of the political power of the stories was that "Arthur had not died but waited to return to overthrow the oppressors. Arthur could therefore be used by rebels trying to replace the king. The name Arthur was a powerful symbol in its own right — for example, Richard I's nephew and Henry II's grandson was called Arthur of Brittany."

Interest in Arthur was further stimulated by excavations at Glastonbury, which discovered Arthur's tomb and body, complete with an inscription on the coffin. Henry II showed great interest in the excavations, and later used Arthur's reputed conquest of Ireland to justify his own conquest of the island.

It might seem from this that the ancient families who had dominated Salisbury Plain and its surroundings for so long had completely lost their hold on power. However, the Wessex line was not completely eliminated. Henry I had married Matilda, niece of the last Anglo-Saxon king, and their daughter, also Matilda, was later to marry Geoffrey of Anjou and become the mother of Henry II, the first king of the House of Plantagenet. Oddly, the name Plantagenet means "broom" (the plant), and recalls one of the ingredients used by Math and Gwydion in the Fourth Branch of the *Mabinogion* to make Lleu's treacherous wife Blodeuedd.

The Wessex capital had been Winchester, and that initially remained a center of power — Daniell notes[63] that the royal treasury was still at Winchester when Henry I became king. However, in 1141, during the civil war that followed the death of Henry I, when Matilda fought the usurper king Stephen of Blois, Winchester was partially destroyed by fire, and was not really rebuilt until the 14th century. In Wiltshire itself, Wilton, the administrative capital, founded in the 8th century, continued to prosper, and the Benedictine abbey of Wilton was, at the time of the Domesday survey, the richest of the women's monasteries.[64] Another important town was Malmesbury, in northwest Wiltshire, not far from the old Roman temple at Nettleton Shrub. Malmesbury was the site of an Iron Age hillfort, and a Benedictine monastery was established there in 656 by Adhelm, a nephew of King Ine of Wessex. In 941, King Athelstan was buried in the Abbey. By the 11th century it contained the second largest library in Europe and was considered one of the leading European seats of learning.

But perhaps the fate of the Wiltshire families after the Conquest can be summed up symbolically in the story of two religious establishments in Wessex. As we said earlier, in 979 a Benedictine monastery had been established at Amesbury, the Abbey of St. Mary and St. Melor. This continued for over a century after the Conquest, but in 1177 Henry II, as part of his penance for instigating the murder of Thomas Becket, invited the French Fontevrault order to set up a double priory at Amesbury.[65] Beatrice, the abbess of Amesbury, who had defied Henry and Theobald, archbishop of Canterbury, in 1160 by refusing to accept their nominee in her church at Froyle (Hampshire), was deposed, and her English nuns dispersed — apparently none chose to remain under the new regime.

The other religious establishment is Glastonbury Abbey, in Somerset. Glastonbury has a very long history of human habitation, dating to the Neolithic. Several timber and brushwood trackways have been discovered, mostly running southward across the wetlands of the Somerset Levels.[66] The oldest and best known of these is the Sweet Track, which was constructed around 3800 B.C. As Koch says, the vast amount of work required to construct such a trackway demonstrates that the Glastonbury area must have been home to a relatively large and well-organized community. Another trackway, that at Meare Heath, was constructed in the second millennium B.C., showing that Glastonbury still had a relatively large population in the Bronze Age. Occupation continued into the Iron Age, and

Glastonbury Lake Village was home to about 100 people between around 300 B.C. and A.D. 100. There is little sign of Roman occupation, though it has been suggested that at least one of the wells in the Abbey — St. Joseph's well in the crypt of the Lady Chapel — may be of Roman date.[67]

The legends of Glastonbury suggest, says Gathercole,[68] that it was

> an important place in the shadowy years between the collapse of imperial government in Britain and the establishment of Anglo-Saxon power in the west. Glastonbury's associations with post–Roman British resistance to the Anglo-Saxon expansion — and in particular with Arthur — may have been exaggerated by the medieval monks, but are not necessarily wholly without foundation. High status dark age occupation on the Tor, perhaps a chieftain's stronghold (though perhaps a monastic site), has been confirmed by archeological excavations.

Finds from these excavations include "reused Roman pottery and building materials and fragments of high quality imported Mediterranean wares, the latter comparable with sherds found at other high status sites — both secular and religious — in the South West. Many of these are the remains of amphorae believed to have been used to trade wine and oil."[69]

William of Malmesbury, the 12th-century historian and monk at Malmesbury Abbey, who had a Norman father and an English mother, provides some interesting details on Glastonbury.[70] He says that the first church at Glastonbury, which the Anglo-Saxons called the "Old Church," was a wattle-and-daub structure, built by the disciples of Christ. Gathercole says[71] that there is evidence of wattle-and-daub structures, but whether they are British, as William implies, or Saxon is unclear. William also says that some of the earliest abbots were British, including a certain Worgrez, who was granted land by a king of Dumnonia, when Glastonbury was known as Ineswitrin (Ynys Witrin, or "Glass Island" in Welsh).

It is possible, says Gathercole,[72] that

> the traditions of a British origin for the Abbey may be based in truth, though this remains more problematical. The first reliable charters for the estates of the Abbey, the driving force of Glastonbury's medieval history, are late 7th century, and there is no *proof*— archeological or documentary — that the Abbey existed before this. However, an earlier charter of 601, though not considered authentic in its present form, may record an actual grant of land by an unnamed British king of Dumnonia to the Old Church. The Saxon charters also show that some (though not the earliest recorded) of the early Abbots had British names, which may support the idea of an existing British tradition, later taken over by the Saxons.

There are signs that Glastonbury Abbey did not prosper in the time of Alfred the Great (871–899), possibly because of Viking incursions into the south of England.[73] However, after Dunstan became abbot in 946 and refounded it as a Benedictine abbey, Glastonbury flourished. Kings Edmund, Edgar and Edmund Ironside were buried there; and for a short time the English treasury was held at Glastonbury. The Abbey became "one of the richest, and at times *the* richest, of all the great Benedictine houses in England." The Domesday Book reveals Glastonbury Abbey to have been "the wealthiest in England in the second half of the 11th century, even though the Conquest had disrupted its economic, and its spiritual, life." In 1184, however, a serious fire destroyed the Old Church and many books, vestments and relics which had been accumulated. It is in this context that in 1191 the monks of Glastonbury apparently discovered the body and tomb of Arthur.

There is, it seems to me, a symbolic connection between the removal of the English nuns from Amesbury and the discovery of Arthur's grave at Glastonbury. The nuns at Amesbury had been custodians of the relics of St. Melor, whose silver prosthetic hand recalls the ancient god of Lydney Park, Nodens, and his successor Lludd Llaw Ereint. In honoring the relics of St. Melor, the nuns were paying tribute to a pre–Christian ancestor, just as the Christians of Uley honored their pre–Christian ancestor by taking good care of the head of Mercury/Lugus in the century after the end of Roman rule. When the monks discovered the grave of Arthur at Glastonbury, they were seeking to pay their respects to an ancestor in the same way. Arthur may have begun life as the Druids' Arcturus, a powerful star-god, and the real Arthur may have been, as Reno proposes, Ambrosius Aurelianus, but by the 12th century the monks could not separate fact from legend, and honored this important figure by putting his relics on display. The Druids had long since disappeared, but their monster-slaying hero managed to live on at Glastonbury — and that may be the Druids' most enduring legacy.

Chapter Notes

Chapter 1

1. Geoffrey of Monmouth, *History of the Kings of Britain*, trans. J.A. Giles (London: Henry G. Bohn, 1848), Book 8, Chapters 14–17, http://www.lib.rochester.edu.

2. Edward Gibbon, *The History of the Decline and Fall of the Roman Empire*, ed. David Womersley (London: Penguin), 577. Chinese records mention the appearance of Halley's Comet in 530 A.D., and record another notable comet in 539 A.D.

3. Nennius, *History of the Britons*, trans. J.A. Giles (London: Henry G. Bohn, 1848), Chapter 56, http://www.fordham.edu.

4. *Ibid.*, Chapter 73.

5. Sarah Higley, trans., *The Spoils of Annwn*, http://www.lib.rochester.edu.

6. "What man is the gatekeeper/porter?" Mark Adderley, trans., http://www.markadderley.net.

7. "Culhwch and Olwen," in *The Mabinogion*, trans. Lady Charlotte Guest (London: J.M. Dent, 1910), http://www.maryjones.us.

8. Julius Caesar, *Gallic Wars*, trans. W.A. McDevitte and W.S. Bohn (New York: Harper and Brothers, 1869), Book 6, Chapter 13, http://classics.mit.edu.

9. Diodorus Siculus, *Historical Library*, trans. C.H. Oldfather (Cambridge, MA: Harvard University Press, 1935), Book 5, Chapter 31, http://penelope.uchicago.edu.

10. Strabo, *Geography*, trans. H.L. Jones (Cambridge, MA: Harvard University Press, 1932), Book 4, Chapter 4.4, http://penelope.uchicago.edu.

11. Hippolytus of Rome, *Philosophumena*, trans. F. Legge (London: Society for Promoting Christian Knowledge, Macmillan, 1921) Book 1, Chapter 22, http://www.archive.org.

12. Clement of Alexandria, *Stromata*, trans. William Wilson (Buffalo, NY: Christian Literature Publishing, 1885), Book 1, Chapter 5, http://earlychristianwritings.com.

13. John T. Koch, *Celtic Culture: A Historical Encyclopedia* (Santa Barbara, CA: ABC-CLIO, 2006), 612.

14. John F. Healy, *Natural History: A Selection* (London: Penguin), 216.

15. John Bostock and H.T. Riley, trans., *The Natural History of Pliny*, vol. 5 (London: Henry G. Bohn, 1857), 41–2.

16. Ammianus Marcellinus, *Roman History*, trans. J.C. Rolfe (Cambridge, MA: Harvard University Press, 1950), Book 15, http://penelope.uchicago.edu.

Chapter 2

1. Tacitus, *Annals*, trans. Alfred John Church and William Jackson Broadribb (New York: Random House, 1942), Book 14, Chapter 30, http://www.perseus.tufts.edu.

2. Ammianus Marcellinus, Epitome of Book 32.

3. "Curse Tablets from Roman Britain," at the website of the Centre for the Study of Ancient Documents, http://curses.csad.ox.ac.uk, provides excellent information on a number of Roman temples, including Uley, Lydney and Pagans Hill.

4. Alexei Kondratiev, "Lugus: the Many-Gifted Lord," *An Tríbhís Mhór: The IMBAS Journal of Celtic Reconstructionism* 1 (1997), http://www.imbas.org.

5. See www.roman-britain.org/nettleton.

6. *Ibid.*

7. Wiltshire and Swindon Sites and Monument Record Information: Nettleton Shrub, http://history.wiltshire.gov.uk/smr/getsmr.php?id=2096.

8. David Blamires, *Herzog Ernst and the Otherworld Voyage* (Manchester: Manchester University Press, 1979), 38–9.

9. Miranda Green, *Animals in Celtic Life and Myth* (London: Routledge, 1998), 126.

10. The results of this investigation were televised in *Time Team*, Series 8, Episode 8,

The Bone Cave, Alveston, Gloucestershire, summarized at http://www.channel4.com/prog rammes/time-team/episode-guide/series-8/ episode-8.

11. Jodie Lewis, "Upwards at 45 Degrees: The Use of Vertical Caves during the Neolithic and Early Bronze Age on Mendip, Somerset," *Capra* 2 (2000), http://capra.gro up.shef.ac.uk.

12. Wiltshire Council, "Sites and Monuments Record: Wilsford Shaft, Normanton Down," http://history.wiltshire.gov.uk.

13. Wessex Archaeology, "Remarkably preserved Roman remains from grave," http://www.wessexarch.co.uk/projects/wiltshire/bosc ombe/preserved-roman-remains/index.html.

14. Graham Thomas, *The Romans at Woodchester,* http://grahamthomas.com.

15. Giles Clarke, "The Roman Villa at Woodchester," *Britannia* 13 (1982): 221–222.

16. *Ibid.,* 213.

17. Katherine Dunbabin, *Mosaics of the Greek and Roman World* (Cambridge, UK: Cambridge University Press, 1999), 92–3.

18. Martin Henig, *Religion in Roman Britain* (London: Routledge, 1984), 220.

19. *Ibid.,* 201.

20. Jocelyn Toynbee, *Death and Burial in the Roman World* (Baltimore, MD: Johns Hopkins University Press, 1996), 276.

21. Miranda Green, *Symbol and Image in Celtic Religious Art* (London: Routledge, 1992), 58.

22. *Ibid.,* 57.

23. *Ibid.,* 37.

24. *Ibid.*

25. *Ibid.,* 185.

26. *Ibid.*

27. *Ibid.,* 186.

28. *Ibid.*

29. *Ibid.,* 187.

30. *Ibid.*

31. Stephen Yeates, *The Tribe of Witches: The Religion of the Dobunni and the Hwicce* (Oxford, UK: Oxbow Books, 2009).

32. Hilda Roderick Ellis Davidson, *Myths and Symbols in Pagan Europe* (Manchester, UK: Manchester University Press, 1988), 47.

33. Miranda Green, *Celtic Myths* (Austin: University of Texas Press, 1998), 62.

34. Miranda Green, *An Archaeology of Images* (London: Routledge, 2004), 118.

35. Henig, 49.

36. *Ibid.,* 48.

37. Rachel Bromwich, *Trioedd Ynys Prydein. The Welsh Triads* (Cardiff, UK: University of Wales Press, 1978).

38. Henri Hubert, "Le mythe d'Epona," in *Mélanges linguistiques offerts à M.J. Vendryes,* ed. Jules Bloch (Paris: Librairie Ancienne Edouard Champion, 1925), 187–198.

39. Miranda Green, *The Gods of Roman Britain* (Princes Risborough, Buckinghamshire, UK: Shire Publications, 1983), 56.

40. *Ibid.*

Chapter 3

1. Koch, *Celtic Culture,* 1456.

2. Nennius, Chapter 62.

3. Higley, "The Spoils of Annwn."

4. Julius Pokorny, *Indogermanisches Etymologisches Wörterbuch* (Bern, Switzerland: Francke, 1959), 534, http://www.indoeurope an.nl.

5. Koch, *Celtic Culture,* 1610.

6. Alexander Falileyev, *Dictionary of Continental Celtic Place-Names* (Aberystwyth, UK: CMCS Publications, 2010), entry for *sedo-* "seat, location," http://cadair.aber.ac.uk.

7. Roger D. Woodard, *Indo-European Sacred Space* (Champaign: University of Illinois Press, 2006), 78. Here as elsewhere in the book, I have taken my insights into Sanskrit from the Cologne Digital Sanskrit Lexicon, which is based on Monier-Williams's Sanskrit-English dictionary, and can be accessed at http://webapps.uni-koeln.de.

8. Mary Boyce and Frantz Grenet, *Zoroastrianism under Macedonian and Roman Rule,* Part 1 (Leiden, Holland: Brill, 1991), 477.

9. James Darmesteter, trans., "Vendidad," in *Sacred Books of the East* (New York: Oxford University Press, 1880), 1.17, http://www.av esta.org.

10. Darmesteter, 10.14.

11. Raffaele Pettazzoni, *The All-Knowing God* (New York: Arno Press, 1978), 119.

12. *Rigveda,* trans. Ralph Griffith (Benares, India: E.J. Lazarus, 1897), 1.152.2, http://www.sacred-texts.com.

13. Pokorny, *Indogermanisches Etymologisches Wörterbuch,* 1160–1162.

14. Frank E. Romer, trans., *Pomponius Mela's Description of the World* (Ann Arbor: University of Michigan Press, 1998); Daithi O Hogain, *The Celts: A History,* Part 70 (Woodbridge, Suffolk, UK: Boydell Press, 2003), 25.

15. Thomas Taylor, trans., *Life of St. Samson of Dol* (London: Society for Promoting Christian Knowledge, Macmillan, 1925), Book 1, Chapter 27, http://www.lamp.ac.uk.

16. Geoffrey of Monmouth, *The Life of Merlin,* trans. John Jay Parry (Urbana: University of Illinois, 1925), http://www.sacred-texts.com.

17. "Peredur, Son of Efrawg." In *The Mabinogion*, trans. Lady Charlotte Guest.

18. Roger Sherman Loomis, *The Grail: From Celtic Myth to Christian Symbol* (Princeton: Princeton University Press, 1991), 33.

19. Joseph Clancy, trans., "Y Gododdin," in *Earliest Welsh Poetry* (London & New York: Macmillan, 1970), http://www.maryjones.us. The lines I've quoted come from stanzas VIII, XI, XXXII, and LXI.

20. "Song Before the Sons of Llyr," in *The Four Ancient Books of Wales*, trans. W.S. Skene (Edinburgh: Edmonston and Douglas), http://www.maryjones.us.

21. Will Parker, *Mabinogi: Branwen, Daughter of Llyr*, http://www.mabinogi.net.

22. Ernest Brehaut, *An Encyclopedist of the Dark Ages: Isidore of Seville* (New York: Columbia University, 1912), http://bestiary.ca.

23. Pokorny, *Indogermanisches etymologisches Wörterbuch*, 855.

24. Giraldus Cambrensis, "De principis instructione," in *The Journey through Wales; and, The Description of Wales*, trans. Lewis Thorpe (London: Penguin, 1978), http://www.britannia.com.

25. Giraldus Cambrensis, "Speculum Ecclesiae," in *The Journey through Wales; and, The Description of Wales*, trans. Lewis Thorpe (London: Penguin, 1978), http://www.britannia.com.

26. Nennius, Chapter 13.

27. "The Sick Bed (Wasting Sickness) of Cuchulain," in *Cuchulain of Muirthemne*, trans. Lady Augusta Gregory (London: John Murray, 1902), http://www.sacred-texts.com.

28. "Hostile Confederacy," in Skene, *Four Ancient Books*.

29. "The Chair of the Sovereign," in Skene, *Four Ancient Books*.

30. "The Dialogue of Gwyddno Garanhir and Gwynn ap Nudd," in Skene, *Four Ancient Books*.

31. Chinua Achebe, *Things Fall Apart* (London: Heinemann, 1996), 108.

32. Lewis Spence, *The Mysteries of Britain* (Pomeroy, WA: Health Research Books, 1996), 123.

33. Pokorny, *Indogermanisches Etymologisches Wörterbuch*, 1042.

34. John R. Hinnells, *Mithraic Studies* (Manchester, UK: Manchester University Press, 1975), 9.

35. Carl Huffman, "Philolaus," in *Stanford Encyclopedia of Philosophy*, ed. Edward N. Zalta, http://plato.stanford.edu.

36. Huffman, "Pythagoreanism," in *Stanford Encyclopedia of Philosophy*.

37. Richard G. Geldard, *The Traveler's Key to Ancient Greece: A Guide to Sacred Places* (Wheaton, IL: Quest Books, 2000), 60.

38. Koch, *Celtic Culture*, 1470.

39. W.J. Gruffydd, "Mabon ab Modron," *Revue celtique* 33 (1912): 459–460.

40. Dan Merkur, *Fruit of the Terrestrial Paradise: The Psychedelic Sacrament in St. Ephrem the Syrian and Celtic Christianity*, http://www.danmerkur.com.

41. Koch, *Celtic Culture*, 195.

42. Giraldus Cambrensis, *The Topography of Ireland*, trans. Thomas Forester (London: Henry G. Bohn, 1863), 96–7.

43. Dorothy Watts, *Christians and Pagans in Roman Britain* (London: Taylor & Francis, 1991), 142–3.

Chapter 4

1. Patrick K. Ford, *The Mabinogi and Other Medieval Welsh Tales* (Berkeley: University of California Press, 2008), 3.

2. Pokorny, *Indogermanisches Etymologisches Wörterbuch*, 636–7.

3. Parker, http://www.mabinogi.net.

4. Koch, *Celtic Culture*, 79.

5. Parker, *Mabinogi*: "Pwyll, Prince of Dyfed."

6. *Ibid.*

7. *Ibid.*

8. *Ibid.*

9. Ifor Williams, *Pedeir Keinc y Mabinogi* (Cardiff, UK: Gwasg Prifysgol Cymru, 1974).

10. Joseph Baudis, "Mabinogion," *Folk-Lore* 37 (1916): 51.

11. Parker, *Mabinogi*: "Branwen, Daughter of Llyr."

12. Ranko Matasovic, *Etymological Lexicon of Proto-Celtic*, entry for *liro-*, http://www.indo-european.nl.

13. J.G. Oosten, *The War of the Gods: The Social Code in Indo-European Mythology* (London: Routledge, 1985), 86–9.

14. Koch, *Celtic Culture*, 238.

15. Pausanias, *Description of Greece*, trans. W.H.S. Jones (Cambridge, MA: Harvard University Press, 1918), 10.23, http://www.theoi.com.

16. Diodorus Siculus, 22.9.

17. Strabo, Book 4, Chapter 4.1.

18. John T. Koch, "A Welsh Window on the Iron Age: Manawydan, Mandubracios," *CMCS* 14 (1987): 17–52.

19. Koch, *Celtic Culture*, 200.

20. Nennius, Chapter 19.

21. Koch, *Celtic Culture*, 196.

22. Parker, *Mabinogi*: "Manawydan Son of Llyr."

23. *Ibid.*

24. *The Metrical Dindshenchas*, ed. Edward Gwynn (Dublin: Dublin Institute for Advanced Studies, 1991), http://www.ucc.ie.

25. Pokorny, *Indogermanisches Etymologisches Wörterbuch*, 4.

26. Koch, *Celtic Culture*, 606–7.

27. John Carey, "A British myth of origins?" *History of Religions* 31 (1991).

28. Parker, *Mabinogi*: "Math, Son of Mathonwy."

29. *Ibid.*

30. *Ibid.*

31. *Ibid.*

32. *Ibid.*

33. *Ibid.*

34. Henri d'Arbois de Jubainville, *Les Druides et les dieux celtiques à forme d'animaux* (Boston, MA: Adamant Media Corporation, 2005), 160–162.

35. Dimitri Nikolai Boekhoorn, "Mythical, Legendary and Supernatural Bestiary in Celtic Tradition: From Oral to Written Literature" (PhD diss., Université Rennes 2/University College Cork, 2008), 82.

36. Koch, *Celtic Culture*, 867.

37. *Ibid.*, 83.

38. John Rhys, *Celtic Folklore: Welsh and Manx* (Boston, MA: Adamant media Corporation, 2004), 645.

39. Koch, *Celtic Culture*, 1166.

40. Elizabeth Archibald, *Incest and the Medieval Imagination* (Oxford, UK: Oxford University Press, 2001), 54–55.

41. Christopher R. Fee and David Leeming, *Gods, Heroes and Kings: The Battle for Mythic Britain* (Oxford, UK: Oxford University Press, 2004), 47.

42. Sarah Higley, *Between Languages: The Uncooperative Text in Early Welsh and Old English Nature Poetry* (University Park: Penn State Press, 1993), 291–2.

43. "The Battle of the Trees," Skene, *Four Ancient Books.*

44. Mary Jones, "Notes to The Battle of the Trees," http://www.maryjones.us.

45. Koch, *Celtic Culture*, 1484.

Chapter 5

1. Geoffrey of Monmouth, *History of the Kings of Britain*, Book 6, Chapter 15, and Book 8, Chapter 10.

2. Julian Thomas, *Understanding the Neolithic* (London: Routledge, 1999), 204.

3. *Ibid.*

4. *Ibid.*, 206.

5. Barry Cunliffe, *The Oxford Illustrated History of Prehistoric Europe* (Oxford: Oxford University Press, 2001), 254.

6. David Field, *The Investigation and Analytical Survey of Silbury Hill* (Swindon, Wiltshire, UK: English Heritage, 2002), 12.

7. David Field, "Great sites: Silbury Hill," *British Archaeology* 70 (2003), http://www.britarch.ac.uk.

8. Field, "Great sites: Silbury Hill."

9. Field, *Investigation*, 74.

10. Field, "Great sites: Silbury Hill."

11. Mike Parker-Pearson, *Stonehenge Riverside Project*, http://www.shef.ac.uk/archaeology/research/stonehenge.

12. Brian John, *The Bluestone Enigma* (Newport, Pembrokeshire, UK: Greencroft Books, 2008); O. Williams-Thorpe, P.J. Potts, M.C. Jones, and P.C. Webb, "Preseli Spotted Dolerite Bluestones: Axe-heads, Stonehenge Monoliths and Outcrop Sources," *Oxford Journal of Archaeology* 25 (2006): 29–64.

13. The Amesbury Archer, http://www.wessexarch.co.uk.

14. The Boscombe Bowmen, http://www.wessexarch.co.uk.

15. Cunliffe, *Oxford Illustrated History*, 251.

16. *Ibid.*, 253.

17. *Ibid.*, 254.

18. See Durrington Walls: a Time Team Special, summarized at http://www.channel4.com/history/microsites/T/timeteam/2005_durr_t.html.

19. Parker-Pearson.

20. *Ibid.*

21. Stuart Needham, Andrew Lawson, and Ann Woodward, "Rethinking Bush Barrow," *British Archaeology* 104 (2009), http://www.britarch.ac.uk.

22. *Ibid.*

23. James Dyer, *Discovering Prehistoric England* (Princes Risborough, Buckinghamshire: Shire Publications, 2001), 192.

24. Mike Pitts, *Hengeworld* (London: Arrow Books, 2000), 295–8.

25. A.F. Harding, *European Societies in the Bronze Age* (Cambridge, UK: Cambridge University Press, 2000), 190.

26. Lidia D. Sciama and Joanne Bubolz Eicher, *Beads and Bead Makers* (Oxford, UK: Berg Publishers, 1998), 254.

27. Mike Baillie, "Irish Tree Rings and an Event in 1628 B.C.," in *Thera and the Aegean World III*, ed. David A. Hardy (London: Thera Foundation, 1990), 160–166.

28. Barry Cunliffe, "Landscape with People," in *Culture, Landscape and the Environ-*

ment, ed. Kate Flint and Howard Morphy (Oxford, UK: Oxford University Press, 2000), 120. In *Iron Age Communities*, Cunliffe calls these fields "coaxial field systems." They are popularly — and erroneously — known as "Celtic fields."

29. Cunliffe, "Landscape with People," 121.

30. *Ibid.*

31. *Ibid.*

32. *Ibid.*

33. *Ibid.*

34. *Ibid.*

35. *Ibid.*

36. Cunliffe, "Landscape with People," 122. In *Iron Age Communities*, Cunliffe implies that some ranch boundaries were constructed late in the 2nd millennium, but that others were constructed some time after 900 B.C.

37. *Ibid.*

38. *Ibid.*

39. *Ibid.*, 124.

40. Mike Baillie, *A Slice Through Time: Dendrochronology and Precision Dating* (London: Routledge, 1995), 77–8.

41. Cunliffe, "Landscape with People," 124–5.

42. David McOmish, "Landscapes Preserved by the Men of War," *British Archaeology* 34 (1998), http://www.britarch.ac.uk.

43. Rodney Castleden, *The Making of Stonehenge* (London: Routledge, 1993), 227.

44. English Heritage, National Monument Report, SU14SW67, SU14SW68.

45. Kurt Hunter-Mann, "Excavations at Vespasian's Camp Iron Age Hillfort, 1987," *The Wiltshire Archaeological and Natural History Magazine* 92 (1999): 39–52.

46. Ian Plimer, *Heaven and Earth* (Ballan, Victoria, Australia: Connor Court, 2009), 57; Charles A. Perry and Kenneth Hsu, "Geophysical, Archaeological, and Historical Evidence Support a Solar-Output Model for Climate Change," *PNAS* 97.23 (2000): 12435.

47. Trevor Bryce, *The Kingdom of the Hittites* (Oxford, UK: Oxford University Press, 2005), 356.

48. Herodotus, *The Histories*, trans. A.D. Godley (Cambridge, MA: Harvard University Press, 1920), 7.170–171, http://perseus.tufts.edu.

49. Michael Wood, *In Search of the Trojan War* (Berkeley: University of California Press, 1998), 217–8.

50. Herodotus, 1.94.

51. Robert Beekes, The Origins of the Etruscans, http://www.knaw.nl.

52. Cunliffe, *Iron Age Communities in Britain* (London: Routledge, 2005), 247–8.

53. *Ibid.*, 92.

54. *Ibid.*, 90.

55. *Ibid.*, 92.

56. John Barrett and David McOmish, All Cannings Cross, http://www.allcannings.org.

57. David McOmish, "East Chisenbury: Ritual and Rubbish at the British Bronze-Age-Iron Age Transition," *Antiquity* 70.267 (1996): 68–76.

58. Cunliffe, "Landscape with People," 125–6.

59. *Ibid.*, 126.

60. Cunliffe, *Iron Age Communities*, 65.

61. *Ibid.*

62. *Ibid.*, 66.

63. Cunliffe, "Landscape with People," 126.

64. *Ibid.*

65. *Ibid.*

66. *Ibid.*

67. *Ibid.*

68. *Ibid.*

69. Timothy Darvill, *Prehistoric Britain* (London: Routledge, 1997), 135; Kristian Kristiansen, *Europe Before History* (Cambridge, UK: Cambridge University Press, 2000), 300.

70. Kristiansen, *ibid.*

71. Darvill, 135.

72. *Ibid.*

73. *Ibid.*

74. *Ibid.*, 136.

75. *Ibid.*

76. *Ibid.*

77. *Ibid.*, 136–7.

78. Cunliffe, "Landscape with People," 126.

79. *Ibid.*, 128.

80. Anne Ross, "Ritual and the Druids," in *The Celtic World*, ed. Miranda Green (London: Routledge, 1996), 439.

81. *Ibid.*

82. Cunliffe, *Iron Age Communities*, 85.

83. *Ibid.*, 98.

84. *Ibid.*, 98–9.

85. Darvill, 137.

86. *Ibid.*

87. *Ibid.*

88. Cunliffe, *Iron Age Communities*, 149.

89. *Ibid.*

90. *Ibid.*

91. *Ibid.*, 178.

92. *Ibid.*, 189.

93. *Ibid.*

94. *Ibid.*, 127.

95. Dennis Price, *The Missing Years of Jesus: The Greatest Story Never Told* (London: Hay House, 2009), 227–8.

96. Diodorus Siculus, 2.47.

Chapter 6

1. Nennius, Chapter 10.
2. Geoffrey of Monmouth, *History of the Kings of Britain*, Book 1, Chapters 15–16.
3. The Parish and Priory Church of St. Mary, Totnes, Devon (Diocese of Exeter), http://www.churchcare.co.uk.
4. Prehistoric Dartmoor, http://www.dartmoor-npa.gov.uk.
5. *Ibid.*
6. Herodotus, 1.94.
7. Beekes, *Origins of the Etruscans.*
8. H.W. Bailey, "Arya II," *BSOAS* 23.1 (1960).
9. *Ibid.*, 34.
10. Pokorny, *Indogermanisches Etymologisches Wörterbuch*, 641–2.
11. Julius Pokorny, "Zur keltischen Namenkunde und Etymologie," *Vox Romanica* 10 (1949): 232.
12. Pokorny, *Indogermanisches etymologisches Wörterbuch*, 818–9.
13. Old Iranian Online, www.utexas.edu.
14. Giraldus Cambrensis, *Itinerary Through Wales*, trans. Sir Richard Colt Hoare (London: W. Miller, 1806), 390–392, http://www.archive.org.
15. Koch, *Celtic Culture*, 1164–5.
16. "Lludd and Llefelys," in *The Mabinogion*, trans. Lady Charlotte Guest.
17. Bromwich, *Welsh Triads.* The Triads themselves can be accessed at http://norin77.50megs.com/triads.htm.
18. Nennius, chapters 40–42.
19. Athenaeus, *Deipnosophists*, trans. C.D. Yonge (London: H.G. Bohn, 1854), Book 6, Chapter 49, http://www.attalus.org.
20. Paul Dunbavin, *Picts and Ancient Britons* (Long Eaton: Nottingham: Third Millennium Publishing, 2001), 1.
21. Dunbavin, 1.
22. *Ibid.*, 93.
23. *Ibid.*
24. *Ibid.*, 94.
25. *Ibid.*, 99.
26. Koch, *Celtic Culture*, 484.
27. Asdis Magnusdottir, *La Voix du cor* (Amsterdam: Rodopi, 1998), 121–2.
28. Jan Bouzek, "Cimmerians and Early Scythians: The Transition from Geometric to Orientalising Style in the Pontic Area," in *North Pontic Archaeology: Recent Discoveries and Studies*, ed. Gocha S. Tsetskhladze (Leiden: Brill, 2001), 38.
29. Herodotus, Book 4.
30. Carola Metzner-Nebelsick, "Early Iron Age Pastoral Nomadism in the Great Hungarian Plain — Migration or Assimilation? The Thraco–Cimmerian Problem Revisited," in *Kurgans, Ritual Sites and Settlements*, ed. Jeannine Davis-Kimball, http://www.csen.org.
31. Kristiansen, 194.
32. *Ibid.*, 193.
33. Bouzek, 36–8.
34. Kristiansen, 205.
35. *Ibid.*, 206.
36. *Ibid.*, 206–7.
37. Hermann Sauter, Definition der "thrako-kimmerischen" Bronzen, http://www.kimmerier.de.
38. Nancy K. Sandars, *Bronze Age Cultures in France* (Cambridge, UK: Cambridge University Press, 1957), 215, 225.
39. Barry Cunliffe, "Understanding Hillforts: Have We Progressed?," in *The Wessex Hillforts Project*, ed. Andrew Payne, Mark Corney and Barry Cunliffe (Swindon, Wiltshire, UK: English Heritage, 2006).
40. Cunliffe, "Understanding Hillforts," 155–6.
41. *Ibid.*, 156.
42. *Ibid.*
43. *Ibid.*
44. *Ibid.*
45. Pokorny, *Indogermanisches etymologisches Wörterbuch*, 539–40.
46. Robert Beekes, *Greek Etymological Dictionary*, http://www.indo-european.nl.
47. Pokorny, *Indogermanisches etymologisches Wörterbuch*, 738.
48. Cunliffe, "Understanding Hillforts," 160.
49. *Ibid.*, 161.
50. Cunliffe, *Iron Age Communities*, 104.
51. Martin Litchfield West, *Indo-European Poetry and Myth* (Oxford, UK: Oxford University Press, 2007), 145–6.
52. Ian Johnston, *The Iliad* (Arlington, VA: Richer Resources Publications, 2006), 218–9.
53. Robert Turcan, *The Cults of the Roman Empire* (Oxford, UK: Blackwell, 1996), 248.
54. Turcan, 249.
55. *Ibid.*
56. Pettazzoni, 179–180.
57. *Ibid.*, 181.
58. Herodotus, Book 5, Chapter 7.
59. Pettazzoni, 184.
60. *Ibid.*, 184–5.
61. *Ibid.*
62. *Ibid.*
63. *Ibid.*, 186.
64. David Rankin, *Celts and the Classical World* (London: Routledge, 1996), 30.
65. John O'Meara, *The History and Topography of Ireland* (London: Penguin, 1982), 110.

66. Daniel Bray, Sacral Elements of Irish Kingship, http://escholarship.usyd.edu.au.

67. West, 28.

68. Susan Guettel Cole, "Greek Religion," in *A Handbook of Ancient Religions*, ed. John R. Hinnells (Cambridge, UK: Cambridge University Press, 2007), 298–9.

69. Philipp Vandenberg, *Mysteries of the Oracles* (London: Tauris Parke Paperbacks, 2007), 27.

70. Vandenberg, 29.

71. Pausanias, 8.38.2.

72. Koch, *Celtic Culture*, 170.

73. Raimo Anttila, *Greek and Indo-European Etymology in Action* (Amsterdam: John Benjamins, 2000), 72.

74. West, 28.

75. N.D. Kazanas, "Indo-European Deities and the Rigveda," *Journal of Indo-European Studies* 29 (2001).

76. J.P. Mallory and Douglas Q. Adams, *Encyclopedia of Indo-European culture* (London: Taylor & Francis, 1997), 265.

77. Green, *Animals in Celtic Life*, 112.

78. *Ibid.*, 52.

79. *Ibid.*, 211–212.

80. Green, *Symbol and Image*, 18.

81. Jan Bremmer, *The Rise and Fall of the Afterlife* (London: Routledge, 2002), 38.

82. Fritz Graf, *Apollo* (London: Taylor & Francis, 2008), 39–40.

83. Morris Silver, *Taking Ancient Myths Economically* (Leiden, Holland: Brill, 1992), 237.

84. Pausanias, Book 10.5.7.

85. Apollonius Rhodius, *Argonautica*, trans. R.C. Seaton (Cambridge, MA: Harvard University Press, 1912), 4.603–618, http://www.omacl.org.

86. Pausanias, Book 10.5.7–10.

87. Herodotus, Book 4.33.

88. Silver, 238.

89. Hesiod, *Theogony*, trans. Hugh G. Evelyn-White (Cambridge, MA: Harvard University Press, 1914), lines 767–774, http://www.sacred-texts.com.

90. Sir James George Frazer, *The Golden Bough: Studies in Magic and Religion* (London: Penguin, 1996), 198–9.

91. Manfred Lurker, *The Routledge Dictionary of Gods and Goddesses, Devils and Demons* (London: Routledge, 2004), 13–14.

92. Norman Oliver Brown, *Hermes the Thief* (Great Barrington, MA: Steiner Books, 1990), 36–7.

93. Bremmer, 30–1.

94. C. Scott Littleton and Linda Malcor, *From Scythia to Camelot* (London, Taylor & Francis, 2000).

95. Thomas Green, The Historicity and Historicisation of Arthur, http://www.arthuriana.co.uk.

96. Bromwich, *Welsh Triads*, 544–5.

97. Graham Anderson, *King Arthur in Antiquity* (London: Routledge, 2004), 28.

98. Richard Hinckley Allen, *Star Names: Their Lore and Meaning* (Mineola, NY: Dover Publications, 1963), 92–4.

99. Allen, 95.

100. Anderson, 29.

101. Allen, 99.

102. Hugh G. Evelyn-White, *Hesiod the Homeric Hymns and Homerica* (Charleston, SC: BiblioBazaar, 2008), 75.

103. Anderson, 32.

104. *Ibid.*, 32–3.

105. *Ibid.*, 33.

106. *Ibid.*, 33–4.

107. *Ibid.*, 34.

108. C. Scott Littleton and Linda Malcor, "The Germanic Sword in the Tree," *The Heroic Age* 11 (2008).

109. Herodotus, Book 4.

110. Ammianus Marcellinus, 31.2.

111. Anderson, 96.

112. Herodotus, Book 4.

113. Anderson, 16.

114. *Ibid.*, 104.

115. Herodotus, Book 8.137.

116. Anderson, 96.

117. Pettazzoni, 181.

118. F. Graham Millar, "The Celestial David and Goliath," *Journal of the Royal Astronomical Society of Canada* 89.4 (1995): 142.

119. Proinsias Mac Cana, *Celtic Mythology* (New York: Hamlyn, 1970).

120. Millar, 144.

121. Allen, 285.

122. Rankin, 59.

123. Millar, 145–6.

124. Allen, 20.

125. *Ibid.*, 147.

126. Mircea Eliade, *Shamanism: Archaic Techniques of Ecstasy* (London: Routledge & Kegan, 1964).

127. Millar, 148–9.

128. *Ibid.*, 149.

129. Allen, 319.

130. *Ibid.*, 318.

131. Millar, 150–1.

132. *Ibid.*, 151.

133. Matasovic, entry for abon-.

Chapter 7

1. West, 287.

2. *Ibid.*, 378.

3. West, 378–9.

4. Kazanas, 257–293.

5. James Hastings, *Encyclopedia of Religion and Ethics* (Whitefish, MT: Kessinger, 2003), 805.

6. John Waterhouse, *Zoroastrianism* (San Diego, CA: Book Tree, 2006), 63.

7. Waterhouse, 65.

8. W.H. Matthews, *Mazes and Labyrinths* (Charleston, SC: Forgotten Books, 2008), 71.

9. W.H. Matthews, 74.

10. *Ibid.*, 79.

11. *Ibid.*, 81–2.

12. *Ibid.*, 87.

13. *Ibid.*, 88.

14. *Ibid.*, 90.

15. *Ibid.*, 92.

16. *Ibid.*, 156.

17. *Ibid.*

18. *Ibid.*, 52.

19. *Ibid.*, 158.

20. *Ibid.*, 160.

21. Johnston, 416.

22. Craig M. Wright, *The Maze and the Warrior* (Cambridge, MA: Harvard University Press, 2001), 130.

23. Plutarch, "Life of Theseus," in *Parallel Lives*, trans. Aubrey Stewart and George Long (London: Henry G. Bohn, 1881), http://www.gutenberg.org.

24. W.H. Matthews, 162.

25. Pokorny, *Indogermanisches etymologisches Wörterbuch*, 1089.

26. Henning Eichberg, "The Labyrinth of the City — Fractal Movement and Identity," in *Nature and Identity: Essays on the Culture of Nature*, ed. Kirsti Pedersen and Arvid Viken. Bloomington: Indiana University Press, 2003.

27. Pokorny, *Indogermanisches etymologisches Wörterbuch*, 276.

28. Price, 104–6.

29. Cunliffe, *Iron Age Communities*, 66.

30. Green, *Historicisation of Arthur*, 10.

31. Thomas McEvilley, *The Shape of Ancient Thought* (New York: Allworth Press, 2002), 99.

32. McEvilley, 100.

33. *Ibid.*

34. *Ibid.*, 101.

35. *Ibid.*, 25.

36. *Ibid.*, 25–6.

37. *Ibid.*, 26.

38. *Ibid.*, 102.

39. *Ibid.*, 104.

40. *Ibid.*, 105.

41. Higley, *Between Languages*, 291–2.

42. "The Battle of the Trees," in Skene, *Four Ancient Books*.

43. *Bhagavadgita*, translated by Sanderson Beck, http://www.san.beck.org.

44. Jane Webster, "Sanctuaries and Sacred Places," in *The Celtic World*, edited by Miranda Green (London: Routledge, 1996), 448.

45. Koch, *Celtic Culture*, 1351.

46. Pokorny, *Indogermanisches etymologisches Wörterbuch*, 764.

47. Homer, *The Iliad*, trans. Samuel Butler, http://classics.mit.edu.

48. Strabo, Book 7.3.

49. Iowerth Eiddon Stephen Edwards, *The Cambridge Ancient History* (Cambridge, UK: Cambridge University Press, 1970), 417.

50. Herodotus, Book 3.73.

51. Edwards, 418.

52. Andrew Bell-Fialkoff, *The Role of Migration in the History of the Eurasian Steppe* (New York: Palgrave Macmillan, 2000), 195.

Chapter 8

1. Thomas O'Sullivan, *The De Excidio of Gildas: Its Authenticity and Date* (Leiden: Brill, 1978), 180.

2. N.J. Higham, *The English Conquest: Gildas and Britain in the Fifth Century* (Manchester: Manchester University Press, 1994), 141.

3. Gildas, *De Excidio et Conquestu Britanniae*, trans. J.A. Giles (London: Henry G. Bohn, 1848), http://www.fordham.edu.

4. Rodney Castleden, *King Arthur: The Truth Behind the Legend* (London: Routledge, 2000), 45–6.

5. Castleden, *King Arthur*, 46.

6. Higham, 45–6.

7. Castleden, *King Arthur*, 81.

8. *Ibid.*, 82.

9. Frank D. Reno, *Historic Figures of the Arthurian Era* (Jefferson, NC: McFarland, 2000), 59.

10. Reno, 69.

11. Nennius.

12. Michael D. Costen, *The Origins of Somerset* (Manchester, UK: Manchester University Press, 1992), 67.

13. Barbara Yorke, *Wessex in the Early Middle Ages* (London: Continuum, 1995), 19–20.

14. Yorke, 20.

15. *Ibid.*, 22.

16. *Ibid.*, 23.

17. *Ibid.*, 24.

18. *Ibid.*, 26–7.

19. *Ibid.*, 26.

20. *Ibid.*, 249.

21. Gelling, "The Effect of Man on the

Landscape: The Place-name Evidence in Berkshire," in *The Effect of Man on the Landscape: The Lowland Zone*, ed. Susan Limbrey and John G. Evans (London: Council for British Archaeology, 1978), 124.

22. David James, "Sorviodunum: A Review of the Archaeological Evidence," *The Wiltshire Archaeological and Natural History Magazine* 95 (2002).

23. Wessex Archaeology.

24. David McOmish, David Field, and Graham Brown, *The Field Archaeology of Salisbury Plain Training Area* (Swindon, Wiltshire: English Heritage, 2002).

25. Reno, 59.

26. *Anglo-Saxon Chronicle*, trans. James Henry Ingram (London: Everyman Press, 1912), http://www.gutenberg.org.

27. Yorke, 36–9.

28. Judith McClure and Roger Collins, *The Ecclesiastical History of the English People* (Oxford, UK: Oxford University Press, 1999), 119.

29. Johannes Hoops and Heinrich Beck, *Reallexikon der germanischen Altertumskunde*, Volume 12 (Berlin–New York: Walter de Gruyter, 1998), 51.

30. Daniel G. Russo, *Town Origins and Development in Early England, c. 400–950 A.D.* (Westport, CT: Greenwood, 1998), 109.

31. Yorke, 29–30.

32. Russo, 109–110.

33. Keith Matthews, "What's in a Name? Britons, Angles, Ethnicity and Material Culture from the Fourth to the Seventh Centuries." *Heroic Age* 4.1 (2001).

34. Reno, 164.

35. Reno, 64.

36. David Dumville, "The West Saxon Genealogical Regnal List and the Chronology of Early Wessex," *Peritia* 4 (1985).

37. Yorke, 32.

38. Jeremy Haslam, "A Middle Saxon Iron Smelting Site at Ramsbury, Wiltshire," *Mediaeval Archaeology* 24 (1980): 58.

39. Haslam, 59–60.

40. Haslam, 60.

41. Martin Biddle, "Winchester, the Development of an Early Capital," in *Vor- und Früh-formen der europaischen Stadt im Mittelalter*, ed. H. Jankuhn, W. Schlesinger and H. Steuer (Göttingen: Vandenhoeck und Ruprecht, 1973).

42. Haslam, 61.

43. *Ibid.*, 63.

44. Koch, *Celtic Culture*, 458.

45. Patrick Sims-Williams, "The Settlement of England in Bede and the *Chronicle*," in *Anglo-Saxon England*, ed. Peter Clemoes, Simon Keynes and Michael Lapidge (Cambridge: Cambridge University Press, 2007), 33–4.

46. Michael Swanton, *Anglo-Saxon Chronicle* (London: Routledge, 1998), 20.

47. Pokorny, *Indogermanisches etymologisches Wörterbuch*, 426–7.

48. *Ibid.*, 327.

49. Green, *Symbol and Image*, 186.

50. Yorke, 58.

51. Russo, 112.

52. *Ibid.*, 112–3.

53. Russo, 113.

54. Yorke, 27.

55. Barry Cunliffe, "Understanding Hillforts," 162.

56. William A. Chaney, *The Cult of Kingship in Anglo-Saxon England: The Transition from Paganism to Christianity* (Manchester, UK: Manchester University Press, 1970), 127–8.

57. This is thought, like the comet of 530, to have been Halley's Comet.

58. Christopher Daniell, *From Norman Conquest to Magna Carta* (London: Routledge, 2003), 13.

59. Daniell, 17.

60. *Ibid.*, 28.

61. *Ibid.*, 29.

62. *Ibid.*, 30.

63. *Ibid.*, 37.

64. Berenice M. Kerr, Religious *Life for Women: c. 1100–c. 1350* (Oxford, UK: Oxford University Press, 1999), 162.

65. Kerr, 70–2.

66. Koch, *Celtic Culture*, 815.

67. Clare Gathercole, *Glastonbury Archaeological Assessment* (Swindon, Wiltshire, UK: English Heritage), 5.

68. Gathercole, 6.

69. *Ibid.*, 23.

70. William of Malmesbury, *Chronicle of the Kings of England*, trans. Rev. John Sharpe (London: George Bell and Sons, 1904), Chapter 2, http://www.fordham.edu.

71. Gathercole, 28–9.

72. *Ibid.*, 6.

73. *Ibid.*, 6–7.

Bibliography

Achebe, Chinua. *Things Fall Apart*. London: Heinemann, 1996.

Allen, Richard Hinckley. *Star Names: Their Lore and Meaning*. Mineola, NY: Dover Publications, 1963.

Ammianus Marcellinus. *Roman History*. Translated by J.C. Rolfe. Cambridge, MA: Harvard University Press, 1950. http://penelope.uchicago.edu.

Anderson, Graham. *King Arthur in Antiquity*. London: Routledge, 2004.

Anglo-Saxon Chronicle. Translated by James Henry Ingram. London: Everyman Press, 1912. http://www.gutenberg.org.

Anttila, Raimo. *Greek and Indo-European Etymology in Action*. Amsterdam: John Benjamins, 2000.

Apollonius Rhodius. *Argonautica*. Translated by R.C. Seaton. Cambridge, MA: Harvard University Press, 1912. http://www.omacl.org.

Archibald, Elizabeth. *Incest and the Medieval Imagination*. Oxford, UK: Oxford University Press, 2001.

Athenaeus. *Deipnosophists*. Translated by C.D. Yonge. London: H.G. Bohn, 1854. http://www.attalus.org.

Bailey, H.W. "Arya II." *BSOAS* 23.1 (1960): 13–39.

Baillie, M.G.L. "Irish Tree Rings and an Event in 1628 B.C." In *Thera and the Aegean World III*. Edited by David A. Hardy. London: Thera Foundation, 1990.

_____. *A Slice Through Time: Dendrochronology and Precision Dating*. London: Routledge, 1995.

Barrett, John, and David McOmish. All Cannings Cross. http://www.allcannings.org.

Bartholomae, Christian. *Altiranisches Wörterbuch*. Strassburg: K.J. Trübner, 1904. http://www.archive.org.

Baudis, Joseph. "Mabinogion." *Folk-Lore* 37 (1916): 31–68.

Beekes, Robert. *Greek Etymological Dictionary*. http://www.indo-european.nl.

_____. *The Origins of the Etruscans*. http://www.knaw.nl.

Bell-Fialkoff, Andrew. *The Role of Migration in the History of the Eurasian Steppe*. New York: Palgrave Macmillan, 2000.

Bhagavadgita. Translated by Sanderson Beck. http://www.san.beck.org.

Biddle, Martin. "Winchester, the Development of an Early Capital." In *Vor- und Früh-formen der europaischen Stadt im Mittelalter*. Edited by H. Jankuhn, W. Schlesinger and H. Steuer. Göttingen, Germany: Vandenhoeck und Ruprecht, 1973.

Blamires, David. *Herzog Ernst and the Otherworld Voyage*. Manchester, UK: Manchester University Press, 1979.

Boekhoorn, Dimitri Nikolai. "Mythical, Legendary and Supernatural Bestiary in Celtic Tradition: From Oral to Written Literature." PhD diss., Université Rennes 2/University College Cork, 2008.

Bostock, John, and H.T. Riley, trans. *The Natural History of Pliny*. Vol. 5. London: Henry G. Bohn, 1857.

Bouzek, Jan. "Cimmerians and Early Scythians: the Transition from Geometric to Orientalising Style in the Pontic Area." In *North Pontic Archaeology: Recent Discoveries and Studies*. Edited by Gocha S. Tsetskhladze. Leiden, Holland: Brill, 2001.

Boyce, Mary, and Frantz Grenet. *Zoroastrianism under Macedonian and Roman Rule*. Part 1. Leiden, Holland: Brill, 1991.

Bray, Daniel. *Sacral Elements of Irish Kingship.* http://escholarship.usyd.edu.au.

Brehaut, Ernest. *An Encyclopedist of the Dark Ages: Isidore of Seville.* New York: Columbia University, 1912. http://bestiary.ca.

Bremmer, Jan. *The Rise and Fall of the Afterlife.* London: Routledge, 2002.

Bromwich, Rachel. *Trioedd Ynys Prydein. The Welsh Triads.* Cardiff: University of Wales Press, 1978.

Brown, Norman Oliver. *Hermes the Thief: The Evolution of a Myth.* Great Barrington, MA: Steiner Books, 1990.

Bryce, Trevor. *The Kingdom of the Hittites.* Oxford, UK: Oxford University Press, 2005.

Carey, John. "A British myth of origins?" *History of Religions* 31 (1991): 24–38.

Cassius Dio. *Roman History.* Translated by Earnest Cary. Cambridge, MA: Harvard University Press, 1927. http://penelope.uchicago.edu.

Castleden, Rodney. *King Arthur: The Truth Behind the Legend.* London: Routledge, 2000.

_____. *The Making of Stonehenge.* London: Routledge, 1993.

Centre for the Study of Ancient Documents. "Curse Tablets from Roman Britain: Archaeological Sites." http://curses.csad.ox.ac.uk.

Chaney, William A. *The Cult of Kingship in Anglo-Saxon England: The Transition from Paganism to Christianity.* Manchester, UK: Manchester University Press, 1970.

Clancy, Joseph, trans. "Y Gododdin." In *Earliest Welsh Poetry.* London & New York: Macmillan, 1970. http://www.maryjones.us.

Clarke, Giles. "The Roman Villa at Woodchester." *Britannia* 13 (1982): 197–228.

Clement of Alexandria. *Stromata.* Translated by William Wilson. Buffalo, NY: Christian Literature Publishing, 1885. http://earlychristianwritings.com.

Cole, Susan Guettel. "Greek Religion." In *A Handbook of Ancient Religions.* Edited by John R. Hinnells. Cambridge, UK: Cambridge University Press, 2007.

Coles, John M., and A.F. Harding. *The Bronze Age in Europe.* London: Taylor & Francis, 1979.

Costen, Michael D. *The Origins of Somerset.* Manchester, UK: Manchester University Press, 1992.

Cunliffe, Barry. *Iron Age Communities in Britain.* 4th ed. London: Routledge, 2005.

_____. "Landscape with People." In *Culture, Landscape and the Environment.* Edited by Kate Flint and Howard Morphy. Oxford, UK: Oxford University Press, 2000.

_____. *The Oxford Illustrated History of Prehistoric Europe.* Oxford, UK: Oxford University Press, 2001.

_____. "Understanding Hillforts: Have We Progressed?" In *The Wessex Hillforts Project.* Edited by Andrew Payne, Mark Corney and Barry Cunliffe. Swindon, Wiltshire, UK: English Heritage, 2006.

Daniell, Christopher. *From Norman Conquest to Magna Carta.* London: Routledge, 2003.

D'Arbois de Jubainville, Henri. *Les Druides et les dieux celtiques à forme d'animaux.* Boston, MA: Adamant Media Corporation, 2005.

Darmesteter, James, trans. "Vendidad." In *Sacred Books of the East.* New York: Oxford University Press, 1880. http://www.avesta.org.

Darvill, Timothy. *Prehistoric Britain.* London: Routledge, 1997.

Davidson, Hilda Roderick Ellis. *Myths and Symbols in Pagan Europe.* Manchester, UK: Manchester University Press, 1988.

Diodorus Siculus. *Historical Library.* Translated by C.H. Oldfather. Cambridge, MA: Harvard University Press, 1935. http://penelope.uchicago.edu.

Dumville, David. "The West Saxon Genealogical Regnal Lists and the Chronology of Early Wessex." *Peritia* 4 (1985): 21–66.

Dunbabin, Katherine. *Mosaics of the Greek and Roman World.* Cambridge, UK: Cambridge University Press, 1999.

Dunbavin, Paul. *Picts and Ancient Britons.* Long Eaton, Nottingham, UK: Third Millennium Publishing, 2001.

Dyer, James. *Discovering Prehistoric England.* Princes Risborough, Buckinghamshire, UK: Shire Publications, 2001.

Edwards, Iorwerth Eiddon Stephen. *The*

Cambridge Ancient History. Cambridge, UK: Cambridge University Press, 1970.

Eichberg, Henning. "The Labyrinth of the City — Fractal Movement and Identity." In *Nature and Identity: Essays on the Culture of Nature*. Edited by Kirsti Pedersen and Arvid Viken. Bloomington: Indiana University Press, 2003.

Eliade, Mircea. *Shamanism: Archaic Techniques of Ecstasy*. London: Routledge & Kegan, 1964.

English Heritage. National Monument Report. SU14SW67, SU14SW68.

Evelyn-White, Hugh G. *Hesiod: The Homeric Hymns and Homerica*. Charleston, SC: BiblioBazaar, 2008.

Falileyev, Alexander. *Dictionary of Continental Celtic Place-Names*. Aberystwyth, UK: CMCS Publications, 2010. http://cadair.aber.ac.uk.

Fee, Christopher R., and David A. Leeming. *Gods, Heroes and Kings: The Battle for Mythic Britain*. Oxford, UK: Oxford University Press, 2004.

Field, David. "Great sites: Silbury Hill." *British Archaeology* 70 (2003). http://www.britarch.ac.uk.

_____. *The Investigation and Analytical Survey of Silbury Hill*. Swindon, Wiltshire, UK: English Heritage, 2002.

Ford, Patrick K. *The Mabinogi and Other Medieval Welsh Tales*. Berkeley: University of California Press, 2008.

Frazer, Sir James George. *The Golden Bough: Studies in Magic and Religion*. London: Penguin, 1996.

Gathercole, Clare. *Glastonbury Archaeological Assessment*. Swindon, Wiltshire, UK: English Heritage, 2003.

Geldard, Richard G. *The Traveler's Key to Ancient Greece: A Guide to Sacred Places*. Wheaton, IL: Quest Books, 2000.

Gelling, Margaret. "The Effect of Man on the Landscape: The Place-name Evidence in Berkshire." In *The Effect of Man on the Landscape: The Lowland Zone*. Edited by Susan Limbrey and John G. Evans. London: Council for British Archaeology, 1978.

Geoffrey of Monmouth. *History of the Kings of Britain*. Translated by J.A. Giles. London: Henry G. Bohn, 1848. http://www.lib.rochester.edu.

_____. *The Life of Merlin*. Translated by John Jay Parry. Urbana: University of Illinois, 1925. http://www.sacred-texts.com.

Gibbon, Edward. *The History of the Decline and Fall of the Roman Empire*. Edited by David Womersley. London: Penguin, 2000.

Gildas. *De Excidio et Conquestu Britanniae*. Translated by J.A. Giles. London: Henry G. Bohn, 1848. http://www.fordham.edu.

Giraldus Cambrensis. *Itinerary Through Wales*. Translated by Sir Richard Colt Hoare. London: W. Miller, 1806. http://www.archive.org.

_____. *The Journey through Wales; and, The Description of Wales*. Translated by Lewis Thorpe. London: Penguin, 1978. http://www.britannia.com.

_____. *Topography of Ireland*. Translated by Thomas Forester. London: Henry G. Bohn, 1863.

Graf, Fritz. *Apollo*. London: Taylor & Francis, 2008.

Green, Miranda. *Animals in Celtic Life and Myth*. London: Routledge, 1998.

_____. *An Archaeology of Images*. London: Routledge, 2004.

_____. *Celtic Myths*. Austin: University of Texas Press, 1998.

_____. *The Gods of Roman Britain*. Princes Risborough, Buckinghamshire, UK: Shire Publications, 1983.

_____. *Symbol and Image in Celtic Religious Art*. London: Routledge, 1992.

Green, Thomas. *A Bibliographic Guide to Welsh Arthurian Literature*. http://www.arthuriana.co.uk.

_____. *Concepts of Arthur*. Stroud: Tempus, 2007.

_____. *The Historicity and Historicisation of Arthur*. http://www.arthuriana.co.uk.

Gruffydd, W.J. "Mabon ab Modron." *Revue Celtique* 33 (1912): 459–460.

Guest, Lady Charlotte, trans. *The Mabinogion*. London: J.M. Dent, 1910. http://www.maryjones.us.

Harding, A.F. *European Societies in the Bronze Age*. Cambridge, UK: Cambridge University Press, 2000.

Haslam, Jeremy. "A Middle Saxon Iron Smelting Site at Ramsbury, Wiltshire." *Mediaeval Archaeology* 24 (1980): 1–68.

Hastings, James. *Encyclopedia of Religion and Ethics*. Whitefish, MT: Kessinger, 2003.

Healy, John F. *Natural History: A Selection*. London: Penguin, 1991.

Henig, Martin. *Religion in Roman Britain*. London: Routledge, 1984.

Herodotus. *The Histories*. Translated by A.D. Godley. Cambridge, MA: Harvard University Press, 1920. http://old.perseus.tufts.edu.

_____. *The Histories*. Translated by George Rawlinson. New York: Dutton, 1862. http://www.fordham.edu.

Hesiod. *Theogony*. Translated by Hugh G. Evelyn-White. Cambridge, MA: Harvard University Press, 1912. http://www.sacred-texts.com.

Higham, N.J. *The English Conquest: Gildas and Britain in the Fifth Century*. Manchester, UK: Manchester University Press, 1994.

Higley, Sarah. *Between Languages: The Uncooperative Text in Early Welsh and Old English Nature Poetry*. University Park, PA: Penn State Press, 1993.

_____, trans. *The Spoils of Annwn*. http://www.lib.rochester.edu.

Hinnells, John R. *Mithraic Studies*. Manchester, UK: Manchester University Press, 1975.

Hippolytus of Rome. *Philosophumena*. Translated by F. Legge. London: Society for Promoting Christian Knowledge, Macmillan, 1921. http://www.archive.org.

Homer. *The Iliad*. Trans. Samuel Butler. http://classics.mit.edu.

Hoops, Johannes, and Heinrich Beck. *Reallexikon der Germanischen Altertumskunde*. Vol. 12. Berlin–New York: Walter de Gruyter, 1998.

Hubert, Henri. "Le mythe d'Epona." In *Mélanges linguistiques offerts à M.J. Vendryes*. Edited by Jules Bloch. Paris: Librairie Ancienne Edouard Champion, 1925.

Hunter-Mann, Kurt. "Excavations at Vespasian's Camp Iron Age Hillfort, 1987." *The Wiltshire Archaeological and Natural History Magazine* 92 (1999): 39–52.

James, David. "Sorviodunum: A Review of the Archaeological Evidence." *The Wiltshire Archaeological and Natural History Magazine* 95 (2002): 1–26.

John, Brian. *The Bluestone Enigma*. Newport, Pembrokeshire, UK: Greencroft Books, 2008.

Johnston, Ian. *The Iliad*. Arlington, VA: Richer Resources Publications, 2006.

Jones, Mary. "Notes to The Battle of the Trees." http://www.maryjones.us.

Julius Caesar. *Gallic Wars*. Translated by W.A. McDevitte and W.S. Bohn. New York: Harper & Brothers, 1869. http://classics.mit.edu.

Kanga, K.E. *Avesta Dictionary*. Bombay: Education Society, 1900. http://www.avesta.org.

Kazanas, N.D. "Indo-European Deities and the Rigveda." *Journal of Indo-European Studies* 29 (2001): 257–293.

Kerr, Berenice M. *Religious Life for Women: c. 1100–c. 1350*. Oxford, UK: Oxford University Press, 1999.

Koch, John T. *Celtic Culture: A Historical Encyclopedia*. Santa Barbara, CA: ABC-CLIO, 2006.

_____. "A Welsh Window on the Iron Age: Manawydan, Mandubracios." *CMCS* 14 (1987): 17–52.

Kondratiev, Alexei. "Lugus: The Many-Gifted Lord." *An Tríbhís Mhór: The IMBAS Journal of Celtic Reconstructionism* 1 (1997). http://www.imbas.org.

Kristiansen, Kristian. *Europe Before History*. Cambridge, UK: Cambridge University Press, 2000.

Lewis, Jodie. "Upwards at 45 Degrees: The Use of Vertical Caves during the Neolithic and Early Bronze Age on Mendip, Somerset." *Capra* 2 (2000). http://capra.group.shef.ac.uk.

Littleton, C. Scott, and Linda A. Malcor. *From Scythia to Camelot*. London: Taylor & Francis, 2000.

_____. "The Germanic Sword in the Tree." *The Heroic Age* 11 (2008).

Loomis, Roger Sherman. *The Grail: From Celtic Myth to Christian Symbol*. Princeton: Princeton University Press, 1991.

Lucan. *Pharsalia*. Translated by Sir Edward Ridley. London: Longmans, Green, 1896. http://www.omacl.org.

Lurker, Manfred. *The Routledge Dictionary of Gods and Goddesses, Devils and Demons*. London: Routledge, 2004.

Mac Cana, Proinsias. *Celtic Mythology*. New York: Hamlyn, 1970.

Magnusdottir, Asdis R. *La Voix du cor.* Amsterdam: Rodopi, 1998.

Mallory, J.P., and Douglas Q. Adams. *Encyclopedia of Indo-European Culture.* London: Taylor & Francis, 1997.

Matasovic, Ranko. *Etymological Lexicon of Proto-Celtic.* http://www.indo-european.nl.

Matthews, Keith. "What's in a Name? Britons, Angles, Ethnicity and Material Culture from the Fourth to the Seventh Centuries." *Heroic Age* 4.1 (2001).

Matthews, W.H. *Mazes and Labyrinths.* Charleston, SC: Forgotten Books, 2008.

McClure, Judith, and Roger Collins. *The Ecclesiastical History of the English People.* Oxford: Oxford University Press, 1999.

McEvilley, Thomas. *The Shape of Ancient Thought.* New York: Allworth Press, 2002.

McOmish, David. "East Chisenbury: Ritual and Rubbish at the British Bronze-Age-Iron Age Transition." *Antiquity* 70. 267 (1996): 68–76.

_____. "Landscapes Preserved by the Men of War." *British Archaeology* 34 (1998), http://www.britarch.ac.uk.

McOmish, David, David Field, and Graham Brown. *The Field Archaeology of the Salisbury Plain Training Area.* Swindon, Wiltshire, UK: English Heritage, 2002.

Merkur, Dan. *Fruit of the Terrestrial Paradise: The Psychedelic Sacrament in St. Ephrem the Syrian and Celtic Christianity.* http://www.danmerkur.com.

The Metrical Dindshenchas. Edited by Edward Gwynn. Dublin, Ireland: Dublin Institute for Advanced Studies, 1991. http://www.ucc.ie.

Metzner-Nebelsick, Carola. "Early Iron Age Pastoral Nomadism in the Great Hungarian Plain — Migration or Assimilation? The Thraco–Cimmerian Problem Revisited." In *Kurgans, Ritual Sites and Settlements.* Edited by Jeannine Davis-Kimball. http://www.csen.org.

Millar, F. Graham. "The Celestial David and Goliath." *Journal of the Royal Astronomical Society of Canada* 89.4 (1995): 141–154.

Needham, Stuart, Andrew Lawson, and Ann Woodward. "Rethinking Bush Barrow." *British Archaeology* 104 (2009). http://www.britarch.ac.uk.

Nennius. *History of the Britons.* Translated by J.A. Giles. London: Henry G. Bohn, 1848. http://www.fordham.edu.

O Hogain, Daithi. *The Celts: A History.* Part 70. Woodbridge, Suffolk: Boydell Press, 2003.

Old Iranian Online, www.utexas.edu.

O'Meara, John. *The History and Topography of Ireland.* London: Penguin, 1982.

Oosten, J.G. *The War of the Gods: The Social Code in Indo-European Mythology.* London: Routledge, 1985.

O'Sullivan, Thomas D. *The De Excidio of Gildas: Its Authenticity and Date.* Leiden, Holland: Brill, 1978.

The Parish and Priory Church of St Mary, Totnes, Devon (Diocese of Exeter), http://www.churchcare.co.uk.

Parker, Will. *Mabinogi.* http://www.mabinogi.net.

Parker-Pearson, Mike. *Stonehenge Riverside Project.* http://www.shef.ac.uk/archaeology/research/stonehenge.

Pausanias. *Description of Greece.* Translated by W.H.S. Jones. Cambridge, MA: Harvard University Press, 1918. http://www.theoi.com.

Perry, Charles, A., and Kenneth Hsu. "Geophysical, Archaeological, and Historical Evidence Support a Solar-Output Model for Climate Change." *PNAS* 97.23 (2000): 12433–12438.

Pettazzoni, Raffaele. *The All-Knowing God.* New York: Arno Press, 1978.

Pitts, Mike. *Hengeworld.* London: Arrow Books, 2000.

Plimer, Ian. *Heaven and Earth: Global Warming: The Missing Science.* Ballan, Victoria, Australia: Connor Court, 2009.

Plutarch. "Life of Theseus." In *Parallel Lives.* Translated by Aubrey Stewart and George Long. London: Henry G. Bohn, 1881. http://www.gutenberg.org.

Pokorny, Julius. *Indogermanisches Etymologisches Wörterbuch.* Bern, Switzerland: Francke, 1959. http://www.indoeuropean.nl.

_____. "Zur keltischen Namenkunde und Etymologie." *Vox Romanica* 10 (1949): 220–267.

Prehistoric Dartmoor, http://www.dartmoor-npa.gov.uk.

Price, Dennis. *The Missing Years of Jesus:*

The Greatest Story Never Told. London: Hay House, 2009.

Rankin, David. *Celts and the Classical World*. London: Routledge, 1996.

Reno, Frank D. *Historic Figures of the Arthurian Era*. Jefferson, NC: McFarland, 2000.

Rhys, John. *Celtic Folklore: Welsh and Manx*. Boston, MA: Adamant Media Corporation, 2004.

Rigveda. Translated by Ralph Griffith. Benares, India: E.J. Lazarus, 1897. http://www.sacred-texts.com.

Romer, Frank E. *Pomponius Mela's Description of the World*. Ann Arbor: University of Michigan Press, 1998.

Ross, Anne. "Ritual and the Druids." In *The Celtic World*, edited by Miranda Green. London: Routledge, 1996.

Russo, Daniel G. *Town Origins and Development in Early England, c. 400–950 A.D.* Westport, CT: Greenwood, 1998.

Sandars, Nancy K. *Bronze Age Cultures in France*. Cambridge, UK: Cambridge University Press, 1957.

Sauter, Hermann. *Definition der "thrako-kimmerischen" Bronzen*. http://www.kimmerier.de.

Sciama, Lidia D., and Joanne Bubolz Eicher. *Beads and Bead Makers*. Oxford, UK: Berg Publishers, 1998.

"The Sick-Bed (Wasting Sickness) of Cuchulain." In *Cuchulain of Muirthemne*. Translated by Lady Augusta Gregory. London: John Murray, 1902. http://www.sacred-texts.com.

Silver, Morris. *Taking Ancient Myths Economically*. Leiden, Holland: Brill, 1992.

Sims-Williams, Patrick. "The Settlement of England in Bede and the *Chronicle*." In *Anglo-Saxon England*. Edited by Peter Clemoes, Simon Keynes, and Michael Lapidge. Cambridge, UK: Cambridge University Press, 2007.

Skene, W.S., trans. *The Four Ancient Books of Wales*. Edinburgh: Edmonston and Douglas, 1868. http://www.maryjones.us.

Skjærvø, Prods Oktor. *Old Avestan Glossary*. http://www.fas.harvard.edu.

Spence, Lewis. *The Mysteries of Britain*. Pomeroy, WA: Health Research Books, 1996.

Strabo. *Geography*. Translated by H.L. Jones. Cambridge, MA: Harvard University Press, 1932. http://penelope.uchicago.edu.

Swanton, Michael. *Anglo-Saxon Chronicle*. London: Routledge, 1998.

Tacitus. *Annals*. Translated by Alfred John Church and William Jackson Brodribb. New York: Random House, 1942. http://www.perseus.tufts.edu.

Taylor, Thomas, trans. *Life of St. Samson of Dol*. London: Society for Promoting Christian Knowledge, Macmillan, 1925. http://www.lamp.ac.uk.

Thomas, Graham. *The Romans at Woodchester*. http://grahamthomas.com.

Thomas, Julian. *Understanding the Neolithic*. London: Routledge, 1999.

Time Team. *The Bone Cave, Alveston, Gloucestershire*. http://www.channel4.com/ programmes/time-team/episode-guide/series-8/episode-8.

_____. Durrington Walls: A Time Team Special. http://www.channel4.com/history/microsites/T/timeteam/2005_durr_t.html.

Toynbee, Jocelyn. *Death and Burial in the Roman World*. Baltimore, MD: JHU Press, 1996.

Turcan, Robert. *The Cults of the Roman Empire*. Oxford, UK: Blackwell, 1996.

Vandenberg, Philipp. *Mysteries of the Oracles*. London: Tauris Parke Paperbacks, 2007.

Wagner, Heinrich. *Studies in the Origins of the Celts and of Early Celtic Civilization*. Tübingen, Germany: Niemeyer, 1971.

Waterhouse, John. *Zoroastrianism*. San Diego, CA: Book Tree, 2006.

Watts, Dorothy. *Christians and Pagans in Roman Britain*. London: Taylor & Francis, 1991.

Webster, Jane. "Sanctuaries and Sacred Places." In *The Celtic World*. Edited by Miranda Green. London: Routledge, 1996.

Wessex Archaeology. "Remarkably preserved Roman remains from grave." http://www.wessexarch.co.uk/projects/wiltshire/boscombe/preserved-roman-remains/index.html.

West, Martin Litchfield. *Indo-European Poetry and Myth*. Oxford, UK: Oxford University Press, 2007.

"What man is the gatekeeper/porter?" Translated by Mark Adderley. http://www.markadderley.net.

William of Malmesbury. *Chronicle of the Kings of England.* Translated by the Rev. John Sharpe. London: George Bell and Sons, 1904. http://www.fordham.edu.

Williams, Ifor. *Pedeir Keinc y Mabinogi.* Cardiff, UK: Gwasg Prifysgol Cymru, 1974.

Williams-Thorpe, O., P.J. Potts, M.C. Jones, and P.C. Webb. "Preseli Spotted Dolerite Bluestones: Axe-heads, Stonehenge Monoliths and Outcrop Sources." *Oxford Journal of Archaeology* 25 (2006): 29–64.

Wiltshire and Swindon Sites and Monument Record Information: Nettleton Shrub, http://history.wiltshire.gov.uk/smr/getsmr.php?id=2096.

Wiltshire Council. "Sites and Monuments Record: Wilsford Shaft, Normanton Down." http://history.wiltshire.gov.uk.

Wood, Michael. *In Search of the Trojan War.* Berkeley: University of California Press, 1998.

Woodard, Roger D. *Indo-European Sacred Space.* Champaign: University of Illinois Press, 2006.

Wright, Craig M. *The Maze and the Warrior.* Cambridge, MA: Harvard University Press, 2001.

Yeates, Stephen James. *The Tribe of Witches: The Religion of the Dobunni and the Hwicce.* Oxford, UK: Oxbow Books, 2009.

Yorke, Barbara. *Wessex in the Early Middle Ages.* London: Continuum, 1995.

Zalta, Edward N., ed. *Stanford Encyclopedia of Philosophy.* http://plato.stanford.edu.

Index

Aeneas 114
Ahura-Mazda 156, 158
All Cannings Cross (pottery) 3, 104, 108, 113, 128, 130–131, 154, 167
Allen, Richard Hinckley 2, 144
Alton Priors 183
Alveston Cave 30–31
amber 97–98, 141, 153
Ambrosius Aurelianus 169, 170–175, 187, 188
Amesbury 171, 172, 174, 175, 179, 186, 188, 190, 192
Amesbury Archer 92–93, 95
Ammianus Marcellinus 16–17, 146
Anderson, Graham 2, 143–144, 145, 147, 149
Anglo-Saxon Chronicle 64, 171, 176, 180, 188
Annwn 7, 42–63, 67, 77
Apam Napat 46, 154, 156
Arawn 67, 77
Arcadia 139, 142, 145
Arcas/Arkas 1, 145, 166
Arcturus (Boötes) 1, 143–145, 147, 149, 151, 142, 153, 154, 162, 166, 168, 170, 175, 187, 192
Arianrhod 77–84
Aristotle 60
Artorius 143
Atrebates 111, 186
Avebury Stone Circle 86
Avesta 46, 156

Barbury Castle 181
bards 12, 78, 124, 138
Bath 35–36, 64, 183
Beaker culture 87, 93–94, 95–96
Bede 55, 64, 124, 169, 176, 177
Bedwyr (Sir Bedivere) 8–9
Belenus 61
Belgae 18, 74, 111–112, 185
Beli Mawr 73–74, 81, 121

Bhagavadgita 165
Blodeuedd 80, 82, 94, 190
Bokerley Dyke 173
Bolgios/Belgius 74, 85
Boscombe Bowmen 93, 95
Boudica (Boadicea) 19–20
Bran 47, 52, 55, 58, 69–74, 162
Branwen 66, 69–74
Brennos/Brennus 72–73, 85
Britain (etymology) 69, 118–119
broom (plant) 80, 190
Brutus of Troy 114–117, 118, 156
bull, cult 39, 55–56, 109
Bush Barrow 96–97
Butterfield Down 31

Cabal (Arthur's dog) 7, 9
Cadbury Castle 172–173, 179, 186
Cadbury Congresbury 172, 173
Caer Sidi 43–44, 52, 59, 61, 63, 162
Cai (Sir Kay) 8–9, 49
Calleva Atrebatum 186
Caratacus 19, 176, 179
Cassiopeia 82
Cassius Dio 20, 125
Cassivellaunus 18, 72, 73, 74, 81, 85
cauldron 9, 36, 41, 47, 49, 50, 51, 61–62, 64, 70–71, 72, 75, 106, 126, 146–147, 148, 161–162
Ceawlin 181, 182–183
Celts 1, 2, 14, 16, 37–38, 47, 53, 57–58, 73, 74, 109–110, 112, 124, 150, 154
Cenwalh 184–185
Cerdic 176, 179, 180, 188
Cernunnos 25, 37–38, 150–151
chthonic deities 108, 131
Cimmerians 126–130
Cirencester/Corinium 22, 27, 33–34, 40, 64, 183, 184
Clement of Alexandria 14
comet 6, 176, 180, 187, 188
Coranians/Coraniaid 121–123, 125

Corona Borealis 82, 151, 152, 153
Crete 98, 102, 159–160
Culhwch and Olwen 8–10, 36, 45, 47, 51, 56, 66, 152, 155
Cunetio 34, 181–182
Cunliffe, Barry 2, 3, 87, 93–94, 100–101, 104, 105–106, 108–111, 112, 129, 130–131, 161, 186
Cunobelinus 19, 74
Cunomaglus 27, 35, 180
Cynegils 184
Cynric 176, 179, 180, 184, 188

Dagda 76, 135, 150
Danebury 2, 100, 107–110, 128, 130–131, 134, 139, 186
Dartmoor 101, 116–117, 118, 157, 167
Delphi 72–73
Diodorus Siculus 12–13, 72–73, 112, 129
Dionysus 34, 134
Dis (Pater) 12, 16
Dobunni 30, 35–36, 49, 64, 111, 186
dog, burials 3, 30–31, 109
dog, cult 27, 28, 133, 139–140
Don (*Mabinogion*) 66, 77, 85, 113
door (to Otherworld) 52–53, 62, 72, 141–142, 162
Dorchester-on-Thames 172, 177–178, 179, 181, 183, 184, 185
dragon 5, 46, 121–122, 171, 188
Durotriges 111–112
Durrington Walls 94–95

eagle 9, 80, 155
East Chisenbury 104–105, 107, 128, 129, 167
Egypt, ancient 103
Elidorus 119–120, 157, 160
Epona 41, 45, 68–69, 140
Etruscans 103, 117–118, 122, 142, 154, 157, 159
Excalibur 145

field-systems 100–102, 103, 116, 167
Four-Cornered (Fortress) 46–47, 52, 61–63, 141, 156, 162

Gawain 8, 148–149
genii cucullati 35–36, 38, 41, 49, 65
Geoffrey of Monmouth 2, 5, 10, 48, 86, 114, 115–117, 120, 158, 161, 189
Gewisse 177, 179, 180, 181, 183, 184, 186
Giants Dance 86, 161
Gibbon's *Decline and Fall* 3, 6
Gildas 64, 168

Giraldus Cambrensis 54, 61–62, 114, 119–120, 135, 157
Glass (Fortress) 53–55, 62
Glastonbury 54, 189, 190–192
Gloucester/Glevum 9, 22, 35, 48–49, 64, 69, 183
Greeks, ancient 2
Green, Miranda 2, 35, 39, 41
Green, Thomas 2, 7, 143
Guinevere 8
Gundestrup Cauldron 36, 47, 55, 129, 151
Gwales 52, 72
Gweir 43–45, 61, 63, 76
Gwydion 77–84, 190

Hengist 86, 179
Hermes 12, 134, 135, 142, 157, 187
Herodotus 102, 103, 117, 126, 134, 140, 141, 145, 146, 148, 167
Hesiod 2, 140, 142, 143, 144, 148, 155
Higley, Sarah 43, 46, 51, 53, 55, 57–58, 82
hillforts 101, 106–111, 115, 128, 133, 136, 172–174
Hippolytus 14, 59
Hittites 98, 102, 117
Holy Grail 49–50, 146–147, 149
Homer 2
horse, burials 3, 109
horse, cult 41, 68–69, 70, 131–132, 135, 166

Iliad 114, 126, 132, 137, 141, 159–160, 166
Illyrian 118, 136–137, 153
Indo-European 3, 44, 47, 56, 59, 77, 118
initiation 58–63
Iranian languages 118, 125, 126, 143, 153, 157, 161, 167
Ireland 70–71, 161
Iron House 71, 75, 126, 161

Janus 142
Jordan Hill 29–30, 72
Julius Caesar 2, 10–12, 18, 24, 38, 57, 125

Koch, John 2, 3, 14, 55, 67, 73–74, 77, 125, 166, 182, 190

labyrinths 158–161
Life of St Samson 47–48
Littlecote 34
Livy 149

Lleu (*Mabinogion*) 79–82, 121, 153
Llud Llaw Eraint 8, 56, 188, 192
Lludd and Llefelys 66, 74, 114, 121–126, 149, 188
Llyr 8, 52, 59, 66, 69–74, 85, 156
Lucan 38
Lugus/Lugh 23–26, 29–30, 51, 72, 82, 135, 149, 152, 153, 187, 192
Lydia/Lydians 117–118
Lydney 26–27

Mabinogion 1, 2, 8, 18, 36, 45, 46, 52, 55, 58, 66–85, 94, 121, 149, 153, 161
Mabon/Maponos 8–9, 26, 39, 44, 66, 69, 155
Macedonians, ancient 2, 139, 148–149
Mahabharata 155–156, 165
Maiden Castle 28–29
Manawydan 8, 66, 69–74, 74–77, 126, 161
Mandubracius 18, 73, 85
Matasovic, Ranko 3, 67, 70, 154
Math (*Mabinogion*) 66, 77–84, 125, 158, 190
McEvilley, Thomas 2, 163–165
mead 51–52, 62, 122
meadowsweet 80, 94
Medea 148, 162
Mercury 12, 22–26, 27, 30, 35, 37
Merlin 5, 48, 192
middens 103–105, 107, 113, 128, 129, 136, 167
Milky Way 82
Millar, F. Graham 2, 149–152
Modron/Matrona 9, 39–41, 64
Mona/Anglesey 19
Mons Badonicus 6, 171, 172, 180
Mound-People 67–69, 74–77, 85, 112–113, 117, 153, 157, 160, 162
Mycenae/Mycenean 97, 102, 136, 141, 166, 167

nemeton 166
Nennius 2, 6, 42, 54, 114, 120, 123, 170–171, 179
Nettleton Shrub 27–28, 35, 180
nine maidens 8, 47–49, 61, 65
Nodens 8, 26, 56, 121, 188, 192
Normanton Down 95–96, 97, 102

oak 15, 79, 80, 82, 137–138, 142, 154, 162
Old Sarum 175, 179, 180
Orpheus/Orphism 32–35, 60–61, 163, 164–165
Ossetia/Ossetic 118, 143, 147–148

Pa gur 7–8, 47, 162
Pagans Hill 28
Parker, Will 66, 76
Pausanias 73, 138, 141
Perceval 48, 49–50
Peredur, Son of Efrawg 48, 66
Pettazzoni, Raffaele 2, 46, 133, 149
Picts 124–125
pits, ritual 108–109, 130–131
Plato 157, 163
Pliny the Elder 2, 15, 55, 71
Plutarch 129, 160
Pokorny, Julius 3, 44, 53, 59, 118–119, 157, 160
Pomponius Mela 14, 16, 47, 49
Potterne 104–104, 107, 128, 129, 167
precession 150–151
Price, Dennis 112–113, 161
Pryderi 43, 45, 61, 66, 67–69, 74–77, 77–78, 81, 118, 157
Prydwen 9, 45
Pwyll 43, 45, 66, 67–69, 124, 158
Pythagoras/Pythagorean 14, 59–60, 139, 140–141, 142, 162–163, 164–165
Pytheas of Massilia 112

Ramsbury 34, 181–182
raven, cult 29, 72, 140
reincarnation 14, 82, 84, 142, 154, 162–166
Reno, Frank D. 2, 170, 175, 179, 192
Rhesus 132, 134, 162, 187
Rhiannon 66, 67–69, 74–77, 124, 135, 162
Rig-Veda (Vedas) 44, 46, 131, 135, 138, 139, 156, 160, 162
Rosmerta 25, 27, 35, 37
Round Table 145

Salisbury Plain 100, 101, 102, 104, 116, 175, 176, 185
Santorini (volcano) 98–99
Sarmatians 143
Scythians 2, 118, 124, 126, 134, 142, 143, 145–146, 149, 167
Sea Peoples 103
shafts, ritual 29, 31–32, 72, 96, 99–100
shoemakers 24, 75–76, 81, 82
sidi/sidh 44, 67, 76, 86, 117, 156
Silbury Hill 86, 88–90
Silures 19, 64
Skene, W.F. 43
sovereignty goddess 52, 68
Spoils of Annwn 1, 2, 7, 36, 42–65, 67, 141, 146, 153, 156, 162

Stonehenge 1, 86, 90–97, 98, 99, 100, 102, 112–113, 142, 154, 161
Strabo 13–14, 73, 129, 150
Sword in the Stone 145

Tacitus 2, 19
Taliesin 7, 42–43, 47, 52, 56, 59, 63–65, 71, 82–84, 156, 165
Taranis 38–39
Tarvus Trigaranus 29, 38, 55
La Tène culture 109–110
Things Fall Apart 58
Thracian 2, 14, 36, 126–130, 142, 153
Thracian Horseman 1, 68, 130–135, 137, 139, 162, 187
Timagenes 16, 73
tor 117–118, 157
Totnes 115–116, 167
Troy (city) 16–17, 102, 117, 120, 158, 167
Troy (dance) 159–160
Troy Town (maze) 158–159
Troynt (boar) 7, 9
Tuatha de Danann 8, 77, 84
Twrch Trwyth (boar) 9–10

Uley 22–23, 35–36, 64, 86, 192

underworld cult 31
Uther Pendragon 3, 5–6, 17

Varuna 46, 59, 154, 156, 157
vates 14, 138–139
Vespasian's Camp 102, 112–113, 175
Viroconium 20, 169, 175, 180, 187
volcanic eruptions 98–99, 101, 187
Vortigern 123, 168, 169, 170–175, 179, 187

Wansdyke 173–174, 176
Welsh Triads 40–41, 44, 74, 81, 114, 123
Wessex, kingdom of 1, 3, 168
West Kennet Long Barrow 86–88
Whitsbury Castle 174
William of Malmesbury 191
Winchester 5, 40, 112, 177, 179, 185–186, 187, 190
Woodchester 33

Y Gododdin 7, 42, 51–52, 166
Yorke, Barbara 2, 173, 174, 177, 178, 180, 186
Ysbaddaden 8–9, 152–153, 187

Zoroastrianism 14, 46, 154, 156, 158, 161